BASIC POLITICAL DOCUMENTS OF THE ARMED PALESTINIAN RESISTANCE MOVEMENT

Selected, Translated and Introduced by Leila S. Kadi

Palestine Liberation Organization Research Center

Beirut Lebanon

December 1969

I would like to extend my gratitude to the following friends and colleagues for the efforts they contributed in helping me prepare this book: Mrs. Rosemary Sayegh, Dr. Sadik J. Al-Azm, Dr. Nabil Shath, Mr. Ian Howard and Mr. Ibrahim Al Abid.

PREFACE

This study is essentially a description of the organizational development of Palestinian resistance together with an examination of the political ideologies of the various groups and their relations with the Arab governments. Due to the exigencies of space and time, I have found myself limited to translating the documents of Al-Fateh, the Palestine Liberation Organization (PLO) I. the Popular Democratic Front for the Liberation of Palestine (PD FLP). and the Popular Front for the Liberation of Palestine (PFLP). The Research Center hopes soon to supplement this work by publishing translations of the documents of other resistance organizations. No attempt has been made to give an account of the activities of the guerrilla groups within Palestine.

The significance of the armed Palestinian resistance is not to be regarded only in terms of a new and effective force in the social and political life of the Arabs. In addition to this there is the heroism of the men who have become guerrillas. There can be no doubt that these men have enkindled within the Arab world a new inspiration and a new awareness of the possibilities that exist for the Arabs. While the Arab world still bitterly remembers its third defeat at the hands of Zionism, these young men of Palestine go out to redress the balance, to restore Arab right and pride.

These men, nearly all of whom are Palestinians, remember and fight because they want to return to the land the land that is theirs and the land that is their patents'! In a random sample taken of 300 men of Al-Fateh who led the fighting in 1968, it was found that their average age was 24 years six months, and 23 percent of them were born after 1948. The memory of Palestine is still strong in the hearts of Palestinians and, while that memory remains, Palestine is not lost to them.

HISTORICAL BACKGROUND

Armed resistance, contrary to appearances, is not new to the Palestinian people. They have taken up arms against foreign rule since the British Mandate. In the following pages a condensed summary of the background to the present Palestinian armed resistance movement will be discussed.

By 1936 the Palestinian people had had enough of British occupation and a revolution broke out. This revolution represented the peak of the Palestinian struggle against both the British Mandate and Zionism. The 1936 revolution followed a long period of political struggle by the Palestinian people exemplified in memoranda of protest, demonstrations, strikes and attempts at dissuading Britain from supporting the Zionist movement.

The distinguishing feature of the 1936 popular revolution is that the traditional Palestinian feudal, religious and bourgeois leadership had nothing to do with its outburst. The man who played a leading role in preparing for the revolution was al-Din al-Qassam, a simple man who had contacted Hajj Amin al-Husseini requesting an appointment as a roving preacher to prepare for the revolution. Al-

Husseini refused this request saying: "We are working for a political solution to the problem.

Such an answer did not discourage Qassam who went ahead and organized secret cells among the poor workers and peasants. On 14 November 1933, Qassam fought his first battle against the British forces in the Jenin area where he was killed. Although the Qassam movement was unable to achieve any of its major aims, yet it challenged the traditional family leaders before the people.

The second phase of the revolution started on 13 April 1936. Qassam's secret organizations renewed their operations from the rural areas and the revolution spread from the north of Palestine to the south. On 19 April, the city of Jaffa witnessed a massive popular uprising. The British forces reacted by blowing up whole quarters of the city. This action on the part of Britain prompted the "national committees" of the people to declare a general strike.

On 25 April, the national committees forced the Islamic Council (Hajj Amin al-Husseini), the Defense Arab Party (Ragheb al-Nashashibi), the Reform Party (Hussein al-Khalidi), the National Bloc Party (Abd al-Latif Salah), the Arab Palestinian Party (Jam al al-Husseini), the Independence Party (Awni Abu al-Hadi), to disband their political organizations and form the Arab Higher Committee to lead the peoples struggle through a general strike and armed revolution. The above-mentioned leaders succumbed to the proposed radical measures under the obvious massive popular pressure generated by the Qassam's armed resistance movement.

When the British failed to crush the revolution or prevent it from spreading, they turned to the pro-British Arab rulers to use their influence to convince the Palestinian people to end the revolution and negotiate peace fully with Britain.

The Arab rulers' response, headed by Nuri al-Said, was positive. Said visited Jerusalem on 26 August 1936 and asked the Arab Higher Committee to take all measures to end the strike and disturbances promising that the Iraqi Government would negotiate with the British Government to fulfill the legal demands of the Arab people of Palestine.

The Palestinian people rejected the principle of Arab mediation and carried on their armed struggle until the rulers of Trans-Jordan, Saudi Arabia, Iraq and the Yemen intervened and sent cables to the Palestinian people calling them to "keep quiet."

In spite of the popular rejection of Arab mediation, the Arab Higher Committee issued a statement announcing its approval of the principle of Arab mediation and urging the Palestinian people to end the strike and the disturbances as of 12 October 1936. With this statement the second phase of the Palestinian revolution came to an end. It clearly revealed the Palestinian peoples readiness to adopt the method of armed struggle and reject the logic of negotiations with Britain by foiling the efforts of the Arab rulers to mediate between them (Palestinians) and the British Government who had refused to stop Jewish immigration into Palestine. Moreover, the second phase gave clear indications of the hesitation and continuous efforts of the traditional Palestinian bourgeois and feudal leadership to agree to any media action to end the revolution and start political negotiations with Britain. The important element which was witnessed during this phase is the interference of the Arab rulers, who belonged to the same class structure as the Palestinian leaders, to impose their attitude on the Palestinian people.

The third phase of the Palestinians armed revolution is marked by the assassination, on 27 September 1937, at the hands of the revolutionaries, of L. Andrews, Acting District Commissioner in Nazareth. The Arab Higher Committee issued a communique condemning this act in this phase the antagonism between the rural masses and the bourgeois feudal family leadership came out into the open. The British authorities reacted by escalating their acts of repression and terror. Members of the Arab Higher Committee were imprisoned and others fled the country.

The peoples revolution spread and was concentrated in the provinces of Nablus, Galilee and the northern district. At the beginning of 1938 the revolutionaries were in full control of the villages of these areas where they had wide influence.

Their point of the revolution was the absence of a unified politically aware leadership which could be responsible for coordinating military action between the different areas. As for the traditional feudal bourgeois leadership,' some of its members were in exile while others were cooperating with the British authorities to destroy the revolution. The revolution suffered under some severe handicaps. First of all there was the constant personal bickering for leadership by the bourgeois and feudal Palestinian parties and their attack on the revolution itself both in terms of condemning it before the Palestinian people and then by conducting negotiations with Britain. Then there was the lack of any proper military coordination on the different fronts. Thus gradually the revolution became weaker and less effective. With the outbreak of World War II the revolution came to an end. The reactionary traditional leadership continued its efforts to solve the problem through negotiations with the British Government. The latter sent commissions of enquiries and then issued the White Paper of
1939 which limited Jewish immigration and promised Palestinian independence in the hope of securing a calm situation in Pales tine throughout the war years.

The occupying power imposed rigorous laws against the Palestinian people. It meant death for a Palestinian Arab to be found carrying a gun.

This penalty, however, was not imposed on the Jews. Thus during the course of the war, it was the Jews who were being armed often with British assistance, while the Palestinians were kept under surveillance.

The war period witnessed in Palestine an alliance between the traditional Palestinian leadership and the other Arab rulers who wanted the Palestinian people to terminate all violence against British rule.

By the end of the war the Zionists were ready to fight the now-unarmed Palestinians. The Palestinians were in no way ready to face the Zionist onslaught that was unleashed against them and the Arab armies that eventually came to their aid were too inefficient and ill-equipped. In addition the Arab feudal and bourgeois regimes were primarily concerned with maintaining close relations with Britain and the United States of America. The Palestinian leadership in turning over the fate of the Palestinian people and their struggle to the reactionary Arab rulers went back to the same tragic course of 1936.

The year 1948 saw the establishment of the state of Israel and the

Arab Palestinian peoples loss of their homeland and dispersal.

The first reaction of the Palestinian people after this disaster was to resist any kind of rapprochement that would lead to a final settlement with the state of Israel. Examples of this opposition are to be found in the following:

1. The publication in 1932 of a secret weekly bulletin Nasbrat al-Tbar by the Committee for Resisting Peace with Israel. This committee was mainly composed of students at the American University of Beirut (AUB). These same students were among the group that formed the nucleus of the Arab Nationalist Movement (ANM) founded by a Palestinian, Dr. George Habash. He obtained his degree in medicine from the AUB in the early fifties. After his graduation Habash practised in Amman for a few years. Then he devoted himself to the ANM and became one of its key figures. Nasbrat al-Tbar was very effective and had a widespread distribution among the Palestinians in the camps up to 1934. It played a role in uncovering various secret attempts to liquidate the Palestine problem on the basis of a final settlement with the state of Israel. Such a settlement could only mean that the Palestinians would remain forever after in a state of diaspora. The bulletin's effect was mainly among Palestinians in Lebanon, Syria and Jordan, while its influence on thorn in the Gaza Strip was negligible.

- During the years 1953-54 UNRW A put forward many projects aiming at the rehabilitation of the Palestinian refugees by constructing permanent residence units. They regarded these projects as having one aim, namely, the liquidation of their problem. Rehabilitation meant the end of their existence as refugees and their acceptance of the state of Israel as a fait accompli. This ultimately meant the loss of Palestine to them. In order to counteract the rehabilitation projects, the Palestinians launched mass demonstrations, organized general strikes, and destroyed many of the housing units set up by UNRW A, thus putting an end to such projects. The rehabilitation projects were put forward again by Dag Hammarskild in 1959 in the form of a plan for the integration of the Palestinians in the economic life of the Middle East. They opposed this plan fay holding the Arab Palestinian Conference in Beirut in 1959. The rejection of the plan by Palestinians compelled the Arab governments to oppose it, thus forcing the UN to withdraw the plan.

• Alongside the political struggle of the masses of the Palestinians, small Palestinian groups residing in the Gaza Strip, Syria and the West Bank took the initiative by undertaking commando action inside Israel. These commando raids, which penetrated deep into populated areas of Israel, prompted the latter to carry out a large scale raid on Gaza on 28 February 1955. It also caused Israel to assassinate two commando leaders, Salah Mustafa and Mustafa Hafez. These guerrilla groups were not based on, connected to, or part of any political organization, but were trained and led by Egyptian army officers. These groups were disbanded after the.1956 tripartite aggression on Suez.

Politically active Palestinian groups considered that the Arab governments were mainly responsible for the 1948 defeat and thus they hers me affiliated to, and actively participated in national Arab parties such as the Bath and the Arab Nationalist Movement. These parties called for Arab unity which Palestinians believed was the road to a strong unified Arab state capable of confronting Israel and liberating Palestine.

With the establishment of the United Arab Republic, 22 February 1958, the Palestinians were convinced that they were on the brink of liberating Palestine. Historical developments proved them wrong. During the three years of unity the UAR Government attempted to build up popular Palestinian organizations such as the Palestinian National Union in Syria and Gaza. These organizations were unpopular and ineffective since they were imposed from aboye.

At the same time, in 1959, a secret monthly magazine of limited circulation Our Palestine (Filistinuna) began publication in Beirut. Our Palestine called for the Palestinization of the Palestine problem. This meant that the Arab governments should give the Palestinians a free hand to work for the liberation of their country. Later on, it became known that the sponsors of Our Palestine were the Al-Fateh group. This group came into existence out of the discussions of Palestinian students in the Gaza Strip who had suffered under the Israeli occupation of 1956 and were concerned with the problem how best to win bade Palestine admitting the Arab governments inability to do it for them. Little by little, they became convinced that the Palestinians must take their cause into their own hands. Yasser Arafat became their leader.

Arafat (his aide name is Abu Ammar) was bom in Jerusalem in 1929. His career, in a way, mirrors the history and thrust of the Palestinian commandos. He spent his early childhood in a house within a stones throw of the W ailing W all. When the Arab-Israeli fighting of 1948 ended A rafat found himself with his parents a refugee in Gaza. He managed to go to Cairo to study engineering at Fuad I (now Cairo) University, where be m ajored m civil engineering. As chairman of the Palestinian Student Federation he helped, in his own words, "to lay the basic foundation for our movement." While studying he also acted as a leader and trainer of Palestinian and Egyptian commandos who fought the British in the Suez area, served the Egyptian army as a demolitions expert and fought against the British and French at Port Said and Abu Kabir in 1956. After a brief period as an engineer in Egypt he obtained an engineering job in Kuwait in 1957, where be stayed until 1965. Meanwhile he travelled among the scattered Palestinians to recruit members for the organization. Soon cells were formed in Kuwait and among students in West Germany. The initial development was slow and went against the trends of the period. This could be linked to the belief that Arab unity was the only road to the liberation of Palestine, and any claims to unity boosted this belief. Thus slogans and aspirations to unite under the leadership of President Nasser, made themselves felt strongly during the years 19371938, culminating in union between Syria and Egypt.

Between 1937 and 1967, talk about Arab unity reached its climax but, at the same time, rivalry between the various Arab governments became even more acute. But aspirations for Arab unity were so deeply held by the people that they constituted a reality which had to be taken into consideration. Also significant was the interaction and confusion of the various political movements: Nasserist, Bathist, Arab Nationalist . . . etc., regardless of their country of origin. In this context, the Palestinian national question was not a simple one, even more so because, through the idea of unity, the listener of Israel nude it possible for many Arab governments to redirect popular aspirations towards external objectives and an outside enemy. Certain Arab states accused the militants of Al-Fateh of being agents of CENTO. One can relate such an accusation to the United Arab Republics and Tunisia's policies during the early sixties. President Nasser realized that the war in the Yemen had dragged on for a much longer period 'than was expected and was thus costing the UAR treasury more than it could afford. This led to pressing internal economic problems which threatened the effectiveness and development plans of his regime. President

Nasser was of the opinion that the industry and economy of the UAR should be more developed before embarking on a war against Israel. The UAR was of the opinion that Al-Fateh was trying to involve it in war with Israel at a time when Arab unity had not yet been achieved and the UARs economy was not yet well developed. Thus in his opening speech to the Second Palestinian National Congress which was held in Cairo on 31 May 1963, President Nasser declared: "We do not have a plan for the liberation of Palestine." Moreover, 1963 witnessed the first Arab leader who publicly declared that the Arabs should solve the Palestine problem by signing a peace treaty with Israel. Thus the strictly clandestine character of various Palestinian resistance movements until 1967 was less due to the Israeli enemy d u n to the attitude of Arab states where Palestinian militants were often put under house arrest, thrown in jail or even worse. To this effect, Al-Fateh still remembers that one of its first partisans was killed in 1963 by the Jordanian army.

With the failure of the Syria-Egyptian union in 1961, the concept of unity as the road to the liberation of Palestine collapsed. Palestinians realized that the attainment of unity was an almost impossible task; and that they could not afford to wait until all of the Arab world was united. They started to talk of an independent Palestinian entity and action. As a result, more than thirty Palestinian organizations, most of which had only a small membership, were set

19

up. This large number of organizations was ample proof of the Palestinians desire to work seriously and independently for the liberation of their homeland. At the same time it indicated that a strong effective organization was lacking.

The triumph of the Algerian revolution in 1962 gave more weight to the principle of independent Palestinian activity. The Algerians were able to recruit material and moral support from various Arab regimes and, through armed struggle, to attain their independence. Some Palestinians thus believed that they could adopt the same kind of policy if they took the initiative and maintained their freedom of action.

During this period Al-Fateh, which is the reverse initials of Harakat al-Tabrir al-Watani al-Filistini (Palestine National Liberation Movement), strove to create the nucleus of a political organization recruited from among the Palestinian intelligentsia. Since 1962 Al-Fateh has concentrated all its efforts on starting military action but was faced with the problem of the shortage of means to embark on such an activity. In 1964 Al-Fateh held a conference to discuss this question and the majority of the members voted for starting military action on 1 January 196$ in spite of the shortage of means. Those who opposed this decision proposed that military operations should be started under another name, rather than Al-Fateh, so that, in the event of failure, Al-Fateh might continue its preparations and its secret activities. The proposal was accepted, and it was agreed to use the name of al-'Asifah for the first military operations. Al-Fateh announced that it was al-Asifah after the tenth military communique. Al-Fatehs leadership decided to continue using the name of al-Asifah because it had become a historic name.

The first Arab summit conference, held in Cairo between 13 and 16 January Arab League Council held on 13 September 1963. At that session, the Council studied the problem of Palestine in a more constructive manner than usual by affirming the "Palestine entity" at the international level; by establishing the bases for action through the organization of the people of Palestine; and by making them assume responsibility for their national cause and the liberation of Palestine.

Thus President Nasser was suspected of having no intention of getting into war with Israel when the latter would start pumping water from the Sea of Galilee down to the Negev. Under these circumstances, President Nasser, in a speech delivered on 23 December 1963 on the occasion of the seventh anniversary of "Victory Day," said: "In order to confront Israel (which put a challenge to us last week, and whose Chiefs-of-Staff stood up and said we shall divert the water against the will of the Arabs, and let the Arabs do what they can) , a meeting between the Arab kings and presidents must take place as soon as possible, regardless of the strife and conflicts among them."

The conference was held, and at the end of its meetings issued a communique in which it decided to organize the Palestinian people to enable them to play their part in liberating Palestine and in determining its future.

The immediate background of this decision can be found in the 40th session of the Arab League Council held on 13 September 1963. At that session, the Council studied the problem of Palestine in a more constructive manner than usual by affirming the "Palestine entity" at the international level; by establishing the bases for action through the organization of the people of Palestine; and by making them assume responsibility for their national cause and the liberation of Palestine.

The first decision taken by the Council of the League was the appointment of Ahmad Shuqairi as the representative of Palestine at the Arab League. Shuqairi is a Palestinian lawyer who had been Assistant Secretary General of the Arab League; had later become a member of the Syrian delegation to the United Nations; and then became the delegate of Saudi Arabia to the UN. The Council also asked him to carry out consultations with representatives of the people of Palestine for the formation of a new general government in exile. Furthermore, he was asked to visit various Arab capitals to discuss the means which the Arab governments would place at his disposal for the fulfillment of this task.

Shuqairi began his tour of the Arab states on 19 February 1964, to discuss with Palestinians and the Arab governments the drafting of the Pales tine National Charter and of the draft constitution of a liberation organization, on which the "Palestine entity" would be based.

Shuqairi visited Jordan, Syria, Bahrain, Q atar, Iraq, Kuwait, Lebanon and the Sudan. He met the then President of the Yemen Republic, Abdullah Sallal, in Cairo. His tour ended on 5 April 1964. Upon his arrival in Cairo, Shuqairi made a statement in which he announced that he had held about 30 conferences with the Palestinian people, during which he had met thousands of them. At these conferences he had captained the Palestine National Charter, and the basic system of the liberation organization.

On 28 May 1964, the Palestine National Congress, in which members of Al-Fateb participated, opened in Jerusalem. It unanimously elected Shuqairi as Chairman of the Congress. It was held under the supervision of the Arab League, and under the auspices of King Hussein, and attended by 242 Palestinian representatives from Jordan, 146 from Syria, Lebanon, Gaza, Qatar, Kuwait and Iraq. The most important resolutions adopted by the Congress were the following:

- Establishment of a Palestine Liberation Organization to be set up by the people of Palestine in accordance with its statutes.
- Appeal to all Palestinians to form professional and labor unions.

- Immediate opening of camps for military training of all Palestinians, in order to prepare them for the liberation battle which they affirmed could be won only by force of arms. The Arab governments were urged to admit Palestinians to their military academies.

- Establishment of a Palestine National Fund to finance the PLO. The sources of revenue would include annual subscriptions, to be paid by every Palestinian over 18 years of age, loans and grants to be offered by Arab and friendly states, contributions to be collected on national occa sions, and the revenue from issuing Palestine Liberation Bonds by the Arab League the PLO.

The second Arab summit conference, which was held in Alexandria from 3-11 September 1964, welcomed the establishment of the Palestine Liberation

Organization. (It also fixed the obligations of each Arab state towards the PLO .) The conference endorsed the decision taken bjr the PLO Executive Committee to establish a Palestine Liberation Army to be stationed in the Gaza Strip and the Sinai Peninsula.

The creation of the PLO raised the hopes of the Palestinian people. It absorbed a number of the small organizations that had been set up earlier in the sixties. Al Fateh, which was at that time operating only on the political level, clandestinely, and the Palestinian branch of the Arab Nationalist Movement (ANM), and a few other small organizations maintained their separate identity, in spite of the fact that they participated in the PLO national congress.

Up to this time Al-Fateh was the sole organization which called for the adoption of the principle of armed struggle as the only means for the liberation of Palestine. Furthermore, Al-Fateh believed that the Palestinians should start armed struggle irrespective of the reaction or plans of the Arab regimes. The Palestinian branch of the Arab Nationalist Movement called for coordination between the Palestinian armed struggle and the plans of the progressive regimes, mainly the UAR. The logic behind this thinking was to avoid a premature confrontation between Israel and the Arab states. They feared that Al-Fatehs action would force the involvement of the Arab states, and the UAR in particular, in a war with Israel. Yet despite this Al-Fateh embarked upon reconnaissance operations inside the occupied territories in 1963. On 14 July of that year Al-Fateh lost its first two casualties, Andah Swailem Sa'd and Salem Salim Sad.

In 1964, the Palestinian branch of the ANM formed a military group to undertake reconnaissance operations inside the occupied territories and to establish network and arms caches. This decision was adopted at a conference held in September 1964 that included representatives of all the Palestinian members of the AN. The basic principles that were adopted at this conference were the following :

- Armed struggle is the only way to liberate Palestine.
- All secondary conflicts should be subordinated to the conflict with imperialism and Zionism.
- The different revolutionary groups should be unified.

On 2 November 1964, the first casualty claimed by ANMK Halid al- Haij was killed by the Israeli army in an unplanned clash. At that time the ANM refused to disclose the name of the man or to give any details about the circumstances that led to his death. This was done to avoid any hindrance of its preparations and to maintain secrecy.

On 1 January 1963, Al-Fateh's first communique was published in the Lebanese press announcing the start of its military activities in the occupied territories. At this early stage these activities were not clearly described for the reason that the Arab regimes and their mass media were tacitly opposed to the principle of Palestinian guerrilla warfare. The Palestinian people remained passive awaiting the Arab states, especially the UAR, to bring a favorable end to their problem. Al-Fateh was an isolated movement trying to prove that Palestinians could fight, could confront their own problem and could escape the control of the various Arab states, especially Jordan which was hostile to any possibility of a change in the status quo.

Jordanian police checks on the refugee population made any political activity extremely difficult. In Cuban terminology, the Palestinian resistance began as a "focus, as a nucleus employing armed violence without any political preparation of the population it was trying to involve. But while the strategy of the focus as applied within the framework of class struggle has shown itself to be ineffective in Latin America, the armed nucleus of the Palestinian resistance, due to the military collapse of the Arab states, has been successful within the framework of a national movement. Naturally this strategy was imposed by the circumstances and by the nature of the national movement of which Al-Fateh is the nucleus.

The Arab regimes continued to oppose independent guerrilla warfare until 3 June 1967, except for Syria which found in Al-Fateh the embodiment of its slogan repeated since 1963 (without being applied), calling for a popular war of liberation.

The military grouping of the Palestinian branch of the ANM came to be known as Abtal al-Audab (Heroes of the Return). It started its military operations in November 1966, under internal pressure from the members of the ANM who urged that the reconnaissance activities should be transformed into actual military operations. A few months after its emergence Amdab. Amdab became associated with the Palestine Liberation Army (PLA) for financial reasons. Shupri welcomed this step because he wanted to bring the commando organizations under the control of the PLO in order to compete with Al-Fateh. The Palestinian branch of the ANM then formed another military group which carried out its first operation in the occupied territories a few days before the June war. This group was called Munazamat Sbabab al-Tbar (Youth of Revenge Organization).

Another organization emerging prior to the June war was Jabbat Tabrir Filistin (Palestinian Liberation Front), headed by Ahmad Jibril and Ahmad Zarur. Jibril is a graduate of the Royal Military Academy, Sandhurst, and a former officer in the Syrian army. Zarur is a form er officer in the Jordanian army. The organization is strictly military.

The Palestine Liberation Army (PLA) did not play an active role prior to 5 June 1967. Yet in the six-day war the PLA troops stationed in the Gaza Strip fought bravely against the Israeli forces. The regimes took the Arab people by surprise. This defeat proved that dependence on the Arab governments and armies for the liberation of Palestine would lead nowhere. It proved that the idea of Arab unity, which was considered to be the road to Palestine, was far-fetched under existing conditions. The Arab masses were isolated and could not play their proper role in the war because the existing regimes feared their people in case they armed and trained them more than the enemy. Thus the role of the people was limited to observing the defeat of their armies, the occupation of the whole of Palestine, Sinai and the Golan Heights. The Palestinians took it upon themselves to act, continue the war against the enemy, rally the Arab people to their side and make them play their proper role in retrieving Palestine, Sinai and the Golan Heights from Israeli occupation. Thus directly after the June war a number of conferences were held (in Damascus) in which representatives of Al-Fateb, Munaxamat Sbabab d-Thar, al-Audab and Jabbot T'abrir Filistin participated. The PLO was in touch with what was going on.

In June 1967 of the Arab these conferences was to formulate a Palestinian response to the defeat The only formulathat was approved was that of armed struggle. Nearly half of the Palestinian Arab people were now under the yoke of direct Israeli occupation. However, these meetings did not lead to any practical results; Al-Fateh renewed its military operations unilaterally in August 1967.

The other three organizations Jabbat Tabrir Filistin, al-Tbar and Abtal al-Audab continued to hold meetings and agreed to merge together into the Popular Front for the Liberation of Palestine (PFLP). PFLP started its military operations on 6 October 1967 and the first military communique was published on 21 December 1967.

The re-emergence of several Palestinian politico-military organizations underlined the need to coordinate and unify their activities.

This prompted Al-Fateh to call on 4 January 1968 for a meeting of all Palestinian organizations, including the PLO and PFLP. The conference was held in Cairo between 17 and 19 January 1968. The PLO and PFLP refused to attend, this conference on the grounds that some of the organizations invited did not have a significant military or political weight. Nevertheless, Al-Fateh held the meeting at the end of which the Permanent Bureau for the Palestinian Armed Struggle was set up. This Bureau included, in addition to Al- Fateh, eight lesser organizations. It ceased to exist on the political level shortly after the convening of the fourth Palestinian National Congress, held in Cairo in July 1968. However, on the military level, the military wings of these organizations merged with al-Asifab.

Early in September 1968, Jabbat Tabrir Filistine (Ahmad Jibril) seceded from PFLP and continued to operate on a limited scale under the name of PFLP General Command. It designed for itself a new emblem to distinguish it from PFLP.

In February 1968, the Palestine Liberation Army (PLA) started its commando activities under the name of Popular Liberation Forces (PLF). This is is a commando organization operated under the auspices of the Palestine Liberation Army within the political framework of the Palestine Liberation Organization.

On 10 July 1968, the fourth Palestinian National Congress was held in Cairo and was attended by representatives of the different commando organizations, including al-Saiqah. Al-Saiqah is a Palestinian group which has very close associations with the Ba'th Party, ruling in Syria. The fourth National Congress was held in the absence of Ahmad Shuquari, who had been forced to resign from the presidency of the PLO after a long struggle between him and the majority of the Executive Committee backed by the rank and file of the PLA in Syria. Some other Palestinian organizations had played a. role in the pressures which caused his resignation. They accused him of having single handed leadership harm ful to the Palestinian struggle. They also believed that he subordinated the struggle to political maneuvering.

The Congress elected Yebya Hammouda as Acting President of the PLO Executive Committee. Formerly he had been president of the Jordanian Lawyers Association, however, since 1957 he had been barred from Jordan because he was accused of being a communist. Hammouda was given the job of contacting the Palestinian commando organizations and holding the fifth Palestinian National Congress within a period of six months.

With the collapse of, Arab military strength, the Palestinian guerrilla movement gained momentum and strength very quickly. This was most obvious in Jordan where there was no fast military build-up of the conventional armed forces as was the case in the UAR. The commando organizations armed themselves with great rapidity and in only 18 months, Al-Fateh, for example, was able to train thousands of combatants while, before the defeat, it had taken the same organization seven years (1958-65) to complete the structure of its first political military nucleus. Soon the commando organizations came to control the mass of the Palestinian population especially in the refugee camps in Jordan. With the battle of Karameh, 21 Match 1968. the commando groups (and particularly Al-Fateh) emerged as undisputed leaders of the Palestinian population. Political education was intensified among the refugees with the aim of rediscovering their Palestinian identity. It was also about this time that the resistance was able to consolidate its military bases, the state of Jordan included, and to turn them into relatively secure bases, first of all in the Ghor mountains where a great number of fighters have been trained. The resistance movement, in short, asserted itself in the Arab world, obliged Israel to take account of its existence, began to mobilize the Palestinian population, and set up the beginnings of an administrative infra structure

The armed struggle, intended to win popular support, began to bear fruit. Soon, the impression made by the resistance to Arab public opinion overtook the influence, of Ba'thism and Nasserism and imposed itself upon the mass of Palestinian. All this led even King Hussein to declare in one of his press

curfew was imposed in Amman by the Jordanian authorities. King Hussein urged Yasser Arafat to negotiate a compromise. Shortly afterwards a Palestinian emergency council was set op which, in principle, was composed of all the Palestinian unions, parties, organizations and armed groups.

This council included a bureau of military coordination which was de pendent upon it. The Palestinian organizations were driven to tighten up their ranks by the political context as well as by the necessity of uniting to form a national force in the face of Israel. The palace made the various Palestinian movements sign an agreement of fourteen points which, among other things, stipulated that there should be coordination between the military forces of the Palestinians and the Jordanians and which called for the formation of a unified staff and prohibited commando operations south of the Dead Sea. The agreement served the purpose of restoring peace between the commandos and the regime and was never implemented.

The guerrilla groups issued a statement announcing that agreement had been reached between the two sides, but without giving any details. On Wednesday evening Al-Fateh, in a broadcast from Cairo, had this to say in the wake of Jordanian events: "Al-Fateh does not accept to commit suicide with Arab bullets. The Palestinian organizations are alone competent to punish those Palestinians who deviate from the revolutionary line and we reject controls which, under slogans of 'coordination and cooperation, are designed to liquidate us. Al-Fateh went on to say that" Arab frontiers must remain open for our operations and we demand the immediate liberation of Palestinian

revolutionaries detained in Arab prisons. The insecurity of Palestinian fighters inside Arab frontiers cannot continue and we cannot guarantee to remain quiet in the future. We shall not pay the price of a peaceful settlement and we call on all Arabs to disown the Jarring mission."

One of the most interesting aspects of the crisis was the attitude taken by Egypt. According to Abram of 7 November, the guerrilla organizations dispatched an open letter to President Nasser asking for his personal intervention to settle the crisis. Nasser, however, took the position that, despite his anxiety at what was going on, he did not wish to interfere for fear that his move would be misconstrued; also Jordanian sovereignty had to be taken into account.

Meanwhile, in Cairo itself, President Nasser addressed a meeting of the Central Committee of the Arab Socialist Union with the following reference to events in Jordan: "Our stand regarding Palestinian resistance and commando action is one of complete support and assistance in their rightful struggle against Israeli occupation. The basis on which we must work is to maintain the unity of the Jordanian front and preserve the relations of confidence between the Jordanian people, government, army and commando organizations, and also to support the unity of the eastern front.

Finally, on 10 November a decree was issued by the Jordanian Minister of the Interior to the effect that arms could only be carried by those given a special perm it by the government. This decree was in blatant contradiction to the agreement concluded between the Jordanian authorities and the principal guerrilla organizations.

In accordance with the resolution adopted by the fourth Palestinian National Congress the PLO Executive Committee held several meetings with the different commando organizations. From these meetings a formula of representation for the National Assembly of the PLO was drawn up. This formula gave 33 seats to Al-Fateh, 12 seats to PFLP, 12 seats to al-Saiqah, 11 seats to the Executive Committee of the PLO, 3 seats to the PLA, 1 seat to the National Fund of the PLO, 3 seats to students, workers and women's organizations, 28 seats to independents.

PFLP rejected the formula and refused to participate. It proposed to establish instead a front for all organizations to be formed on an egalitarian basis, i.e., one organization one vote. Al-Fateh, on the other hand, agreed to the formula and issued an important political statement a few days prior to the convening of the Congress. In this statement Al-Fateh announced its belief in the PLO as a general and

proper framework for Palestinian national unity
and said that it would participate in the
conference and the PLO Executive Committee.

The fifth Palestinian National Congress was
held between 1 and 4 February 1969 in Cairo. At
the end of the Congress a new Executive
committee was formed headed by Yasser Arafat
official spokesman of Al-Fateh. The new
Executive Committee was composed of four
representatives of A l-Fateh/ two of al-Saiqah,
three independents and one from the old PLO
executive committee.

At the end of this Congress a statement was
issued. It declared that the Palestinian cause was
facing the danger of liquidation in the interests
of Zionism and imperialism through the U N
Security Council resolution of 22 November
1967. It further warned against everything that
went under the name of peaceful settlements
including the Soviet project to lay down a time
table to implement the Security Council
resolution. It also rejected any Arab policies or
international interventions which contradicted
the Palestinians right to their country. It objected
to any form of tutelage over Palestinian affairs
and particularly over the development of the
rising Palestinian resistance movement.

The statement called on the Palestinian
masses, in particular, and the Arab masses, in
general, to mobilize all their resources and put
all their forces at the disposal of the armed

Palestinian resistance, and to consider that the Palestine liberation movement was part of the overall Arab revolution.

The statement went on to say that the aims of the fighters should be directed against one target only the Zionist enemy. The fundamental conflict was with Zionism. All other internal conflicts should be shelved because they were secondary.

The statement warned against the "defeatist deviationists who wanted to liquidate the Palestinian cause in favor of a spurious Palestinian entity subservient to Zionism and imperialism. Furthermore, the Congress drew up a plan to augment the effectiveness of the Palestinian resistance. This included, above all, a call for the unification of guerrilla action and financial resources, and the strengthening of the Palestinian Liberation Army.

Since this plan required additional finances the Palestinians were called upon to give more money and the Arab states to meet all their financial commitments to the Palestinian Liberation Organization. It urged Arab states to facilitate the residence, work and movement of Palestinians found on their soil. After the fifth Congress Al-Fateh announced that it would retain its organizational independence.

Towards the end of January 1969 an open conflict arose within the ranks of the PFLP. As previously mentioned the Front had originally consisted of three separate groups which had agreed to operate together. These were Sbabab al-Thar, all of them members of the Arab Nationalist Movement; Abbah Al Andah; and Jabbat Tabrir Fillistine (i.e., Ahmad Jibrils and Ahmad Za'rurs group).

As mentioned before the Jibril and Za'rur group split off from the others, though it continued to use the name "Popular Front for the Liberation of Pales tine" adding "General Command" to distinguish itself from the others. The split took place after the arrest of three of the Arab Nationalist Movement's leaders in Damascus: D r. George Habash, Fayaz Qaddurah and Ali Bushnaq. Ahmad Jibrils group refused to condemn the arrest on the grounds that it might have been the result of party political disputes only. However, this, probably, precipitated the split and did not simply cause it.

Moreover, during the month of August 1969, PFLP General Command witnessed another split. The group led by Ahmad Z a'rur called itself the Arab Palestine Organization, while Ahmad Jibrils group retained the name of PFLP General Command.

Meanwhile, the Arab Nationalist Movement as a whole was undergoing a sharp shift to the left. This did not happen with the same speed and decisive ness everywhere in the Arab world, but it became clear that with the internal splits taking place most ANM members were in the leftist camp, whose organ of expression is the Beirut weekly Al-Hurriyab. It was only to be expected that this conflict should make itself felt in the Popular Front for the Liberation of

Palestine. The conflict persisted until Dr. Habash returned to Amman after being freed from Damascus. However, the Front refused to participate in the Palestine National Congress under the pressure of the left-wing group.

On 10 February 1969, the Beirut weekly Al-Hurriyab carried a statement by the left-wing faction of the PFLP (under the leadership of Nayef Hawatemah who is a Jordanian and a graduate from the Arab University in Beirut, joined the ANM in the fifties, and early in the sixties' became one of its leading members) pointing out that at a decisive PFLP conference held in Amman in August 1968 the progressive-wing gained the day in its call for a revolutionary policy linked with the toiling masses. According to Al-Hurriyab although the moderates had ostensibly approved the conference proposals they had acted in a manner which is contrary to these proposals. For example, on 28 January 1969, they arrested three members of the progressive-wing in the cultural club of one of the refugee camps in Amman. Then five more were arrested in al-Baqa camp, and six others in various places.

The progressives called for an immediate meeting of the coordinating bureau of the resistance which the moderates refused to attend. H ie bureau strongly condemned the arrests and sent a delegation to the moderates to ask them to release the prisoners. The request was turned down.

In a communique published on 15 February 1969, George Habash, leader of the moderate-wing of the PFLP, declared that while the front had been ex posing the reactionaries and petit bourgeois and their luke-warm attitude towards the Palestine cause, while it had been challenging the Zionist enemy in the occupied territory and outside it, "opportunist pockets" had appeared within the Front's own ranks who sought to impede its revolutionary progress. These were a group of "adolescent cafe intellectuals" who subscribed to scientific socialism in name only.

On 24 February, the Beirut weekly al-Hurriyah officially announced that the progressive-wing of the PFLP had broken away and formed an organization to be known as the Popular Democratic Front for the Liberation of Palestine (PDFLP).

The causes behind this split can be summarized as follows:

The Marxist group led by Nayef Hawatemah, who was behind the split, called for breaking off of all relations of subservience with the Arab regimes whether they were progressive or reactionary. Furthermore, this group strongly criticized the other Palestinian organizations, especially the PLO and Al-Fateh, on the grounds that, like the progressive Arab regimes, they were led by the "petit bourgeoisie" and its ideology, which had proved its failure in the 1967 defeat. The new Marxist group called for a long-term war of popular liberation against imperialism and Zionism. They also called for the establishment of a Marxist-Leninist party completely committed to the ideology favorable to the dispossessed peasants and workers (the Asian proletariat).

On the other hand the majority of the PFLP, led by George Habash, while agreeing to the basic analysis of the Hawatemah group, believed in maintaining certain relations with the progressive Arab governments. These relations they see as necessary to secure financial and military support vital for the survival of PFLP and the resistance movement in general.

As for the Palestinian people, Habash maintained that the war with Israel is a national liberation war which requires the recruitment of the widest sec tions of the Palestinian people, a great number of whom are "petit bourgeois. U nis to alienate and antagonize the petit bourgeois class would bring a heavy loss to the national cause. At the same time, Habash stressed that the leading cadres of PFLP should be in the hands of those who are committed to the ideology of the proletariat.

On 3 April 1969, the PLO Executive Committee issued a statement in which it stated that the PLO had established a new command for a number of Palestine guerrilla groups. It would be called the "Command for Armed Palestinian Struggle" (CAPS) and would include al-Asifah, the Popular Liberation Forces, al-Saiqah, and the Popular Democratic Front for the Liberation of Palestine. The PFLP under George Habash has not agreed to participate in the Command for Armed Palestinian Struggle. The establishment of the Com mand was described as an "essential step towards the unification of commando activity and armed struggle. The Executive Committee took this decision because it was profoundly aware of how necessary it was that the Palestinian revolution should be unified in order to escalate and develop guerrilla activity.

The PLO had decided that from now on all reports of the operations of forces attached to the new command would be exclusively issued in the form of statements in the name of a military spokesman speaking for the new command, instead of the communiques hitherto issued by each commando organization individually.

In addition to the above-mentioned Palestinian commando organizations, towards the end of 1968 the Egyptian daily newspaper d-Abram announced that there had been in existence a resistance organization known as the "Arab Sinai Organization." This organization coordinates its activities with other Palestinian resistance groups in the Gaza Strip.

On 10 April 1969, the "National Command" (pan-Arab) of the Bath Party, backing the faction ruling in Iraq and opposed to the party regime in Syria, announced that they had formed their own commando organization called "The Arab Liberation Front."

The new organization was not intended to replace existing commando activity but to give it wider (inter-Arab dimensions). It is formed of Palestinians and nationals of various Arab countries who are members of the Bath Party.

On 10 April, King Hussein addressed the National Press Club in Washington. In his address Hussein presented a six-point program for settling the Middle East conflict. He declared that he spoke for President Nasser as well as for Jordan. The program promised to end the state of belligerency, recognize the existence of the state of Israel, and guarantee Israel freedom of navigation in the Suez Canal and Gulf of Aqaba.

On 1) April 1968, the Popular Liberation Forces of the Palestine Liberation Organization, al-Asifah, al-Saiqah, the Popular Front for the Liberation of Palestine (PFL P), and the Popular Democratic Front for the Liberation of Palestine (PD FLP) issued a statement rejecting King. Hussein's six-point Middle East plan. The statement was distributed lifter a meeting held on 14 April to discuss what was termed as "the grave and dangerous situation through which the Palestine issue is passing due to plans being put forward, especially the latest Jordanian plan, which affects the fate of the Palestine issue and the future of the armed resistance to Israeli occupation.

The statement said that the five organizations decided the following at their meeting:

1. To reject the Jordanian plan in its entirety, and to reject also all plans for the liquidation (of the Palestine issue) as well as all solutions proposed earlier. The organizations have also agreed to a unified plan to face this serious situation.

2. To form delegations which would contact certain Arab countries seeking a clarification of their position concerning the proposed plans rejected by the resistance movement.

In spite of the existence of numerous differing commando organizations there is complete agreement among them concerning the rejection of a political settlement of the Palestine problem to which they do not fully agree. Finally, it should be noted that all these organizations have made it very clear on numerous occasions that their war of liberation is not directed against the

Jews as such but against the Zionist state which has rendered the Palestinians a homeless and dispossessed people.

Yasser Arafat of Al-Fateh in his press conference held in Damascus on 28 October declared: The Palestinian revolution is against Zionism and not the Jews. Our Jewish brothers the sons of the Israeli sect are Egyptians in Egypt, Syrians in Syria, Lebanese in Lebanon, Palestinians in Palestine. We welcome every free and honest person of any nationality and religion to work within the framework of our humanitarian revolution, which aims at liberating our occupied lands and establishing our Palestinian democratic state.

The Popular Democratic Front for the Liberation of Palestine (PDFLP) presented the following proposed solution at the sixth Palestinian National Congress held in Cairo between 1 and 4 September 1949: "The establishment of the peoples democratic state of Palestine in which Arabs and Jews will live without any discrimination whatsoever. A state which is against all forms of class and national subjugation, and which gives both Arabs and Jews the right to develop their national culture . . . The peoples democratic state of Palestine will be an integral part of an Arab federal state in this area, . . . hostile to colonialism, imperialism, Zionism and Arab Palestinian reaction.

The Popular Front for the Liberation of Palestine (PFLP) in its February 1949 Political, Organizational and Military Report states: "The aim of the Palestinian Liberation Movement is the establishment of a national democratic state in Palestine in which both Arabs and Jews will live together as citizens equal both in rights and in duties. The state will form an integral part of the progressive democratic national Arab entity which lives in peace with all the progressive forces in the world.

THE RESISTANCE

A Dialogue between Al-Fateh and Al-Talfah

Lutfi al-Khouli: I think that it would be beneficial to start the discussion from the present state of the battle with the enemy. Can we find out something of Al-Fatehs attitude about this? Perhaps you agree with me that to know this we have to know the enemy's and our own strong and weak points. I mean in particular by "our, Palestinian, and in more general terms, Arab.

Abu Eyad: Naturally any scientific analysis must include both What is weak and what is strong, i.e., the positive and negative. I f we start the discussion with the Palestinian attitude, in Al-Fatehs opinion there are a number of positive things which have been achieved, but at the same time we do cook across negative approaches.

Among the positive factors has been the coming together in guerrilla action of large effective groups. This has found expression in the Armed Struggle Command following the reorganization of the PLO. If this is able to function in an atmosphere devoid of the earlier emotionalism, it will have a great effect in unifying guerrilla action.

The Armed Struggle Command has taken the place of the Military Bureau of Coordination and the guerrilla organizations inasmuch as it is the real unified leadership of four large groups of the guerrilla movement, the Popular Liberation Forces, al-Saiqah, al-Asifah and PDFLP; if the forces of PLA are added, in accordance with the last decision of the Executive Committee of PLO, this means that 90 per cent of the fighters are under the com mands leadership. This is clear indication of the participation of the revolutionary fighting groups in a national front within the framework of the PLO. In reality these positive developments have deprived the enemies of Palestinian action of the justifications with which they used to point out the strife among the Palestinian factions. But this position is still opposed and here I want to make it clear that I am not referring to the Popular Front for the Liberation of Palestine (PFLP). For we judge that it will ultimately agree to the new formula, if it understands the reality of the situation. Since the question is not that of Al-Fateh or others dominating the leadership.

Khouli: Would you explain what you mean by understanding the reality of the situation?

Abu Eyad: Its well known that PFLP's refusal to join the command is based on the principle of percentage of representation. Of course, there are some trying to exploit this to maintain the status quo and keep PFLP out of the command.

Therefore they are putting forward an illusory argument that Al-Fateh and others want to monopolize the leadership and organization. Here I want to make it clear that the question is not one of monopolization but, to be exact, it is one of conformity to Palestine and Arab public opinion. Our aim is to group the largest possible number within the framework of a national front and a unified command.

Khouli: Don't you think that it has become absolutely necessary to demand and insist on unity of action at least, if not complete unity on tactics, strategy and aims?

Abu Eyad: Exactly, we must understand that the outward differences, with regard both to the enemy and to calculations of profit and loss in building up the national front of the Palestinian people, will be ultimately eliminated if our brothers in PFLP understand the real attitude they should adopt towards the organization and the Armed Struggle Command. On the whole building up the national front through the organization, and also the unified military command for action are the essence of positivism in the present phase.

Khouli: What about the negative aspects?

Abu Eyad: In our opinion the negative aspects are confined to the stands adopted every now and then by the small organizations, in attempts to destroy the principal forces of Palestinian action. What can I say? I think this is enough.

Khouli: I don't think it is enough. What you are saying is very important. In my opinion the Arab people have the right to know all about this matter so that they can view from a position of awareness. It's not enough to talk in general and abstract terms because this would mean that this accusation would be without any substantiation and would not indicate who was responsible. The war of liberation cannot endure such things and we should avoid them. What have you to say?

Abu Eyad: Yes, it really is important. For example there are a few groups, such as Fateh al-Islam, who have mobilized reactionary elements under leaders who have been rejected by the Palestinian people. The aim behind Fateh al-Islam or similar organizations is the destruction of guerrilla action. They have no allegiance with the resistance movement and they were formed to support certain regimes.

Khouli: How do you meet this situation?

Abu Eyad: If we complete the building of the front and the Armed Struggle Command and if these two occupy their true places in Palestinian action, we are sure that this abnormality will be destroyed by the convictions of the people concerned. If we don't succeed, then we will have to use other methods.

There are other negative factors connected with aid which is distributed at times, and at other times heavy conditions are put on it. In addition certain quarters attempt to link Palestinian action with the official Arab position. This entails many dangers: first, imposing a mandate by limiting financial aid unless those receiving the aid adopt the official Arab position, and at the same time isolating guerrilla action and the Palestinian revolution from the Arab masses. It is not necessary to have a tax collector who collects money from the people. But it is necessary and important that the Arab citizen should feel that he is participating in the revolution by personal contacts with the active guerrilla forces. In addition there are certain Arab regimes which are waging a psychological war concentrated against the guerrillas, and I mean Al-Fateh in particular. Believe me, and I am not saying this with any conceit or narcissism, but as a result of actual facts, they think that if they can destroy Al-Fateh, they can destroy all guerrilla action. This is because of Al-Fatehs size and popularity. The strange thing is that this campaign has grown more intense following Al-Fatehs entry into the PLO. Al- Fateh was called upon to achieve national unity as it was the basic force in Palestinian action hindering unity. Al-Fatehs duty and this is true was to achieve unity. This unity could have been achieved in different ways. A national front could have been formed in which PLO could have been one of its members and not the framework of the national front as its National Charter stipulates. Al-Fateh could have overlooked this stipulation and considered PLO like any other organization such as PFLP, and then Al-Fateh would have entered the national front on the basis of full equality with PLO. Al-Fateh did not oppose this tendency, on the contrary we were ready to go along with it till the very end. However, there was a different way of viewing the question of the PLO... an objective way which took into account the interests of the Palestinian people before those of Al-Fateh. Thus, the PLO, for the first time, is considered as the representative of the official Arab commitment to the Palestinian people. Considering the PLO as a special force implies weakening it and breaking the commitment. The PLO could become the general framework of the national front, especially so because since its establishment the PLO has not had any political organization, but it has had a military force the Palestine Liberation Army, and basically the Forces of Popular Liberation. If we had insisted on joining the PLO on the basis of the principle of equality, although such an attitude might be unrealistic, it would have paralyzed the PLO. Paralyzing the PLO implies that the equal forces should unanimously agree to enable the PLO to move or take a decision. If a unanimous agreement is not reached this implies that any small organization can veto any decision and we will be going in a vicious circle. The opinion agreed upon was that the PLO should have a steering committee, or what others call a leading force.

This does not at all imply that the other organizations will lose their identity in the PLO or the national front. This is the case because what determines the taking of decisions is not the fact that the PLO has four members and Al-Fateh five members, but the size of the latter in the Palestinian field and its effects on the front. The voice of the representative of any organization will be influenced by its actual size in the field of action. In other words if we decide to carry out a big operation, the one who decides and whose voice will have more weight is the one whose material size is effective in what it offers the operation. Thus the question put forward is not one of voting or imposing an opinion, but it is a question of what the organization in question offers and what its actual size in the field is. I believe, if good intentions, objectively and subjectively, prevail in the relations of a sound front, then it is possible for the organization whose representatives are a minimum, in the event of their putting forward a good proposal which can be executed, to have their way adopted irrespective of other considerations.

This is the case with regard to the Palestinian position. We can summarize this by saying that there are strong positions; guerrilla action has become more popular; Palestinians are joining it in a manner which supersedes the present ability of their organizations; the size, quantity and quality of the operations are developing. I believe that the future will enable the Armed Struggle Command to adopt more positive positions and thus impose itself.

The present program which, I think, is linked with the solutions put forward for the area, is the question of the small organizations, and this is a new danger facing guerrilla action.

Khouli: I notice that in your discussion of the negative aspects you concentrate on the phenomenon of the establishment of new resistance organizations. No doubt this is not a healthy sign and causes continuous restlessness among the Arab people who are looking forward to both the military and political unity of the Palestinian people. It is noticeable that this phenomenon comes at a time when efforts are made to establish the national front of the Palestinian people and their commando forces. These efforts have given positive results. There must be a quick and final solution to this phenomenon. Here it does not suffice to say that these organizations exist but their causes, roots and aims must be known. Would you clarify for me how Al-Fateh explains this phenomenon? How does Al-Fateh evaluate it and what is its solution?

Abu Eyad: Of course it is an unhealthy sign, and we think that it is linked, in different forms, to the internal situation of guerrilla action in order to destroy it. The method of destruction is not overt and direct, but covert and indirect. The small organizations are well-known for their intelligence. Each organization carries special slogans, as if it attempts to convince^ the masses that these slogans are not found among the other Palestinian groups. For example the organization of Fateh al-Islam carries the slogan of Islam for a special and particular aim, and it attempts to point out to the masses that Al-Fateh is not Muslim or that it does not stem from Islam. Thus Fateh al ls! am appears as if it complements this missing part in the Palestinian action in accordance with its claims which are ill-founded. There are also other organizations. I referred to Fateh al-Islam because it uses the particular name Fateh. However, there are other small organizations which are founded on the basis that Al-Fateh, and other teal guerrilla organizations, have a regional or unclear view of matters, and still others outbid each other in leftist claims lacking any reality.

Khouli: To determine the size of this phenomenon, how many new organizations have been formed during 1969?

Abu Eyad: Three organizations have been formed, one on the basis of religion, another regionalism, and the third on a leftism which makes gross claims. If we analyze this phenomenon, we notice that our people do not believe in force as a principle and basic method; especially since Palestinian action has not yet taken final form. As a result, we have followed, and we are still following, the method of persuasion and direct dialogue. In our opinion the cadres of these organizations are honest but the deviation comes from the leaders. Thus it is necessary to go over the heads of the leadership and contact directly the cadres and make them understand the harm that these small organizations can inflict upon the Palestinian movement. We should not get tired of discussing with these cadres until we negate all justifications put forward by their leaders for the establishment and existence of such organizations.

Khouli: How do you carry out this discussion?

Abu Eyad: It can be carried out through information or direct contact. It is our conviction that the revolutionary struggling youth, when they know the truth, will come bade and join one of the real branches of Palestinian action which have proved their real existence in the struggle against the enemy.

Khouli: Have you achieved any positive results in this way?

Abu Eyad: Some positive results have been achieved and more will be achieved as a result of increasing the contact and deepening it.

Khouli: Tbe method which you have adopted to solve the phenomenon of small organizations in the Palestinian field leads ns to the following question: Why do you not use the same method with the PFLP since you consider it to be a teal guerrilla organization, in order to overcome the obstacles hindering it from joining the PLO, or the national front, or the Armed Struggle Command? I believe I am right when 1 say that it is Al-Fatehs responsibility to achieve

57

this since it is the biggest organization in the Palestinian field of action?

Abu Eyad: As far as the PFLP is concerned we have always carried on a dialogue with it, and we will never disrupt it. We started the dialogue before PFLP was divided into three different groups. The first division resulted in secession of the National Liberation Front which is known as Ahmad Jibril's group. This was followed by ideological differences within the PFLP which resulted in its division into two groups. One of these groups proclaimed to have led by ai-Hurriya group and that Nayef Hawatcmah. It called itself the Popular Democratic Front for the Liberation of Palestine (PDFLP). The other, which also proclaims Marxism but differs in its method of application, is led by D r. George Habash. These circumstances the internal divisions of the PFLP continuously-hindered the dialogue. Instead of carrying on a dialogue with PFLP with regard to its participation within the framework of Palestinian unity of action, the dialogue pertained to the resumption of talks among the two splinter groups. Frankly speaking this was a matter of great importance and took a long time. When events took the shape of a struggle between the two groups, great effort was required from us to put an end to the resort to arms by the quarrelling fighters in the streets of Amman and other places. We had to exert every effort to prohibit armed struggle among the different splinter groups of PFLP. Thus the dialogue was continuous; but it could not bring about the unity of PFLP with Al-Fateh, or PFLPs joining the Armed Struggle Command, unless the principal problem among the members of PFLP was solved. As a result, discussing the unity of PFLP took long days and nights. It is true we succeeded in hindering armed struggle; differentiating between PDFLP, PFLP which basically represents the Arab Nationalist Movement (ANM), and the Ahmad Jibril group which distinguished itself by the name of General Command. In the first phase which took almost three months of it was Marxist-Leninist and was Al-Hurrryd is a weekly publication which used to be the organ of the Arab Nationalist Movement discussion, we succeeded in differentiating between the three groups by giving them different names. Actually when the question of the last National Congress of the PLO came up, none of the PFLP members was in a position to discuss this question. Some groups in the PFLP requested the postponement of the date of the congress, others, such as Ahmad Jibril's group, requested increasing their percentage of representation, the third group, namely PDFLP, rejected the principle of considering the PLO as a meeting ground for the different Palestinian organizations. Later PDFLP withdrew from its position and joined the Armed Struggle Command. As you can see the dialogue with PFLP has never been discontinued but has been related to questions of primary importance pertaining to the PFLP itself. In spite of all this, after matters had been settled in the PFLP and after the convening of the National Congress and the election of the new Executive Committee we undertook to contact the three branches of PFLP. PDFLP asked to join the Armed Struggle Command. The condition put forward by the Executive Committee was that PDFLP must recognize, in writing, the National Charter of the PLO. PDFLP complied with this condition and declared that it adheres to the contents of the National Charter "as a minimum program" to govern the internal relations of the Armed Struggle Command. As far as Ahmad Jibril's group is concerned, negotiations center around an important subject of a special nature which must not be discussed new. It includes a definite attitude which needs clarification after which we decide to continue negotiations or not. As for the ANM group, the PFLP, we have contacted them through the PLO Executive Committee. All the reservations of PFLP regarding the PLO were put forward. As I understood there were no differences on the question of PFLP joining the PLO except with regard to general unspecific matters. It was agreed to prepare for another meeting to discuss specifically all these matters. Another meeting between Al-Fateh and PFLP was held to convince the latter to job, as a first step, the Armed Struggle Command, so it does not have any conditions or aspects which involve sensitive issues. The Commands field of activity is that of unified military action which is not directly linked to the PLO b its present form. Our brothers in the PFLP declared that the nature of the composition of the National

Congress must be reviewed to enable them to join the Armed Struggle Command. The implication being, as we have said before, that the meeting inside the National Congress will be granting PFLP an equal percentage along with the other organizations. As the discussion progressed to the subject of the small organizations and the method of their representation, PFLP put forward a condition that all the small organizations should have an equal percentage of representation in the congress. This brings bade anew the question of the national front and its formation. On the whole the dialogue is still going on and will continue.

Khouli: This is what we want, and we hope that you will achieve positive results through such a dialogue, the minimum of which in my opinion is unity of action. There are other points pertaining to the Armed Struggle Command which I would like to tackle. As I see it, this Command came after what was known as the Military Coordination Bureau. The first question is the following: Is the Armed Struggle Command, as its name implies, a more developed formula, with regard to the unity of resistance action, than the Coordination Bureau? The second question is: If the Armed Struggle Command is more advanced than the Coordination Bureau, what are the more advanced features? The third question: Is the Armed Struggle Command in the opinion of Al-Fateh the final step on the road to unity of action of the resistance or are there other steps, and what are they in the light of what can be published and announced?

Abu Eyad: The Armed Struggle Command is an important step on the road to the unity of guerrilla action. It is also without any doubt more advanced than the Coordination Bureau.

The Coordination Bureau was a committee composed of representatives from the different organizations. Also I frankly tell you, we believe that we must discuss our problems frankly, the bureaus activities were limited to coordinating relations among the guerrilla organizations and attempting to solve the problems that might arise among them. The bureau did not discuss, in any of its meetings, a military operation or plan, or a common act to be planned and executed under one leadership. Yet the different organizations, independently, carried out common operations on the battlefield in the face of the enemy's challenges.

It is true that the Coordination Bureau was a first step on the right toad, yet. I believe and scientific experience has proved it was not enough, unsatisfactory, and the wrong way to achieve a general command for armed struggle for the Palestinian people. When the new Executive Committee of the PLO was elected, it was interested in drawing up a new basis for establishing the National strong relations among the organizations participating in Congress and the leadership of the PLO. Care was taken to ensure that the leadership would not only be on paper or nominal with a flashing name, nor would it only inherit the Coordination Bureau. It must be a teal leadership in action for all the participating groups in the leadership.

As we know any action must be studied in detail and objectively : firstly, the reality and the potentialities; secondly, a plan should be drawn up on the basis of this reality and these potentialities; and thirdly, the actual execution of this plan. It can be said that we have almost completed the first two steps and we are embarking on the third.

Khouli: Can we understand from the above-mentioned that we are on the verge of carrying out common resistance actions in which all the forces of the organizations who have joined the PLO participate under the unified leadership of the Armed Struggle Command?

Abu Eyad: Yes. There will be common training in the operations under a unified leadership in which side by side the fighters of al-Asifah, PLA, the fighters will carry out al-Saiqah and PDFLP will participate. All common operations according to a unified system of allocation, ability, sufficiency, and work conditions. This means that at times and within the framework of the plana group, from e.g. al-Asifah, would be chosen to carry out a definite operation, or a group from al-Saiqah and al-Asifah, or al-Asifah and the Popular Liberation Forces, etc. In other words operations would be carried out according to what the leadership sees fit from the point of view of training, sufficiency, experience with the land, etc.

I am not telling a secret when I say that the Armed Struggle Command will start its activities at an important level in the near future.

And I do not tell a secret when I say that the latest "Himmah" operation was carried out according to plans drawn up by the Armed Struggle Command, in spite of the fact that al-Asifah forces carried it out J alone, yet the planning for the operation resulted from a new way of thinking 1 among the members of the Armed Struggle Command.

Khouli: I notice that you have used the expression "new way of thinking" with regard to the planning of the Himmah operation. Does it imply that this operation represents in your opinion a new development in resistance action?

Abu Eyad: There is no doubt that the Himmah operation represents a point of departure and a new development in guerrilla action.

Khouli: How?

Abu Eyad: As you know, our commando action remained limited to the general classical theory of guerrilla warfare hit and run. In spite of the necessity of adhering to this general theory, especially in the early stages of guerrilla action, we have actually carried out a kind of limited confrontation with the enemy in certain phases which were not dominated by the theory of "hit and run. An example of such a confrontation, on a wide scale proportionally speaking, is the Israeli aggression on al-Karameh in March 1968.

After al-Karameh we carried out other operations of the nature of limited confrontation such as that of Wadi al-Oilt and others.

These limited confrontations were an introduction to the Himmah operation. What does the latter operation mean? It means the occupation of a post under the control of the enemy for a limited period to dear it of the enemy forces and their capabilities. Thus with the Himmah operation we are embarking on a new phase of guerrilla warfare, namely, occupying certain positions and completely daring them of enemy forces. Of course, we choose these posts very carefully and according to very complicated considerations in order to inflict the heaviest losses on the enemy in addition to the political, military, economic and psychological effects that will result in the enemy front.

In turn this phase is a preparation for the next one, namely, the permanent occupation of the enemy posts. Such a phase will start after we complete the movement of our bases into the occupied territories, when the act of organic link becomes total, deep, and moves effectively among all the forces inside the occupied territories.

Khouli: Does it mean control of liberated areas as known in guerrilla warfare?

Abu Eyud: Exactly.

Khouli: There is no doubt that if the resistance was capable of taking "liberated areas" from the enemy by force then it would enter the phase of total liberation. But allow me, since we have agreed to face our problems frankly, to ask a question. The question takes into consideration what has been reiterated by observers, foreign correspondents and Israeli sources that Israel has been successful in combatting the resistance movements operations as a result of its use of electronic devices and electric wire in certain occupied areas. Moreover Israel has discovered many cells of the resistance movement inside the occupied territories. I am sure that this news is exaggerated for psychological reasons, yet it is true that electronic devices and electric wires have been set up and that a number of cells have been discovered by the enemy. Thus the question is to what extent has this actually affected commando operations and the required development toward the phase of liberated areas that we have talked about? Naturally-historical experiments have proved to us that the progressive resistance movements have been confronted with these difficulties and finally have been able to overcome them.

Abu Eyad: Naturally, not everything the enemy or foreign observers say is true. Exaggerations are made on purpose for psychological effects.

Yet honesty and responsibility require us to say that some of what is said is true. We do not deny or hide this fact; on the contrary we face it and try to overcome it. We cannot compare our human, technical and military capabilities when we embarked upon the armed struggle before the June 1967 war with our present state of readiness. What I want to point out is that we are aware of the enemy's strength and capabilities, especially since the experience of imperialism in the area is put at its disposal. The enemy benefits from Nazism and the American experience in Vietnam. We all know that Dayan stayed with the American army in Vietnam to benefit from its experience there in confronting the Vietnamese Liberation Army and guerrilla warfare. In addition the enemy acquires new weapons all the time, and benefits from the colonialist experts in combatting popular armed resistance all over the world. As a result we are facing an enemy which has well-developed education, technique and experience. Thus, we are aware that the resistance movement must have these three basic conditions.

I would like to raise the complicated question of Arab support of the resistance movement. The latter now depends solely on itself, in the sense that the Arab mentality, education and experience are far from actually and effectively participating in solving the problems that they face. They are now called upon the electronic line and the fortifications which Israel has set up along the borders, the narrowness of our land, the regulations pertaining to the occupied territories such as dividing Palestine into security zones. The first thing that Israel has done in the West Bank and the other occupied territories is to open roads to make it easier for its security units to move quickly to any area where a clash or a guerrilla operation takes place. This is the reason behind the quick movement of Israelis and not the result of the strength of its intelligence services. I can affirm here, from experience and with total responsibility, that the rumors about the strength of the Israeli intelligence services is a myth. Israel is not particularly advanced in its intelligence as such. But this is not to deny the fact that it benefits from the simple information it gets and immediately diffuses it among its units to get the full benefit from it to participate

The truth that we must stress here is that the resistance movement is in need of Arab support on the level of education and technical experience in order to confront and defeat the well-advanced Israeli education and experience.

Khouli: Naturally this is the duty of all the educational establishments and technical experts in the Arab world. In this connection the resistance movement could have technical experience bureau composed of Arab volunteer scientists and experts. But you have not answered my definite question pertaining to the effect of the electronic devices and electric wires on guerrilla action. What is the extent of their effect? And does it greatly prohibit the entry to the occupied territories?

Abu Eyad: No it does not. Naturally it has affected the entry, and thus we changed our tactics. We still enter the occupied territories; the proof is the daily operations of our forces inside the occupied territories.

Here I would like to point out a fact which you have always referred to in your articles, namely, the exaggerations in the resistance movements communiques with regard to its operations. What is the source and reality of the exaggeration? Actually exaggeration is absent in the communique issued by Al-Fateh or the Armed Struggle Command when they carry out an operation. But exaggeration results from the totality of communiques issued by the big and small organizations together.

I shall give you a live example. In the Jordan Valley every week five or sextants are actually blown up by the principal organizations. Yet every small organization claims these operations for itself. If the minimum number of these organizations is six or seven, the total number of tanks blown up according to the communiques will be at least 24. This is the basis of the regrettable exaggeration. You as an Arab citizen sense the general exaggeration in the military communiques of the principal organizations. Yet these communiques tell the truth without exaggeration or falsification.

Khouli: How do you calculate the losses of the enemy resulting from the operations your carry out? I recall that during a discussion with Che Guevara in 1965), he declared that calculating the real losses of the enemy is one of the most difficult problems of any armed resistance movement or guerrilla warfare.

Abu Eyad: This is true. That is why in Al-Fate hand maybe you noticed it we decided not to specify the total number of the losses of the enemy in al-Asifah communiques prior to its joining the Armed Struggle Command. That is, we said a number of men were killed and wounded. In spite of the fact that it is a standard expression, its effect on the Arab citizen is lighter than saying we have killed 10 or 20 and wounded 30 or 40. It was also agreed in the Armed Struggle Command not to specify the number of the killed and wounded although we are often sure of the real numbers. This does not hinder us from evaluating the actual losses of the enemy in every operation we carry out, and that is based on the reports of the fighters who have participated in it. Each fighter submits to his command a detailed report on the operation and the losses; an average then is calculated from the reports. These precautions are taken to avoid exaggeration. We know that our people are sensitive with regard to this point.

Khouli: Now perm it me to shift the discussion to another point which, in my opinion, is very important How does Al-Fateh conceive of the relationship between military and political action? In other words how does it conceive of the military and political leadership, and which directs the other? Who takes the decisions? Who has the final say when differences arise vis–vis main issues? Perhaps you are aware of the accusations directed against Al-Fateh that its activities are limited to the military field without miring them to definite political viewpoints of definite programs and organized popular mobilization of the Palestinian people. Such a criticism in my opinion is very important and we need to know your opinion of it, especially as Al-Fateh was the first organization to embark upon armed struggle in the Palestinian field.

I hope that in answering this question you will clarify the following points: Firstly, how was Al-Fateh organized, or what are the objective conditions which resulted in the adoption of the line of armed struggle? Secondly, does Al-Fateh believe that armed struggle is an end in itself, a strategic aim, or one method among others in its struggle? I f it is one method how does it relate to the others? Thirdly...

Abu Eyad: One by one.

Khouli: Dont you think that it is better to give you a comprehensive idea about the subject?

Abu Eyad: It is so. But the second point of your question pertaining to armed struggle as an end in itself or a method needs clarification.

Khouli: I mean, does Al-Fateh in viewing the methods of struggle against Zionism and its Israeli entity end with armed struggle alone, or does it consider that other methods alongside armed struggle are necessary and vital for its direction? Thus what leads Al-Fateh: military thinking or comprehensive political thinking equipped with different kinds of experience among which is military experience?

Abu Eyad: Understood. Actually Al-Fateh is a reaction to a totality of Arab circumstances, error of Arab politics and Arab parties. This had led a great number of the Palestinian youth to realize that partisanship, dissipation and fragmentation are not the toad that will lead to the solution of their problem.

This was a strange phenomenon in the fifties. In those days you rarely found a Palestinian who was not affiliated to a party or a political movement, and those who were not were considered a burden on society and were not respected. The affiliations of the Palestinian youth tanged from the extreme right to the extreme left. Some of them thought that religious affiliation could solve their problem. Others thought that communism could achieve this end. A third group adopted a nationalist line, namely, the nationalist parties represented in the Bath Party and later in the Arab Nationalist

Movement (ANM), the movement which erupted on the basis of revenge, blood, iron and fire. A group of this youth who have joined the above-mentioned parties and movements and were unable to discover the toad to liberate their homeland, actually withdrew as a result of the and awareness movements. It might not be correct to claim that the withdrawal pertained to the thought but it was from partisan affiliations which, in their view, could not achieve any positive results. The world is suffering from the experiences that are tearing the left to pieces. We hear of the left of the left, and a third left might erupt. These were the objective conditions. Actually they are the conditions of the Arab homeland which is boiling with restlessness. In the early stages this feeling of restlessness was expressed by the Palestinian people through the formation of a great number of secret organizations. It can be said that the victory of the Algerian revolution played great role in this dunking when the Palestinian youth felt that they were as capable as their Algerian brothers; that they, too, were capable of raising the slogan of armed struggle and putting it into effect. Yet the totality of the Arab circumstances was against this slogan and its application. Thus the Palestinian youth had no choice but to take refuge in secret action. There was a conviction that the aim behind the establishment of the PLO was to absorb the faith which began to spread among the Palestinian people and express the feeling of true restlessness and belief in building up a Palestinian national revolutionary movement. In short the attempt to establish the PLO at the beginning was to abort the true feeling of revolutionary restlessness. This was the reason behind our objection to the PLO at the beginning. It was imposed from above and represented a super-structure. The people did not create it. Under these circumstances we began to think of secret Palestinian action. Of course secrecy has its shortcomings and its advantages. If we analyze a great number of these organizations we find that they are part of a plan to strike at the true revolutionary movements. A number of Arab embassies established such organizations. Palestinian personalities whose historical role had ended at a certain stage also established organizations. At the same time a number of they acquired from their membership in these parties.

Arab parties attempted to establish secret organizations in order not to be outdone by the true revolutionary organizations. Al-Fatehs thought realized that words are of no use and serious and practical struggle must be carried out even with meagre resources. This is bow we started.

Khouli: At this starting point what was Al-Fateh, and who was Al-Fateh?

Abu Eyad: At that time Al-Fateh represented a group of Palestinian youth who had revolted against existing conditions as exemplified by the divisions among the Arab states, especially after Syria's secession from the

UAR, and by the failure of the Arab parties to take up any struggle. The youth, who have lived through this experience, established Al-Fateh.

Khouli: What is the social background of these youth who have organized Al-Fateh and led it? I think that they are basically Middle class educated Palestinians.

Abu Eyad: Of course they are basically educated Palestinians who wanted to open up the road and change these conditions. In order to accomplish such a change they had to carry out armed struggle, which depended on meagre resources.

I will not be telling a secret if I say that at that time there were two viewpoints. One believed that it was impossible to embark on armed struggle until Al Fatehs popular and military roots had become stronger so that its strength and continuity could be ensured. The other believed that armed struggle must begin even with the minimum resources, as these, through action, would develop, become stronger and deep rooted. The latter viewpoint was the one that was adopted.

Like any other true revolutionary action, in its early stages, Al-Fateh was strongly attacked. The nature of the attack depended on the circumstances of each of the Arab states. The Arab progressive circles considered Al-Fateh as a reactionary movement. The Arab reactionary circles accused Al-Fateh of being communist and Marxist.

Khouli: In reality it was . . . ?

Abu Eyad: This is a secret which only God knows. On the whole a decision was taken to start the armed struggle in spite of the limited resources.

Actually prior to the start of military action, we published a simple magazine "Filistinuna" (Our Palestine). It used to express the view of the members without bluntly mentioning Al-Fateh or al-Asifah. When this magazine declared that the Palestinian people must have an independent entity with a will and a personality of its own, we were faced with another accusation that we were regionalists. This accusation came from the national parties. Of course they began to review their stand with regard to this question. We were also accused of Nazism and Fascism. We realized the necessity of proving ourselves to the Palestinian and Arab people by undertaking a national progressive armed action that would lead them to liberation. As I have already said the viewpoint favoring the start of military operations won in spite of limited resources, and this coincided with the establishment of the PLO.

Khouli: Before we move to another subject, would you perm it me to enquire about the financial sources of Al-Fateh in this early stage that enabled it to embark on its military operations. There is no doubt, however limited were the resources, that the question of financing is relevant.

Abu Eyad: Al-Fateh was financed by its Palestinian members. In reality, and because of our desire for secrecy, we decided not to take one penny except from members of Al-Fateh. We can now declare and it is no longer a secret we aspired to technical work and activity in rich Arab oil areas such as the Arab Gulf. This might have also resulted in surrounding Al-Fateh with a special atmosphere. This did not frighten us because our aim was to secure total self-dependence for the revolutionary movement especially so with regard to financing. The members used to deprive themselves of the simple things which one can buy in the Gulf area, in order to save as much as they could from their salaries for the movement; a minimum of half the salary or more than that.

Before embarking on military action now we can announce this secret we levied a heavy tax on all our members which they paid to a special fund. Those who did not have the requited sum had to borrow it. The reason behind this step was to secure for the families of those who the in the military operation's financial assistance in case the movement fails. We deposited this fund with certain trustworthy Palestinian personalities to be responsible for the distribution of the money.

Khouli: Al-Fateh started the armed struggle in January 1963. Is this true?

Abu Eyad: Yes, on 1 January 1963.

Khouli: Can we know something about the first military operation of Al- Fateh? Precisely what was its aim militarily and politically speaking?

Abu Eyad: The first operation was a confrontation with an Israeli armed patrol. Actually the second operation of Al-Fateh was of value. Its aim was to attack the installations set up to divert the Jordan River. As you know, the basic issue in 1963 was the diversion of the Jordan River and for this purpose the Arab summit conferences were convened. We held the view that through the diversion issue we could erupt the beginnings of the Palestinian revolution. A revolution which can continue and leave its effective landmarks on the Zionist, racist, imperialist presence in our homeland; and thus develop the partial issue, namely that of diversion, into a whole that of liberation by blowing up the Israeli diversion operations with our limited potentialities. We carried out this operation in which the first fighter of al-Asifah, Mahmoud Hijazi, was captured. He was tortured and imprisoned. He was captured because his gun was rusty and was of no use to him.

Also in this operation our first martyr, Ahmad Musa, was killed not by the enemy bullets, but by those of an Arab upon his return after the operation was carried out. The groups which entered the occupied territories were given orders not to shoot the Arab soldiers under any circumstances, even if the latter fired on them. The aims behind this were that a commando must not kill an Arab even if he were defending himself, and that guerrilla action must express the tragedy of the Palestinian people.

Khouli: What were the reactions to your first operation?

Abu Eyad: The truth is that we felt that the Palestinian and Arab people reacted positively to our action, with the exception of a few groups and individuals. Some of these attacked us directly, such as certain Arab newspapers which accused the commandos of being agents of CENTO in the area.

Others directly admitted that such action is good and beneficial but reprimanded it for not having coordinated its activities with the progressive Arab states before embarking on it. Yet others requested the implementation of a common plan between the commandos and the Arab states at that time. A third group said that the timing was wrong. And a fourth said that these are one or two adventurous operations and such action has no future. Yet the operations continued and the communiques too. Those who carried the attack against guerrilla action were silenced and the people began to reciprocate on a larger scale. Yet at the same time obstacles in the face of Al- Fateh and its movement began to increase. In addition to limited arms the national organized forces did not support the armed struggle of Al-Fateh, contrary to expectations.

The majority of the Arab governments were against Al Fateh. This hostility was expressed in several ways. The Unified Arab Command, for example, recommended and gave orders, which we now possess, requesting the Arab governments to discourage the commandos and not to broadcast or publish any military operation of al-'Asifah forces.

Khouli: What do you think was the aim behind that?

Abu Eyad: I believe that the aim was not to link the masses with the armed struggle by knowing about it, so that they would take it as their own and assist it. To be fair you should mention that certain Arab newspapers tried to publish the Israeli communiques about our operations when they were incapable of publishing the military communiques of Al Fateh. Of course we did not keep quiet in face of this wall of silence. We tried to penetrate it by issuing secret publications which were distributed all over the Arab world. In spite of the great number of pamphlets that were distributed, as regards the Arab homeland, it was still limited.

Khouli: In your estimation when was the wall of silence removed, before or after the June 1967 defeat?

Abu Eyad: It was removed in 1966 at the time of the Israeli aggression against al-Samu village. The Jordanian people strongly expressed their support of guerrilla action and called for freedom for such action. The country witnessed large and spontaneous demonstrations which expressed the consciousness of the people. The national and progressive forces could not understand these demonstrations and did not have a unified program to reap their advantages. That was the reason behind the failure of the demonstrations, and guerrilla action was subjected to more severe persecution and counter propaganda through press conferences and broadcasting services pointing out that the subject of commandos does not pertain solely to Jordan but to a general Arab attitude in accordance with the decisions of the Arab Unified Command. Of course, this command was exploited in an organized manner because it included, in addition to Jordan, certain Arab progressive regimes at the time.

The most important result was that the wall of silence surrounding guerrilla action was broken. The number of people who were arrested in Jordan was great. They were not all from Al-Fateh but included every nationalist who was accused of being a member of Al-Fateh, or a guerrilla or a supporter of guerrilla action.

Khouli: What happened after the June defeat?

Abu Eyad: The defeat has resulted in a feeling of bewilderment among the Arab masses who have refused, at the same time, to surrender. The six-day war did not end with the Israeli victory on 10 June, because on the second day al-Asifah men attacked the occupied territories for the first time after the defeat. The value of carrying out military action on 11 June was to overcome the feeling of despair and bewilderment and manifest the determination of the Arab people in general and the Palestinian people in particular not to surrender and to carry on the war against the enemy.

Following that, our fighting patrols increased their visits into Palestine. I will not be telling a secret if I disclose that the great majority of Al-Fateh leaders entered the occupied territories, in addition to those who were there already, to organize the popular Palestinian resistance movement. Such an operation was not easy at the beginning and we met many difficulties. For example, it was difficult to train fighters under occupation in spite of absolute secrecy. The enemy's ability to move its intelligence services was quick at a time when our intelligence services had not yet been trained actively to con front that of the enemy as is the case now. As a result the enemy was able to discover, every now and then, some of our training cells in the mountains. The enemy used to attack these cells fiercely, and the commandos, at that time, were not yet able to hit back effectively because they had primitive weapons. Consequently, a number of them were killed faring training.

Khouli: Without interfering with military secrets how did you then face the problem of modem arms?

Abu Eyad: The set-back, in spite of its bitterness, has helped us in solving the problem of armament. After the defeat we sent special patrols to the battlefields of the occupied territories with one aim, namely, to collect the largest amount possible of the arms left behind by the Arab armies. We can bluntly say that Al-Fateh took amounts of arms from the occupied Arab territories after the defeat which superseded, qualitatively and quantitatively, the arms it possessed throughout the earlier period of its struggle, even after the Arab state's recognition of Palestinian resistance and its struggle. This was our main source of armament.

Khouli: But the need for arms is continually increasing in proportion to the growth of the resistance movements operations. Naturally other sources must be found. Yet, in accordance with the historical experiments of the resistance movements, an important source is the enemy itself. Have you taken this into consideration? If the answer is yes what is the approximate ratio?

Abu Eyad: Our basic emphasis was on training. The enemy's arms is a basic principle in guerrilla warfare. This was, still is, and will continue to be a part of our evaluation. But, in order to be realistic, I should declare that we consider the amount of arms captured from the enemy far below the required quantity. It does not form more than 10 per cent of our arms. Naturally such a percentage is double what it was once. We have taken this into account.

Khouli: With your permission, let us go back to the general trend of the conversation. How did you face the complex situation directly after the defeat?

Abu Eyad: Our first emphasis was on guerrilla warfare training, on the the one hand, and reorganizing Arab rule, I mean in Jordan, and establishing new cells to confront the requirements of the new situation after the whole of Palestine had fallen under the Israeli occupation. The number of people who joined the resistance movement was greater than expected, and the enthusiasm of the people enhanced our activity. the cells which had existed during

We can say that the phase of training and organization of cells was completed precisely, on 29 August 1967, and a new phase of organized resistance operations on a grand soak was embarked upon.

Khouli: Why specifically 29 August 1967?

Abu Eyad: Prior to this date we had completed a great deal of training. We had organized our main cells and moved the largest amount of arms possible from the Arab occupied territories.

Here I would like to clarify an important point. We could have postponed the starting of organized resistance on a wide scale for a few weeks after 29 August in order to complete the training of the greatest number, enlarge our cells, develop more and make more than one level of our organizations politically aware, but we were forced to start our operations on that date in Jerusalem, Tul Kann and other places.

Khouli: Why?

Abu Eyad: For a number of important considerations. First, it was not healthy from the political, military and psychological points of view to freeze the organizations and the fighters after the degree of training we had reached. Second, freezing with no movement made us more vulnerable to dangers. Third, the enemy began to sense and hear about a number of our secret bases.

For these reasons we decided to strike so that the enemy could not surprise us with a counterattack. Actually we started, and Al Fateh continued, to fight alone until December 1967. Our brothers in PFLP started their armed struggle in the first half of January 1968. Of course following that date the operations continued and the establishment of small organizations continued until we reached the situation which I have discussed earlier. These are, as far as can be published, the principal points with regard to the formation, ideology and action of Al-Fateh.

Khouli: Permit me here, before we proceed to another subject, to ask a question; How was the decision taken to start organized resistance on 29 August 1967? Who took the final decision? In other words, was this derision adopted on political grounds and a comprehensive analysis of the situation or was it taken on military grounds to prevent a counterattack by the enemy and to unfreeze the cells and fighters? Who took the decision: the political leadership or the fighters? If it is possible, I hope that the answer will cover a more detailed definition of the- relationship between political action and military action in Al-Fateh?

Abu Eyad: I am grateful for being given the opportunity through this question to explain Al-Fateh's understanding of such an important question. Evidently you are aware of the accusation that Al-Fateh is only interested in military action; that it is composed of a group of adventurers and this was actually said who are only interested in hitting, killing and frightening the enemy; and that Al-Fateh is a prisoner of this traditional role which it cannot overcome to indulge in political activities.

I am still unaware of the reasons on the basis of which such an accusation is made. Is it possible that military action in an armed resistance, a guerrilla warfare, or a liberating movement be separated from political action?

On the whole we in Al-Fateh clearly recognize that military action is of no value if it does not serve a political program and is not a part of a comprehensive political plan. The first nucleus of Al-Fateh was formed on a political basis which rejected a specific political situation and developed its own political beliefs, which they believed, and still believe, will lead to the accomplishment of their aim. Out of the political attitude of Al-Fateh emerged the military action of the armed resistance movement as a concrete manifestation of such a line. Military action follows Al-Fatehs political orientation. We thus believe that we have placed political action in its right place. We in Al-Fateh struggle in the political and military fields. Either one of these two fields serves the other within the general framework of the strategic plan of Al-Fateh. Thus we do not separate or distinguish between political and military action. To ensure the implementation of such a policy we do not admit to the armed struggle movement any fighter unless he is recommended by the political organization.

Khouli: Does this imply that all the fighters in al-Asifah have been members in the political organization of Al-Fateh and the latter has recommended them for military action?

Abu Eyad: This is the principle we follow and apply. But in order to be honest with you, there have been exceptions to this rule for special reasons and on the basis of our political evaluation. I do not deny that in spite of the fact that we have been forced to do so and it has erased us some trouble which I cannot divulge and discuss eight now. Yet such an exception has strengthened our belief in the necessity to adhere to the general rule, namely, that a member in Al-Fateh is in the first place political and in the second a fighter. The exception took place in the first difficult phase of the development of Al-Fateh, following the defeat, when we were forced to accept volunteers for direct fighting without their passing through the membership of its political organization. Almost two months after the battle of al-Karameh we reapplied the general rule, no fighter is accepted unless he is recommended by the political organization. This clarifies the point that the political organization and mentality is at the head.

Khouli: A question for clarification. For example, when an operation is thought of, the fighting unit might have an idea . . . Can its military leadership carry it out directly or has it to discuss its political implications in addition to the military ones? Thus will the final decision be taken by the political leadership?

Abu Eyad: It might be helpful if I answer this question by giving you a specific example which up till now has been a secret. When we decided to embark on organized armed resistance on a wide scale, our brothers inside the occupied territories demanded that it should start on 20 August 1967, yet those who were outside the occupied territories thought otherwise. What did we do? We called all of the political leaders, including those of the occupied territories such as Abu Imad, in order to discuss carefully the problem from both the political and military points of view. We requested the leadership inside the occupied territories to postpone starting operations until the leadership took a decision. The discussions lasted for nine days and it was decided to start military operations. For that reason operations started on 29 August. This explains that we do not carry out military action except in the light of comprehensive political orientation. Operations carried out by the resistance movement are military in nature yet they are political and have definite political aims. If they were simple military operations, then they would become demagogic and the work of adventurers. These false impressions might have resulted from our emphasis, in the face of the political circumstances, that our method in the struggle is that of armed struggle. Will you be amazed if I tell you that in Al-Fateh there is no professional military man or leader. There is no fighter in Al-Fateh who is not a university student, an engineer, nationalist intellectual, or a worker. We do not have classical military men. Some people considered this situation a short-coming which Al-Fateh should be criticized for. Our differences with some of our brothers in the Palestine Liberation Army (FLA) pertained to this point. They used to ask us: W here are the officers? W here are the lieutenants? W here are the captains? We told them that we are fighting a war of liberation in which the fighters and the leaders leant the tactics of war from the war itself. Unless they become an army and leadership, a true and active force through practicing and leading armed struggle over a long period and according to plan. We do not have a military leader who is a graduate of a military college. All the leaders were trained during the war and learnt the art of war from the war with the enemy, itself.

In the general command of Al-Fateh, within the central committee, there is a distribution of responsibility. There are colleagues who have political responsibilities and others military. Yet all of them represent one unit. In 1963, when we started our activity, we issued a political statement; and in 1967 we did the same.

I would like to take this opportunity to clarify one point, in Al-Fateh there is nothing in the name of the military wing as reported by the newspapers and broadcasting services.

Khouli: How is this? What about al-Asifah?

Abu-Eyad: This is precisely the point. How did the word al-Asifah emerge? The principle and only thing we have is Al-Fateh. Yet when we embarked upon our military operations in January 1963, the majority of those who attended the congress which we called for this purpose supported the view that operations should be started. The minority which opposed this view suggested that operations should be carried out under another name so that if they fail, Al-Fateh would not be affected. Consequently we used the name of al-Asifah.

We did not announce that al-A sifah was actually Al-Fateh except after the 10th military communique and the success of the operations. We decided to continue the use of the name al-Asifah since it has become a historic one, but in reality Al-Fateh and al-Asifah are synonymous.

Khouli: Can we know something about the organization of Al-Fateh, the nature of the relationship between the commandos on different levels from the base to the top, if it is not to be kept secret.

Abu Eyad: The organizational structure of Al-Fateh is actually a secret. Yet I would like to assure you that relationships have developed, since the secret development of Al-Fateh, from a narrow form of centralization into a revolutionary democracy governed by specific organizational regulations to which all members adhere from the base to the top.

Khouli: There is another point. I have noticed through my contact with you that you are all careful in portraying the nature of collective leadership in Al-Fateh. Then you decided to appoint Abu Atomar as the official spokesman of Al-Fateh. What is the principle idea behind this decision and bow does it reflect itself on the principle of collective leadership and its implementation?

Abu Eyad: As you have pointed out, collective leadership is a basic and essential principle of Al-Fateh. This conclusion was not reached as a result of being outwardly fascinated by revolutionary expressions, but as a result of the suffering that we and our youth have gone through. Individualism was one of the causes of failure, hesitancy, etc... The principle of collectivism, especially with regard to leadership, expressed our extreme reaction against the principle of individualism in all its forms. Al-Fateh may have succeeded in maintaining its unity~~and cohesiveness as a result of its adherence to the principle of collectivism. Al-Fateh was originally a secret movement and its leaders were unknown. Their names remained secret. If it were not for the necessity of personal contacts to carry on the work, none of its members would have been publicly known. We were forced to announce a number of the names of its members. A section of our leadership, who might be better and more virtuous than those of us whose names are known, remains secret. Moreover, the widening scope of action and responsibilities compelled us to put forward to the masses an official responsible man. This is especially so since in Beirut pamphlets and communiques began to be issued in the name of Al-Fateh, at a time when it had nothing to do with them and they did not express its point of view. Who could stand up and declare publicly to the people in the name of Al-Fateh what belonged to it and what did not? There was no one. Moreover, the Israeli broadcasting service and press began to stress the name of Abu Animar as one of the leaders of Al-Fateh in the occupied territories. In addition he was a commando who carried both political and military responsibilities. A t one of its meetings the leadership chose him as the official_ spokesman of Al-Fateh. He was not present at the meeting and knew of the decision as others did. There is a special reason for choosing Abu 'Ammar, besides other reasons pertaining to his long standing struggle, and that is of us all he is the least garrulous. Actually the idea was to announce three names as the official spokesmen of Al-Fateh, but they all refused. Since Abu Ammar was the only absent one, he was chosen.

The decision was announced publicly and he could not but accept. Evidently any member of a liberation movement prefers secrecy, unless it is necessary to act otherwise. You are aware of the difficulties we encountered in nominating colleagues of ours in the leadership to the executive committee of the PLO in its new form, because this implied the disclosure of their names. Thus, there is no relationship between nominating Abu Ammar as the official spokesman of the movement and the collective leadership. It was merely an answer to urgent necessities.

Khouli: You explained in your discussion that military action is subject to and in the service of the political programs of Al-Fateh, can we know the main characteristics of these programs?

Abu Eyad: We cannot discuss the political programs of Al-Fateh without including the objective circumstances pertaining to its establishment and through which it operates. Generally speaking, it is a national liberation Movement which works for the realization of the Palestinian people's potentialities through their armed struggle for the liberation of all of Palestine from the imperialism of Zionist colonization. Al-Fateh has declared from the start that it is a national liberation movement. This implies that Al-Fateh considers itself to be a part of the whole Arab revolution, the signs of which are beginning to Appear in certain parts of the Arab homeland. Moreover, Al- Fateh considers itself to be a part of the progressive world movement against imperialism, in spite of the fact that the actual conscious application of this clear political content is caused by objective circumstances which are known to the Arab citizen. Al-Fateh is criticized, and this may indirectly shed some light on its political line, because it calls only for the liberation of the land and does not tackle the problem of man and society. We say that this is nonsense. Liberation of the land cannot be achieved except through the liberation of man. A revolution cannot raise the banner of liberation and practice the method of armed struggle, unless it is a progressive revolution. We have never heard in the history of the world of a rightist who carried arms in the face of imperialism. In other words, since Al-Fateh, at the phase of its formation, admitted and accepted grouping all of the Palestinian youth who were engulfed in Arab politics and were members of different parties in order to express their sufferings as Palestinian refugees, it opened the way, without complications, for this youth to reconsider their unproductive political activity and practice productive, effective and armed political activity. Al-Fateh opened the door for the youth who believed in the theories and ideology which might belong to this front or that, to group them within the framework of armed struggle. Armed struggle purifies the soul, wipes out sensitivity and makes them follow a truly revolutionary progressive course of action. Thus Al-Fateh from the beginning was interested in grouping people from the extreme right to the extreme left. Through interaction within the revolution and through armed struggle the true revolutionary youth will emerge.

Khouli: What were the conditions for their joining Al-Fateh?

Abu Eyad: The Palestinian youth had to dissociate themselves from their ideologies and party affiliations and believe in liberation. This was the bask condition. At this point we should differentiate between strategy and tactics. The past and present announcements of Al-Fateh may be considered as a tactic more than a long-range strategy. For example, the question of non-interference in the internal affairs of the

Arab states to which Al-Fateh is committed has aroused criticism such as that of being a rightist slogan. I believe that this slogan is, objectively speaking, sound. It requires of Al-Fateh to be disinterested in who is the prime minister of this state or that. In reality there is an interconnection between Palestinian action and Arab action, and for this reason we have always declared that we are part of the Arab revolution. From where did tills interconnection stem? We believe that the progressive slogans of the Arab nation cannot be achieved except through the war of Palestine and its liberation. Even socialism and unity cannot be achieved except through a true war of liberation of Palestine because Arab efforts are of necessity directed to that course of action. This is the case irrespective of whether such production is fruitful or not yet. The most important thing is that Arab efforts in the field of production must be directed to the war of liberation. How can we build an advanced social life in our countries at a time when all our material efforts (money and means of production) are channeled towards the war machine against the aggressive colonialist enemy? From here the slogan of non-interference in the internal affairs of the Arab states stems. It does not imply non-interference between the Arab states and Palestine. Thus it helps in bringing the objective circumstances of the Palestinian Liberation movement to fruition by grouping the Arab forces with no diversionary side issues. At the same time it creates a revolutionary atmosphere along the

Arab borders with Israel and among the Arab people living near the borders. Such a revolutionary atmosphere may spread all over the Arab world. Thus Arab hopes and progressive thoughts will be achieved through a revolutionary atmosphere along the Arab borders with Israel and among the Arab people living near these borders. Such a revolutionary atmosphere may spread all over the Arab world. Thus Arab hopes and progressive thoughts will be achieved through a real war inside Palestine itself. If it is necessary to give examples, we can take Jordan or Lebanon in which the national and progressive forces, irrespective of their differences, can move. Another example is the idea put forward by some that the "petit bourgeoisie" has failed and does not have the right to struggle. Al-Fateh has by-passed these matters as a result of its experiences. It said that every Palestinian has the right to participate in the war of liberation, but the leadership of Palestinian action must be in the hands of honorable national people who will not sell or bargain or transfer this action for the benefit of any reactionary forces. The leadership could limit action to a certain class. But such action is not the privilege of any one class, in addition it would weaken the liberation movement. There are classes and groups which were not known at the time of Karl Marx. Did Karl Marx discuss the question of the class of refugees that has emerged among the Palestinian people? The refugee was a laborer working in his country but now is unemployed. There are refugees who were peasants but now are unable to do this work. How can we evaluate this and that. Evidently there is a class of refugees that imposes itself upon us and cannot be defined according to classical lines even if they were revolutionary. This is what we are facing openly and fearlessly.

There are some who criticize Al-Fateh for not adopting a Marxist- Leninist course, or something similar that is defined as progressive. I say that if we ask those who are at present propagating such a course what their background was and former practices were, we find that they are very firm Marxist-Leninists. Al-Fateh, which has not declared that it is a Marxist-Leninist movement, was the first to undertake armed struggle, offered martyrs and opened the long way for the war of liberation. Uttering words is not enough. Action is the determining factor. We say that Al-Fateh's actions are related to progressive thought more than those who merely declare their support for such thought. The important thing in any revolution is not propagating an ideology but actual action. Ideology alone is meaningless if it is not put to the test.

Khouli: This will lead us to discuss the social structure of Al-Fateh. If you want to explain more, 1 say that at the early stages of its development the more dominant feature in Al-Fateh was that of the educated intellectuals meaning that the majority of its members and leaders were educated Palestinians. The question is: Is this still the dominant feature even after the development of Al-Fateh and the increase in its membership, or have other social groupings joined it after June 1967, such as workers, peasants and craftsmen and thus changed this feature?

Abu Eyad: This is closely and organically linked to the principal slogan of national liberation which was raised by Al-Fateh and which it is still raising. Such a slogan is a wide one and can encompass all the national forces, groups and classes which believe in national liberation. Yet a person cannot deny the clear fact that the majority of the people who participate in the armed struggle are workers, peasants and revolutionary intellectuals.

Khouli: In training its members for the struggle does Al-Fateh pay attention to the political aspect alongside the military fighting aspect? Do you have the opportunity to educate political-military cadres in special schools for organizing the cadres? How is this carried out if such schools exist?

Abu Eyad: Naturally the political and military education of the cadres is an essential question in Al-Fateh. In the absence of such an education Al- Fateh would not have been able to survive, develop and be strengthened. This is accomplished within the limits of the phase of national liberation. For such a purpose our cadres are taught the Palestinian reality, problems and aims in addition to both the Arab and international realities. We also pay great attention to the reality of the enemy. Knowing the enemy's policies, economy, parties, thought, method of living and armed forces is a principal matter for every commando in Al-Fateh. Moreover, we acquaint our cadres, without complications, with world experiences in national liberation. We believe that we should benefit from such experiences, but at the same time we believe that attaining victory necessitates that we produce from our actual circumstances a national experience which will also enrich world experience. We study the experiences of the world and we have published them in pamphlets which are regularly distributed to our cadres and discussed. As for the cadres' schools, we have such schools, but we are dissatisfied with them, and we are studying the possibility of improving and strengthening them. Some of these schools have been closed for reasons which are beyond our control, and that was during the stage of transferring our activity and its leadership from Damascus to Jordan.

Khouli: Actually the spatial movement you have discussed reminds me of certain opinions uttered about the Palestinian resistance, which I do not personally agree with, but I will put them forward in order to know your opinion about them. A summary of these opinions is that resistance, or guerrilla warfare, or a liberation revolution must stem from the occupied territories. According to such views the Palestinian resistance movement is located outside the occupied territories. Naturally these

100

ideas are classical and do not take into consideration the nature of the circumstances of the Palestinian movement. I do not want here to expose in detail my opinion, but I would like to get acquainted with your opinion and the extent to which the forces of the Palestinian people can be mobilized inside and outside the occupied territories.

Abu Eyad: These opinions evidently confuse two things. In the first place there is a difference between the leadership of the armed liberation and the revolution. It would be true to say that some of the leaders are outside Palestine that is to say they are located outside it. But the revolution itself both in terms of people and the way it is carried out stems from and actually exists inside it. This is historically known and a natural phenomenon of all the national liberation revolutions.

As for our action or revolution, objectively speaking, the Palestinian people are carrying out, under objective circumstances, a revolution which differs from the rest of the world revolutions. Why? Because the people, as it is clear, are socially, politically and geographically dispersed. Such a situation imposes the application of methods for the struggle. In spite of that within the general framework ours is not an innovation among the world revolutions. Let us, for example, analyze the Yugoslav revolution. This revolution had wide stretches of land, and areas fortified by their geo graphical position, at its disposal it was in the Blade

Mountain as far as I remember that the leaders of the revolution headed by Tito were to be found, i.e., inside Yugoslavia. Another example is the Algerian revolution whose leadership was found outside the country in spite of the nature of the wide land and geographic fortifications, and in spite of the fact that the Algerian people were all inside the country. This did not arrest the revolution and prevent it from attaining victory.

In our Palestinian revolution we are located both inside and outside the occupied territories. This is natural. In the inside we are in our occupied country, because we do not recognize the Zionist-Israeli entity. Thus our revolution is in a natural form and cannot be compared as in some foreign newspapers with the French resistance, which was led from London, against the Nazi occupation. Only a few meters separate the leadership, which Is located outside, from the occupied territories.

Colonial Zionist imperialism has expelled a great number of our people from part of their land. By virtue of such expulsion, those who were not expelled and kept their land will initiate resistance. From where will the revolution emanate? It will emanate from the West Bank and the Gaza Strip. These are two parts of Palestine we do not recognize a land called Israel. The revolutionary movement must be located in it because we consider it, in its totality, Palestine.

Israel with the whole of the Arab land bordering Palestine constitutes one unit, the land of the Palestinian revolutionary bases are located in this area, and we have many bases inside the occupied territories. If it were not for these bases, we would have been unable to carry out any military action. In the absence of such bases, the revolution would be completely isolated. The principle bases are those located inside the occupied territories, and those which are located outside constitute a continuous source of supply for the revolution by virtue of the Palestinian peoples circumstances, which I have already discussed.

Khouli: Don't you think that the Arabs inside Israel have been continuously neglected and that the difficult circumstances under which they are living have not been appreciated?

Abu Eyad: The truth is that I cannot say that there was any negligence or lade of appreciation. The evidence is our recognition that the best of our modem poetry is that of our brothers in the occupied territories, eg. Samih al-Qasim, Mahmud Darwish, Tawfiq Zyad, e tc .. All of them have contributed to the enrichment of the Arab revolution in general, and the Palestinian revolution in particular, by their humanitarian, honest and good words. This is the aim of revolutionaries in their struggle.

At the same time we appreciate their conditions and we do not attempt, either directly or indirectly, to provide the Zionist-Nazi force with motives to torture them more. Such is the nature of the torture which they are facing courageously that we do not ask them to carry arms and they are not required to do so.

At the same time we deeply appreciate the demonstrations of the Palestinians men and women in Nazareth and the surrounding areas of the Galilee District. This proves their adherence to the land and country in spite of the suffering, terror, arrest, imprisonment, eviction, confinement to quarters, confiscation of property, etc., inflicted upon them by the Zionists. For this reason we do not endeavor to organize them according to Al-Fatehs system of organization.

Abu Eyad: Here I do not need to say more than that they are being mobilized. Evidence will be found in daily demonstrations and the numerous different forms of passive resistance to the occupation. At this point we should mention, with great appreciation, the role of the Palestinian women which has reached the level of armed resistance. The Israeli prisons are full of thousands of the sons and daughters of our people who reject occupation and resist it in every way and bear all kinds of psychological and physical torture. In this connection I would like to tell you of an incident which took place more than two months ago in Nablus. Under pressure from world public opinion the Israeli authorities permitted a Red Cross delegation to visit our imprisoned sisters in the jail of Nablus. They received the delegation with a song, "My country, my country, Al-Fateh is the revolution against the aggressors. The prison guards were unable to stop them. The representatives of the Red Cross could not hide their impression.

Actually one of the most important results of the armed Palestinian revolution is the emergence of the Palestinian woman and her role as a commando equal to the Palestinian man T h armed action and sacrifice. The important feature in all this is that the Palestinian woman, through the revolution, was able to overcome all the traditions according to which she was brought up in old Palestine. Nothing stands in her way for the liberation of her country, neither death, nor imprisonment, nor torture. Thus, the Israeli intelligence services, which have depended in their psychological propaganda on old traditions against the progress of the Palestinian woman in the field of struggle, failed because in reality the Palestinian people men and women have overcome these traditions. The enemy has propagated accusations of assaulting honor, etc., but this did not prevent women from joining the revolution en masse and carrying arms against the enemy.

Khouli: This is natural because national armed struggle always achieves teal equality between man and woman through struggle and resisting the enemy. This took place in the colonized or occupied countries which had been underdeveloped in social relations and in which armed liberating revolutions broke out; such as Algeria, the under-developed areas of

Yugoslavia, the under-developed southern areas of Italy and now Palestine.

Abu Eyad: This is true.

Khouli: With your permission, let us move to discuss another point. From reading Al-Fateh's statements and documents, and through discussions with its leaders, it becomes clear that Al-Fateh is intent on careful distinction between Judaism and Zionism , and although it fights Zionism it does not harbor any animosity towards the Jews as human beings and Judaism as a religion. What is the practical meaning of this?

Abu Eyad: The meaning is that the Palestinian revolution is a revolution against racism, fascism and colonialism. Thus it is totally purified from racism, fascism and colonialism. On this basis it does not act or carry arms against the Jews as human beings and people. Al-Fateh is against the fascist, racist Zionist movement, which practices colonial imperialism in the homeland of the Palestinian people. Thus Zionism is a colonialist movement closely linked with imperialism. This is the movement, with its concepts and entities, which polarizes our animosity and which we confront with anus until our last breath. The strategy of the Zionist movement is based on:

- Exploiting what happened to the Jews, as individuals and groups in Europe at the hands of the Nazis to nourish the complex of persecution among them in order to enmesh them in the traps of Zionism. Under the influence of this complex, and for other reasons, the Zionist movement pushes the Jews to join its organizations and emigrate to Palestine awakening in them the evil feeling of revenge.
- The Jews cannot be absorbed in Palestine without expansion, not only at the expense of Palestine but also at the expense of Pales tines neighboring Arab countries.

These two elements of the policy of the Zionist movement are continuously interacting with each other. The proof is that whenever immigration to Palestine reaches a low ebb or is obstructed, Zionism and its organizations create secret societies composed of its terrorist members. These embark on campaigns of persecution of the Jews in order to terrorize them and deepen the persecution complex among them, thus forcing them to immigrate to Palestine. It has been possible at certain times to expose the reality of these organizations and their organic association with the Zionist movement. This happened in Brazil and other parts of the world where anti-Semitic movements made their appearance. As a result we talk and act on the basis of a deep awareness of the necessity of distinguishing between Judaism and Zionism. We are true to our long

Arab history and traditions. In the gloomiest ages the Arabs and Jews lived in peace and equality without any kind of prejudice. Since the Zionist movement's interference in the affairs of the Jews and Arabs it has poisoned the atmosphere, planted obstacles and practiced, against our people, all the barbaric methods it had learnt from Nazism, in addition to its colonialist usurpation of our homeland and the eviction by it of the Palestinian people. In the name of "the chosen people of God Zionism has implemented its racist colonialist plan. Zionism s endeavor to exploit religion to the maximum is very dear, it is forged and counterfeited religious bodes to prove to world Jewry that their place is in Palestine. In this context, all the non-religious Zionist parties, such as Dayan who declares that he is non-religious, concurred in rushing to the W ailing W all to exploit religion and the appearance of religion in order to convince the Jews. From here we realize that the question of Judaism and the Jews is separate from that of Zionism and its colonialist racist movement. Thus when we declared that through our struggle we aimed at the establishment of a Palestinian democratic state, it was not a tactic but a true and honest manifestation of our strategy. This is based on our conviction that among the Jews there are individuals of a good calibre with whom we can live in peace. In our opinion those who are fighting against our way of thinking are the Zionists. Take for example, the Zionist Israeli newspapers. After every operation we carry out, they publish comments on it in the following manner: These are the terrorists of Al-Fateh who want to establish a Palestinian democratic state. They always do that even if we are not responsible for the operation.

Khouli. What does Al-Fateh exactly understand by "Palestinian democratic state?

Abu Eyad: We have always believed and declared, and will continue to declare, that armed struggle is not an end in itself. It is a means for a great humanitarian aim. Since 1917 Palestine has been subjected to w an, revolutions and bloody fighting. The time has come for this land and its people to live in peace as other human beings. We carry arms in order to achieve a truly peaceful settlement of the problem, and not a false settlement based on the imposition of aggression and racism. Such peace cannot be achieved except within the framework of a democratic state in Palestine. What are its details? I believe that through the development of the struggle and fighting the details of such a state will be drawn up. But this is the wide strategic course which will encompass all these details.

Khouli: Within the framework of this wide strategic course will the Palestinian democratic state accept the Jews as equal citizens with the Arabs?

Abu Eyad: Of course we accept the Jews as equal citizens with the Arabs in everything. The meaning of the Palestinian democratic state is very clear. It only aims at eliminating the Zionist racist entity in Palestine.

Khouli: For the sake of more clarity, will Al-Fateh guarantee in word and deed the right to citizenship in the Palestinian democratic state to the anti- Zionist Jews who will declare their agreement with Al-Fatehs aim of establishing the new Palestinian democratic society? Is the right to citizenship guaranteed to the anti-Zionist Jews whether they have been in Palestine before or after 1948?

Abu Eyad: I repeat that this right will be guaranteed by Al-Fateh, as a liberation movement with humanitarian dimensions, not only to every anti- Zionist Jew but also to a Jew who has purified his soul of Zionist Ideas, meaning one who has been convinced that Zionist ideas are alien to human society.

Khouli: How does Al-Fateh view Israeli society? Does it still view it as a conglomeration of racism, colonialism, reaction and aggression? Or does Al Fateh see the emergence of certain progressive forces and tendencies in Israeli society even if they are small and weak opposing aggression, Zionism and racism? If Al-Fateh is aware of the existence of such forces and tendencies, what is its opinion of and attitude towards them?

Abu Eyad: There is no doubt that Israeli society, in its present form, is a colonialist, imperialist and racist society. We are attempting with all the means at our disposal to liquidate such a society and create its substitute, namely, a democratic anti-racist society open to humanity and the world. Actually Israeli society is closed to humanity and to every progressive movement in the world. Israel has not supported any liberation cause in the world. Thus when we said that we want to live with the Jews in a non-racist democratic Palestine, we primarily call on the progressive forces, if they exist, to strengthen their stand. There are certain forces in Israel which claim progressiveness, but in reality, they are false, Zionist, racist and imperialist.

Yet this does not prohibit us from saying that there is a small nucleus of progressive forces which have started to emerge and we sense their existence. They call for the liquidation of the Zionist entity, and we are sure that if their voices were heard and met with a positive reaction, they would suffer even more torture and persecution than that suffered by Al-Fateh. The truth is that there are signs of progressiveness, small beginnings. We hope and wish that such beginnings will grow and assert their belief in the right of the Palestinian people to live on their land. When I say the Palestinian people I mean all the people with all their sects: Christians, Muslims and Jews; but without the Zionist entity that is linked with colonialism. A country in which there will be no racism, no Zionism and no religious fanaticism.

Khouli: In accordance with the principle of frankness which we have agreed on, I perm it myself to ask the following question: Some

111

people say in spite of their appreciation of Al-Fatehs valor and its leadership of the Palestinian armed struggle that it is concerned with malting propaganda about itself and its action so that it has begun to appear in papers and broad casting services to be of a greater stature than it really is. What is your opinion of such an accusation?

Abu Eyad: 1 do not want to start by declaring that such a statement is un objective and contrary to the truth. But let us view the matter step by step and unemotionally. Has Al-Fateh started to concern itself with the propaganda aspect? The answer is yes. But if one says that the interest of Al-Fateh in propaganda is superseding that of the military aspect, then there is a basic error in the analysis in which such statements are uttered. Why? Because the question of propaganda for us, as a resistance movement, is one form of political action which complements and accompanies military action. Thus it is not action merely for the sake of propaganda. Propaganda basically revolves around persons; we refuse and resist this because it harms our struggle and movement. If this has happened unfortunately it is happening t is not Al- Fatehs fault but that of certain Arab journalists and newspapers whose enthusiasm and the necessities of incitement in journalism have blinded them. We in Al-Fateh do not agree with the journalists on that point and we have told them our opinion more than once; actually at times we have told them that such incitement is a disease and some Arab newspapers should get rid of it. Abu Ammar, in his capacity as the official spokesman of Al-Fateh, expressed frankly our stand vis–vis this question, and his opposition to publishing his picture if the occasion arises or in the absence of a time when they avoided publishing anything about the fighters as a group and a movement. I would like to assert once again that publishing the picture of the leaders will harm our work because it hinders their freedom of movement. The three oi four members of the leadership whose pictures have been published are greatly distressed. This is not an attempt to defend thank God my picture has not been published but it is the actual truth with regard to the necessities of work. On the other hand, I would like to assure you that publishing the picture of one or more of the leaders of Al-Fateh does not create any kind of sensitivity because the structure of collective leadership of our movement is so deep that the individual melts in the group. Thus the picture of Abu Ammar or any other member, as far as we are concerned, is that of Al-Fateh as a whole.

Khouli: You have said that information for Al-Fateh is not propaganda but political activity, what do you mean by that?

Abu Eyad: I mean that it is a part of the whole bottle of liberation, because the battle is not merely military statements which are announced and published without a continuous effort to explain Al-Fateh's thought and aims. There is an important matter which should not be neglected, namely that before the June war we met with great obstacles in the dissemination of information. All means of informing and contacting the Arab masses to explain our ideas, aims and methods of struggle were closed in our faces. Now these vistas have been opened and we have had to put ourselves forward to the masses and deepen our political ideas and the principles of our struggle, otherwise we would be greatly neglecting the rights of our movement and the Palestinian struggle as a whole. This required contacting people, dis closing names, etc. As for the fact that certain newspapers have deviated, and I stress the word deviated in presenting all this for the purpose of incitement or individualism; this is not in the least the fault of Al Fateh.

Khouli: If Al-Fatehs information is a political activity directed at the non-Arab people of the world, namely, the capitalist and socialist people, what are Al-Fatehs principal broad lines in this field?

Abu Eyad: The principle broad lines are based on presenting Al-Fateh to the world as a national liberation movement hostile to racism and colonialism, and one which, in its struggle, distinguishes between Judaism and Zionism. Thus our movement is a part of a humanitarian movement, whereas Zionism, which we have taken it upon ourselves to fight and liquidate, is the enemy of humanitarianism and not of the Arabs alone.

If you review what has been published lately about Al-Fateh in the foreign press whether in the West or East the success of Al-Fatehs plan will become clear. If we and this is not our fault have failed with regard to the press of the socialist camp which has not clarified Al- Fatehs aims in a satisfactory manner, the fault is not ours but theirs. I am saying that with regret and I am not attacking or alluding to the socialist camp or its press.

Khouli: Does Al-Fateh, within the framework of its plan of political information, envisage winning world Jewish public opinion which is against colonialism and Zionism? If this is the case, what steps have so far been adopted in this field?

Abu Eyad: Naturally we are concerned with this. Our concern stems from our principal point of view which distinguishes between a Jew and a Zionist, Zionism and Judaism. Thus we try to have relations with all the Jews who do not participate in consolidating, the Israeli colonialist, racist, closed society the Zionist society. I shall give you practical examples to prove the true meaning of my words. In January 1969 the Second International Conference in Support of the Arab Peoples was held in Cairo. All the departments, forces and Arab and foreign individuals among whom there were Jews who attended the conference were of the opinion that Al-Fateh's stand vis–vis this problem saved the conference, since it urged every progressive Jew, outside or inside Israel, to work for the liquidation of Zionism and its entity, and called for. the establishment of the Palestinian democratic state.

Another example. In February 1969 the Palestinian Theatrical Troop gave a play in Rabat in Morocco for the benefit of Al-Fateh. The Moroccan police forbade the Moroccan Jews from attending the play to protect their lives against the enthusiastic Moroccan masses. Our friends over there took it upon themselves to protect the lives of the Moroccan Jews and convinced the policemen to allow them to attend the play and see for themselves, through the play, the reality of the racist and non-humanitarian nature of the Israeli state. During the play the Moroccan citizens contributed to Al-Fateh expressing their support for its armed struggle. Among those who contributed was a Moroccan Jew, Ibrahim al-Sarafad, a professor in the School of Engineering at Muhammad Fifth University. He contributed one thousand dirhems as a token of his support for Al-Fateh in its struggle for the establishment of a democratic state in Palestine. He wrote us a letter in French explaining his stand and the reason for contributing to Al-Fateh in particular. His wife translated it to Arabic and gave her wedding ring to the resistance movement struggling against Zionism and its racist entity. Such stands towards Al-Fateh have become popular in a great number of European countries.

This Arab orientation towards the Jews who are against colonialism and Zionism, in addition to being an untactical action, could not have taken place if Al-Fateh had not carried arms. Through the armed struggle for liberation such an orientation was possible. If such a call had been put forward before Al-Fatehs armed struggle, it would have been fiercely opposed by Arab public opinion in general, and Palestinian public opinion in particular. The liberation weapon of Al-Fateh and its strength in the political and military fields gave this strategy the opportunity of being implemented.

Khouli: This is, to a great extent, true. 1 have other remarks which I would like to discuss with you in order to know Al-Fatehs opinion. From the time Al-Fateh embarked upon armed struggle in January 196$ up until 1967 ,1 can distinguish two phases in its history: first, the difficult phase of the starting point before June 1967 when Al-Fateh was isolated as a result of the press blockade and accusations of adventurism.

Abu Eyad: Unwillingly.

Khouli: Naturally. After June the blockade was removed, and the Arab masses and nation became aware of the existence of Al-Fateh. This was followed by the battle of Al-Karameh, March 1968, in which Al-Fateh proved itself politically and militarily. From that date the great and important phase of resisting the enemy started. Can you, through these two phases and the experience of August 1968, explain what Al-Fateh has precisely gained? Has the totality of the experience gained resulted in particular changes with regard to Al-Fatehs methods of resistance and activity?

Abu Eyad: With regard to the first phase Al-Fateh has benefited from organizing its cadres, or what we can call the nucleus of the real Palestinian struggle' which gave birth to the growing forces of the armed resistance movement. The most important thing which we have concentrated on and acquired from experience, during this phase, is educating the guerrillas to reject individualism and egoism, adhere to the group, get used to the most difficult work pertaining to the struggle, and offer sacrifices in difficult circumstances. In this phase you would start a battle and only few would support you, even the forces which were supposed to be our heirs did not support us at this time. Thus Al-Fateh was able to get rid of all the diseases of society, such as individualism, showing off and substituting action with futile discussions. When the post-June war phase began Al-Fateh had benefited from the earlier phase and was ready to confront it with cadres that were politically and militarily aware, In spite of all that certain errors were committed. Such of Al-Fateh, after the June battle could be traced bade to the opening war, to the Palestinian and Arab masses on a scale that its organizational and military apparatus was not yet ready to cope with. We went through a phase full of problems and difficulties which we had to overcome before we could enter the phase of wide-scale organized resistance in August 1968.

In all these phases there is one truth which has been revealed through beneficial experience, namely that a vanguard group, who believe in something stemming from the will of the people, on which they insist and for which they struggle, will be able to fulfill their aims despite the sacrifices and difficulties. I do not know if I have fully answered your remarks or not.

Khouli: I think you have but let us complete the picture. On the basis of Al-Fatehs position as a symbol of the aim ed Palestinian struggle internationally speaking, what does Al-Fateh have to say to the Palestinian people in general, and the other resistance organizations in particular?

Abu Eyad: I do not have any objections to answering your questions. But I fear that in answering this question I will appear as a preacher and adviser. Yet through my education in Al-Fateh I refuse to take such a position. I mean I do not w ant to stand and preach saying: My brothers this and that. With your permission, let us reformulate the question in the following manner: What can Al-Fateh contribute in the light of the present circumstances which are witnessing the emergence of numerous resistance organizations, and how can healthy relations be established for the benefit of Palestinian action aiming at liberation in spite of the present circumstances?" Do you approve this formulation?

Khouli: Yes.

Abu Eyad: There is a truth which should be admitted by our brothers in the different guerrilla organizations. Such an admission should be preceded by an admission on the part of Al-Fateh to the effect that it is not an ideal and infallible organization. Since in Al-Fateh there are wrong things, it is the duty of the other guerrilla organizations and honest critical outside observers to point out the mistakes to the members of Al-Fateh who cannot discern them in order to get rid of the mistakes which any national liberation movement commits. On the other hand, our brothers in the other guerrilla organizations should admit that the colonial and Zionist departments, the intelligence services of the imperialist countries, in addition to other counter revolutionary forces, work according to one plan to sabotage and deface Al Fateh. Evidently, they attempt to fight it directly using material and tangible means. They attempt to wage psychological warfare on Al-Fateh from both within and without. Sometimes sabotage is done by exaggerating Al-Fateh through the information media, or by attributing to Al-Fateh statements which it does not support, or by misinterpreting the essential policies which Al-Fateh adopts in its relations with the Arab states: they in these ways fight against Al-Fateh. Our brothers in the other organizations should comprehend that the destruction of Al-Fateh means the destruction of the totality of Palestinian guerrilla action, the movement of the Palestinian people, and the Arab progressive movement.

Khouli: I believe that we have reached the point where you can explain Al-Fatehs vision of the present Arab attitude vis–vis the battle of liberation on the one hand, and the armed Palestinian resistance movement on the other? I do not know if it is beneficial to divide the discussion into phases or not? Of course, this is left up to you.

Abu Eyad: Here are a number of remarks to be made in this connection. The first and basic one is that we did not fully and effectively mobilize all the Arab forces. At times and under certain circumstances not few we feel that certain aspects of the Arab reality are not involved in the fierce battle in all its dimensions.

Khouli: In your opinion what is the reason for that?

Abu Eyad: In my opinion the Arab masses participation in the battle implies their living and objectively understanding the realities of the battle without concealment or exaggeration and that they are assigned their proper role. The role of the masses when the country is under occupation is known mobilizing, training and giving arms to the people, and their participation in different forms in the battle. The Arab masses, up till now, have not been given this proper role. The implication behind this is that rebuilding the regular armies is not enough if the Arab masses role is neglected.

This is a reality which we should remember and it is not shameful to say it. The shame lies in hiding it, became we are all supposed to live for the battle. This is the first remade.

As for the second remark, it is that there is a difference between the Arab states adjacent to Israel and those far from it. If we feel the separation between those who live on the front and those who live in the duty in the same country, we feel greater separation among those who live in areas far from the borders. The Arab masses who are far away should know the reality of the Zionist danger; for it does not aim at certain areas in Pales tine, or this part of the Arab land or that, but it aims at the whole Arab nation. Thus the Arab individual who is living in areas far from the states adjacent to Israel does not have the right to say that the battle is not his. I believe that the Arab masses who are geographically separated from the land of the battle want to participate in the battle with all the power at their disposal.

Thus the duty of national leaders who are aware should be to develop the attitude of their government in order actually to participate in the battle. I do not say anything more than that.

The third remade concerns Palestinian resistance. Palestinian resistance is requited to develop and gradually escalate its activity inside the occupied territories. These are duties which the Arab people request. But we should ask a question: Is the escalation of the resistance a mechanical action; you press a button and Palestinian resistance is escalated, you press another one it is de-escalated? Not is not a mechanical action. It is a process of interaction on the part of the Arab people, providing the fighting people with Arab expertise. H as the Arab nation provided Palestinian resistance with what it requires?

I frankly say that the Arab people are ready to help, but certain obstacles are put between them and Palestinian resistance. If the resistance has the chance to meet the Arab masses without complications and formalities, the Arab people might play a great part in the battle alongside Palestinian resistance. It is not true that Palestinian resistance is regional. When we talk about Palestinian resistance and Palestinian people we do not separate the Palestinian people from the unified Arab nation which has the same destiny. National unity does not deny the existence of an Egyptian people or Iraqi people, etc. The Palestinian people have the right to appear after 20 years of burial and after having been charged with 1,000 different accusations. The appearance of the Palestinian people implies that of the Arab people. There is absolutely no contradiction between the appearance of the Palestinian people and their being a part of the large Arab nation. Thus Palestinian resistance is neither regional nor isolationist. It demands that the Arab people with the totality of their capacities should adopt it. Take for example the question of material aid, has any Arab government allocated in its budget a sum for Palestinian resistance? I say it frankly, is there one Arab state? On the contrary, the Arab governments have begun to interfere with the popular subscriptions which the resistance movement used to carry out, by setting up government committees for the support of guerrilla action to which collection of contributions is limited. These committees are headed by a minister or a government official. The collection of contributions has been subjected to state regulations, if the state has wanted the committee to continue its work, then contributions will continue, if not, they will stop. The government has turned the collection of contributions into a new tax to be paid by the people. We believe that the continuation of the operation on this basis will hinder the interaction between the resistance movement and the Arab people which is the essence of the operation.

These are my three remarks on the Arab reality. What do we hope for? We hope that the reasons for the three afore-mentioned remarks will disappear and that the masses will be effectively mobilized for the battle. We do not fail to pay due regard to the danger nor to dilute the battle. What do we mean by dilution? We can dilute the battle by confusing political and military action. We should explain to the people the meaning of political action and military action. The masses who participate in the battle will not be observers, and I say the participation of the masses is possible and it is a necessity. We should believe in the role of the peoples militia which can greatly hinder the enemy's effectiveness. We hope the subject of Palestinian resistance will be given enough attention and concern, materially and financially. At the same time we should show the people the truth without deception.

Khouli: Based on what you have said, I understand that Al Fatehs concept of the battle of liberation is Palestinian in its initiation, Arab in its dimension and essence. Isn't it so?

Abu Eyad: Exactly. The national dimension in the Palestinian revolution is essential and basic It is not mere words uttered in order to incite or reach the press. We cannot be separated from the struggle of the Arab nation and its struggling forces, otherwise we will be our own enemies before anything else.

Khouli: Don't you agree that it has become necessary to manifest, in a practical way, the national dimension of Palestinian resistance in order to be able to maneuver and surmount obstacles in its way? With regard to this I have three specific points. Firstly, hasn't it become necessary to work for the establishment of a comprehensive Arab popular front to rally around one specific aim, namely the protection and support of the resistance movement? Secondly, what is the attitude of Al-Fateh to the desire of many non-Palestinian Arab nationals who want to join the resistance movement and participate in the armed struggle? The third point pertains to the question of coordination between Palestinian armed resistance and the regular Arab armies. With reference to this point, there is a view which says that Palestinian resistance cannot alone liberate Palestine, thus the Arab regular armies should out of necessity intervene.

Objectively speaking, to what extent can a phase of the struggle be achieved in which the two forces and methods are used guerrilla warfare and the movement of regular armies without infringing the freedom of action and independence of the resistance movement?

Abu Eyad: Actually Al-Fateh has declared that one of its direct short-range aims is the establishment of the Arab front. Al-Fateh is not solely responsible for the creation of such a front. It is the responsibility of all the Arab national forces in addition to Al-Fateh. Al-Fateh had made contacts, more than once, for this purpose. It seems that the multiplicity of the Palestinian organizations has obstructed the formation of the front in an organized manner.

On the information side, Al-Fateh called for the creation of an Arab front for the support of guerrilla action. Practically speaking, Al-Fateh considered a great number of the Arab youth in the Arab states, especially in the national and progressive circles, to be the front. It is true that such a front was not organized, and it is necessary and our duty to organize it. But, as I have pointed out, the responsibility is that of Al-Fateh and the other national and progressive forces. Actually we have witnessed, in certain cases and at certain times, that the response of some people with regard to the establishment of the front was vitiated with unbelief as a result of the local differences existing in this or that state.

It is our duty and very necessary to think of a practical way of forming the front. I recall the proposal which you have put forward and which was published more than once and was calling for the conveying of a preparatory conference for this front to be attended by all the national and progressive forces in the Arab homeland. What can we do when these forces are divided against each other? For example, in Lebanon the national and progressive forces have not yet been able to form a unified powerful and effective front. Each one of them wants to be the sole supporter of armed struggle, or of Al-Fateh in particular, without the participation of the others. The different trends inside the national and progressive forces in the Arab homeland are hindering the creation of the front. We hope that in the near future these forces can develop their attitudes and lessen the sensitivities and existing differences among them for the sake of the Arab struggle in general, and the Palestinian struggle in particular, and agree on a minimum program , namely supporting the armed Palestinian struggle, irrespective of the organization. The important thing is to support the concept of armed struggle for liberation in order to stop the recurrence of what happened in an Arab state against us and comprehend the reality of our stand through this front.

Khouli: I believe that under the present circumstances we are capable of overcoming all these problems and differences and, thus, of creating the Arab front. This is our role in the struggle. The nucleus for building the front is the Palestinian armed struggle, which has become the true and practical way for the liberation of

Palestine and the establishment of the Palestinian democratic state and which is offering a great service for the liberation of the Arab homeland from the different forms of colonial bases. In the final analysis, Israel is a colonial base in the form of a state opposed to the Arab states. Thus the front should be opened to all the national and progressive Arab forces without exception and in spite of their thought and social and political tendencies with regard to the other problems confronting the Arab home land or the individual Arab states. The most important thing is that it should support and aid the Palestinian armed struggle. I believe that the PLO can take the initiative and call for the convening of the preparatory conference of the popular Arab front.

Abu Eyad: There is no disagreement on this point. We fully support it. Al Fateh, as a part of the PLO, can actually participate in realizing this great and necessary aim.

In your discussion you tackled the question of the non-Palestinian Arab youth volunteering to join the resistance. I take this opportunity to stress in the name of Al-Fateh that it accepts without reservation any Arab youth who wants to volunteer. We accept him, but there are obstacles put by the circumstances of Arab officialdom. If these circumstances are eliminated, we are ready, as of this moment, to accept the Arab youth among us.

In this context there is a point which should not be neglected, namely that volunteers come in great numbers, for example 12,000 volunteered from one Arab country. How could the resistance movement arm 12,000 with its present capabilities? Again the necessity for creating an Arab front which could play its role in supporting, aiding and widening the resistance movement emerges. Through the front we can organize all these matters so that volunteering will not become a hindrance but a driving force.

Khouli: Some Iraqis and Sudanese have expressed their desire to volunteer with their arms?

Abu Eyad: Such men are welcome.

Next we come to the point of coordination between the resistance and the Arab regular armies. Our concept with regard to coordination is a specific and clear one, from which we will not deviate. Coordination in our view is, firstly, whatever is contributed to the resistance in the field of support, aid and training. We are ready to be part of a national plan for liberation. But we are not ready to be part of a regional plan for coordination. In other words, if we find Arab regimes which have a serious plan for the liberation of Palestine and which want us to be part of that plan, we do not have any objections. But if certain Arab regimes aim at containing us in the name of coordination and maintaining their regional boundaries, we frankly reject this. We reject coordination if it means containment and mandate; we accept it if it means a plan on the national level of liberation.

Khouli: You want to say that, as you respect the independence of each Arab state, you require each Arab state to respect the independence of the Palestinian armed resistance movement.

Abu Eyad: Exactly, in order not to indulge in irrelevancies. This is our concept of coordination and our view of blending guerrilla warfare with regular armies. When, in 196}, we raised the slogan of armed struggle and said that the Palestinian people want to carry out this action, we realized that blowing up a bridge could not be a determining factor with regard to liberation. Yet we realized that blowing up a bridge would recruit 10 other people to join Al-Fateh. We were aware of the fact that b l o w in g u p a bridge will enlighten 10 other people and make them believe in the armed struggle. We did not understand the struggle in terms of profit and loss. We blow up one bridge and the Zionists will blow up 10 of our bridges. The concept of profit and loss has been entrenched in our system of thinking by colonialism, to restrict our movement. We should not think, as in the past, in a manner which always fears retaliation. We believe that the Palestinian popular armed struggle should, in fighting any serious battle with the forces of Zionism , indulge in a popular liberation war on the Arab level. In the present phase and under the present Arab circumstances, we could be the losers if a regular war is waged against Israel. Yet this does not imply that the Arab states are not required to have strong armies. On the contrary we want strong armies to defend the borders. However, if we calculate the battle of Palestine on the basis of loss and gain tank for tank, combat plane for combat plane, pilot for pilot, etc. there is no doubt that the Zionist state in Palestine is more capable than us since it is supported by world imperialist forces, in addition to being better armed and more scientifically educated.

Khouli: You are against mechanical calculation.

Abu Eyad: Exactly, mechanical calculation is rejected. At this point, in our opinion armed struggle is required on the Palestinian level. But it is well known that Israel does not allow itself to lose one battle, even if it is a partial one. It must always take revenge, because this false state cannot survive unless it is always victorious. Any defeat, even a partial one, will affect the morale of its people. This explains the continuous Israeli threats. Any small operation on our part will be answered by 10 in order to terrorize the Arab people and tell them that their endeavor is a hopeless one, and that the Israeli army is a legend which cannot be defeated. We should let our people get used to the idea that a conventional war is not the only kind of war they can fight. As Palestinians we hope that the capabilities of the Arab armies will be very high, and that they will coordinate with us for a dual battle in which guerrilla warfare and regular armies will have a part. Are we truly prepared for this? Or is it because we are not prepared to let the fighters feel that they are fighting in emptiness? Here lies the danger of saying that the Palestinian question will not attain victory except through regular armies. We know, and reality forces upon us this know ledge, that the regular armies cannot achieve this end now.

We must plant it firmly in our minds that the war is that of a guerrilla warfare which should be developed into a popular war of liberation in which the Arab masses by means of the Palestinian question will be prepared to confront the Zionist enemy and its policy and expansionist war. In future, things may change, and the regular Arab armies become capable of fighting successfully the War of liberation. But we are living the present reality and its conditions. Thus the vanguard of the Palestinians will be the same as that of the popular war of liberation in its entirety in term s of the Arab homeland as a whole. This is mainly what frightens Israel, Zionism and the other counter-revolutionary forces. Why? Because calculations will not be made on the basis of a tank for a tank and a combat plane for a combat plane. The calculations are based on the will of a struggling people their land and terminate the Zionist existence. who want to fight, defend term war. We do not believe that our war will We believe that it is a long end in victory in one or two years. In the war many of our fighters will the. Thus we are not against the idea of strengthening the Arab regular armies. On the contrary they should get stronger and stronger. Yet the regular armies are not a substitute for the Palestinian peoples struggle and their fight on their land. The implication behind this is that the

Palestinian people's struggle is a tactical trump card in the hands of the Arab armies, or Arab regimes. If we consider it as a tactical trump card then I will be gam bling with and selling these men who are dying each day for a tactical plan of certain Arab countries. This is a fundamental factor. Even the struggle of the regular soldiers falls within the framework of armed struggle. I do not want to discuss here the international circumstances and the link of the regular Arab armies, through their states, with the official international status and its effects if we declare the war to be that only of the regular armies.

Khouli: I noticed that in your discussion of the Arab states you distinguished between the Arab states bordering Palestine and the remote Arab states. Such a distinction on your part must have the meaning that each group has a special role to play in the battle of liberation. What is your evaluation of the role of each group? What has been accomplished until now? What has not been accomplished and why?

Abu Eyad: Briefly I say that the fundamental role of the Arab states bordering the occupied territories is to shoulder whatever results from the resistance operations in the form of Israeli counter-attacks, in addition to rebuilding their armed forces and modernizing their armies. This is what is happening to the UAR, Syria, Jordan and Lebanon. They are supposed to shoulder the Israeli counter-attacks. Israel tells lies when it claims that it is attacking

133

guerrilla bases in the East Bank or other places. Actually Israel attacks civilians, their cars, and homes in order to intimidate the Arab masses, in Jordan for example, and attempts to make them believe that support for the commandos is futile and will cost them great sacrifices. Israel knows that it cannot destroy all the bases of the commandos because it does not know and will never know their location. Furthermore, Israel attempts to make world public opinion believe in the futility both of resistance itself and of any world feeling for it. What is requited of the Arab states bordering Palestine is the following: to mobilize and strengthen their armies, to mobilize and organize the masses for the battle, and to prepare themselves to bear the consequences of the resistance movement. This was the case with Algeria and Tunisia with regard to the Algerian resistance movement. Egypt also in 1936 shouldered the consequences of its support for the Algerian resistance and successfully confronted the tripartite aggression on the Suez.

As for the remote Arab states their role centers on continuously providing financial aid. They are not deposed to direct danger so they should compensate for not having to mobilize their armies by mobilizing the masses and providing the bordering states, in addition to the resistance movement, with the necessary financial assistance. We are confronting a Zionist state which receives and continuous assistance from imperialism and world Zionism.

Khouli: Let us have a look at the international attitude vis–vis the problem and the battle of liberation after the two years which have elapsed since the June 1967 defeat. What is your analysis of the present international position of the Palestinian aimed struggle? Has it proved its existence and forced the world to recognize it?

Abu Eyad: Actually, this question has been always buzzing in our minds. All the people of the world only respect strength. And I do not mean by strength the mere possession of vast military equipment, I mean the determination and for forces there. It is my belief that on the basis of this understanding in the last two years - we have made up for the past 20 years when all our activity and propaganda centered on the wretched refugees queuing at UNRW A soup kitchens. This picture of refugees has been transformed into one of fighters carrying arms to win their freedom. At the outset many asked what can such a weak few do in the face of a state so strongly supported by imperialism and which has defeated Arab armies. We were accused of adventurism. But now the world and its political information have become interested in us after Palestinian resistance has proved that it is a growing and effective force in the area, politically and militarily. They are now facing a new political development in the area. A force which is carrying arms to liberate its homeland. resolution of groups of organized people to strive for their right at any expense, summoning up their inner forces.

We know the world is almost divided into three parts: the countries of the eastern camp, those of the western camp, and those of the third world. As far as we are concerned, I believe that we have succeeded in different degrees and up to an extent, in explaining our case in these three camps. H ie support of the peoples of the world is continuously growing. The Second International Conference in Support of the Arab Peoples, which was held in Cairo on 23 January 1969 and in which a number of forces of differing tendencies participated, was a great test for the strength of our movement and struggle. The delegates who attended the conference expressed their support for the problem as put forward by Al-Fateh. Naturally this did not result from a plan drawn up for the conference but was a positive result of political effort prior to the convening of the conference. We are now hoping that the information media in the socialist bloc and the countries of the third world will show more readiness to present our case. Isn't it strange to find the means of information in the western countries more open to us than that of the socialist countries?

Khouli: How do you explain this phenomenon?

Abu Eyad: I relate it to the inadequacy of the Arab progressive forces, which are supposed, in this context, to carry the burden of the Palestinian socialist resistance movement to the country as a whole.

Khouli: I think that this explanation is insufficient. Why don't you explain it on the basis that the resistance has not seriously put itself forward in this sphere? In other words, why do you only explain it by blaming the others and denying that you have also erred?

Abu Eyad: What does the other side accuse us of?

Khouli: They say that you distinguish, in an unobjective manner, between political action and military action, and that you always prefer military activity to any political activity. Furthermore that you make the accusation that any political activity, exerted for the sake of the Palestinian problem at different levels and within the scope of securing the national rights of the Palestinian and Arab people, is bargaining.

Abu Eyad: I believe that the problem is different. The question of the remissness of the socialist information media with regard to the resistance is a reality. I would like to assert that our discussion of this point is initiated by reprimand and argument and not intimidation or attack on the socialist bloc, to whom we have friendly feelings and appreciate the huge and valuable assistance they offer to certain Arab states. But we would not be friends if we did not discuss the issues frankly. I think that this remissness is related firstly to the Palestine question itself because the socialist camps stand, at the beginning, was not proper and was unobjective. The reasons for such a stand could be traced in the unfriendly relations we had with this camp because of our circumstances, especially in the years 1947, 1948. In addition the Arab communist parties failed to explain the reality of the problem and situation. The socialist camp was of the opinion that a progressive revolution could only be launched with the support of around 60 percent of the local inhabitants. Since this was not the case in Palestine, the socialist camp did not recognize the Palestinian revolution. Let us suppose that the socialist camp wanted now to apply this theory to the present situation in Israel, it would find that the number of the local inhabitants who wanted the revolution and the elimination of the Zionist entity would not total 60 per cent. We are of the opinion that such a view of the Palestine question is not sound. The subject is prim arily that of the existence of a racist fascist state as a result of an outright and direct usurpation of the land of another people through colonial imperialism. The essence of the problem is that colonial imperialism was able through the methods of the fascist Zionist movement to expel and drive out the indigenous inhabitants in a manner similar to what is happening in Rhodesia and South Africa. This is the real problem which the socialist camp did not comprehend very well. In addition, we did not seriously attempt to make the socialist camp understand it.

Khouli: In your opinion the failure was both their responsibility and our own. How can we overcome it?

Abu Eyad: There is no doubt the failure was the responsibility of both them and ourselves. There are two important points to be considered here: Firstly, the attitude of the socialist camp towards the Palestine problem. I believe that one of the basic reasons behind the weakening of the communist parties in the Arab world is their wrong stand vis–vis the Palestine revolution, by limiting its development and expansion and by alleging that the num ber of those supporting it do not constitute a majority. This might not apply to the Communist Party of Egypt but it applies to the other Arab countries.

Khouli: It applies to Egypt.

Abu Eyad: The second point is that the socialist camp, after the June war, did not attempt to understand the reality of our attitude towards the November 1967 Security Council resolution.

Khouli: Here you should explain why Israel rejects the implementation of this resolution.

Abu Eyad: Israel simply rejects this resolution because the victorious wants to achieve results from its aggression which it has not yet achieved. The aggression as understood by our enemy aimed at terminating the existence of anything called Palestine and Palestinian. The enemy could have made many of the Arab regimes fall. It could have put the Arabs in a position of defeat and surrender so that they would accept its existence. All these matters were not accomplished as a result of the aggression. Thus, victory was one of paper and maps but not a real one. The Palestinian resistance movement grew and became stronger. Certain regimes which were supposed to fall did not do so. Many other things, the peace treaty which the enemy requested was not agreed to by any Arab country. I think that the importance of the Khartoum Summit Conference was suppressed in the decision calling for no peace, no recognition and no negotiations. Thus the aggression did not achieve anything. The Security Council resolution calls for w withdrawal; it is true and natural that the Israelis do not want to withdraw, not even with secured boundaries. The Arab governments might accept on paper the concept of secure boundaries, but in reality, the Israelis want more guarantees. What are they going to lose? They are occupying territories which might solve their economic problems, since the reality of the Zionist aggression is always linked with Israel's daily requirements. If we go back to the Israeli official yearbooks, we find that in 1956 unemployment totaled 36 per cent; in 1967 it totaled 39 per cent. In both cases they had to wage wars to curb unemployment.

Khouli: Can't we say that the Palestinian resistance movement fears that if the Security Council resolution was implemented and I think that this will not be the case the attitude of the

Arab governments, or a number of them at least, might change with regard to the resistance movement?

Abu Eyad: Actually I did not, purposefully, tackle the question that one of the conditions of the colonialist countries for the implementation of the Security Council resolution is the liquidation of Palestinian resistance. But and I am not being conceited it has become a popular movement and cannot be liquidated. It cannot go backwards.

Khouli: At least it will be faced with unsettling problems?

Abu Eyad: Even so, at present the Palestinian resistance, in spite of the numerous loopholes within it, has become the property of the Palestinian people and all the Arab people. It is not feasible to destroy a movement which has such deep roots, which has been adopted by the masses, and which belongs primarily to the logic of the present age. Of course, when colonialism thinks of implementing the Security Council resolution, it does so according to its own wants and interests. These require the destruction of Palestinian action and guerrilla action, even if by putting forward, the outward form of our alternative. Consequently, we hear, every now and then, of the idea of the Palestinian state which aims at aborting the liberation movement of the Palestinian people and their armed resistance. That is a Palestinian state which is completely subordinate to Israel and colonialism to be established on the West Bank and the Gaza

Strip with a corridor connecting these two parts. That will end the fighting. You want a Palestinian state. H ere is the Palestinian state and the war is over. According to our sources of information on the discussion of the four great powers in New York, such a "forged Palestinian state" is under consideration. The strange thing is that the American delegation is the one presenting and defending this project.

Khouli: What is so strange about that?

Abu Eyad: The strange thing is that, in the past, the Americans have been refusing to recognize the Palestinian people and now they are showing such interest in the Palestinian state.

Khouli: Exactly as they understood the destiny of socialism in Czechoslovakia. Why don't you have a dialogue concerning these questions and differing points of view with the socialist camp?

Abu Eyad: What I can say is that we have asked them, and we are still asking, to have such a dialogue. We are always ready to have a dialogue with all the world forces. We are open to every kind of unconditional aid and discussion. But, as you know, the opening from one side is insufficient It should be from both sides.

Khouli: Alright. What is the attitude of the states and peoples of the third world towards you?

Abu Eyad: Actually their attitude is one of great and growing support. Naturally the internal problems of the third world limit its capabilities. We realize that.

Khouli: As for the peoples of the capitalist world?

Abu Eyad: We are continuously winning over friends from among them. We cannot say that we have won the support of a great and important part of public opinion, but it is continuous, especially in the Scandinavian countries, France and Britain. The new left supports us totally.

Khouli: Last week while discussing the resistance with foreign journalists, some of them said that if the present situation continues as it is in the area and Palestinian resistance continues in its rejection of any peaceful solution, the area will blow up and this time it will lead to a world war. In their opinion the Palestinian resistance movement should realize its responsibility concerning the question of world peace.

Abu Eyad: We are puzzled with these people. At times the resistance is weak and carries no weight, and it is not necessary to contact it to know its opinion and position. At others its role grows to such an extent that it begins to threaten world peace!

These people should define their position concerning the resistance. Is it weak and unworthy of contact? Or is it a primary movement and of weight in the area?

Moreover, is our armed resistance against a racist-fascist enemy which occupies our homeland, a threat to world peace, or a threat to colonialism and racism, the cause of wars? We are a liberation movement. W hy are such words concerning world peace not uttered with regard to, e.g., the Vietnamese liberation movement? Vietnam also could be regarded as a cause of a world war. Why are we alone accused of threatening world peace? What threatens world peace is the continuation of the squandering of the right of the Palestinian people to their land and country, and the continuation of the Zionist colonialist entity in our country. Peace and progress will not be realized in our country unless the Zionist entity is liquidated from the Arab homeland. The peoples of the world should comprehend that when the Palestinian people carry arms, they are working seriously for peace in the world.

Khouli: Meaning that Palestinian resistance is causing a liberation war to burst out against colonialism and racism. Thus, like every liberation movement in the world, it objectively serves the question of world peace. This is true. Let us discuss another problem. It has been noticed that during the last few weeks the Voice of al-Asifah, which belongs to Al-Fateh, has harshly and unobjectively criticized the Soviet Union. Don't you think that differences in viewpoints should not hide an important fact, namely that the Soviet Union is an important friend and objective ally of the national liberation movements in the world. And that such differences must be settled in terms of friendship.

Abu Eyad: We totally agree that the Soviet Union must be viewed as a friend of the Arabs. This friendship has been actually expressed in the form of material aid to and strong moral support for the Arab states especially after the June war. Yet this does not prevent us from declaring the differences in our viewpoints with regard to the situation. I believe that in this context there must be direct relations between the Soviet Union and the Palestinian people. The fact that the relations are indirect is not our fault.

The Soviet Union must appreciate our sensitivity to the meetings of the great powers. We have always, as a people, had to put up with our destiny being decided in our absence. In our criticism, we wanted to clarify to the Soviet Union, the friend and yet at the same time participant in these discussions, this essential point which we believe is supported by Soviet Unions principles. Our criticism was the sort that wants to bring the enemy nearer and not send him farther away.

Khouli: Then it should have been essential that the method of criticism should have differed and not equated the Soviet Union, United States and Britain.

Abu Eyad: No. We did not equate the Soviet Union, United States and Britain. Please re-read the criticism to be sure of that. We said that the United States and Britain participated in the creation of the Zionist entity and are still strongly supporting it. While the Soviet Union, the friend of the Arabs, is supposed not to maintain its previous 1948 stand vis–vis the Palestine question.

Khouli: Now I would like to get acquainted with your outlook concerning the enemy. What was it prior to and after the implementation of armed resistance?

Abu Eyad: From the start, I would like to clarify a general element. The Zionist movement has attempted, and is still attempting, to convince the Arabs and its followers that it cannot bear any defeat whether in a partial battle which would have psychological repercussions on its people, or in a great battle which would lead to the liquidation of the Israeli entity and Jewish masses. It has succeeded in this attempt to a great extent. It is noticeable with regret that in the same way that we minimized the ability of the Zionist soldier before 1948 by portraying him as a non-fighter and a coward, so now have we exaggerated the picture of this soldier after the June war.

We feel that the individual in Israel, as far as being a man is concerned, especially the soldier if we exclude the leaders who work within the framework of the Zionist colonialist movement plan is not convinced of the war except from the viewpoint of self-defense. If we were able, through our behavior, to reach the heart of this individual and convince him that we are truly not butchers who want to slay him and throw his women and children into the sea, as Zionism portrays us, we can make a psychological separation between the human being and the Zionist, the Jewish soldier and military Zionist colonialist establishment.

We have proposed to the Arab governments that they announce officially that they are ready to receive all the Arab Jews who have immigrated to Israel, that they will return to them all their property and civil rights and treat them as Arab citizens equal to the other Arab citizens. I believe that if we succeed in this and clarify our humanitarian stand vis–vis the Jew as a human being, we are sure that the military Zionist colonialist establishment will be automatically defeated. The Jewish soldier who is under the influence of the belief that if he does not fight and shed Arab blood, he is bound to get killed and the, will lose such a belief. We have been made profoundly aware of this implication. After the Karameh battle 300 Israeli officers and soldiers were tried for refusing to participate in it. It is regrettable that, in our newspapers, we distorted the attitude of these soldiers and officers by accusing them of being cowards and running away from the battle. If we had looked carefully into the matter and reviewed what they had written before and after the battle we would have discovered the great humanitarian implication behind it, namely that they were not convinced of the war of aggression, nor even of the destruction of Palestinian resistance. On this basis, if our propaganda is able to express the reality of our humanitarianism, and can convince the Jewish soldier and officer, and the Jewish human being in general, that our resistance under no condition aims at him but aims at Zionism and its entity, the myth will disappear, and our battle for the liquidation of Zionism and its entity will become easier and possible with fewer sacrifices.

Perhaps in my discussion 1 have concentrated on the military aspect and its establishments. In fact this is the enemy's source of strength and weakness. We have recently met a foreign progressive journalist who has come from Israel, we asked him: What are your main observations? He said that there is a basic understanding among progressive and sometimes unprogressive circles, even if their size is small, of why the Palestinian carries arms and resists. The Israeli intelligence services are after these people and constantly watch them. It is regrettable that our newspapers do not know much of what is happening inside Israel, and this in turn makes the Arab citizen ignorant with regard to these important facts. The implication behind this is that the truth about the Palestinian resistance has reached the Jewish human being, and it is not strange anymore that a Palestinian throws a bomb at an Israeli patrol. On the contrary, the attitude of the Zionist military authority with regard to blowing up Arab houses and the maltreatment of captives and prisoners has become strange and is sometimes condemned.

Our view of the enemy covers the social structure and the social situation within it Up till now Israeli Zionist society has not experienced a real sense of belonging or assimilation. It is an alliance of interest based on confronting danger as portrayed by Zionism. The only thing that unites a Jew coming from Syria with one from Iraq or Europe is a feeling of persecution and the necessity to be grouped together to face the danger. Such a society cannot be humanitarian, nor is it capable of any permanence. The eastern Jews are, generally, treated as second class citizens. There is obvious discrimination between them and the European Jews (Ashkenaz). Harmony between the two groups is difficult and does not exist at all at some levels. Only the European Jews are first class citizens and enjoy all privileges; they alone occupy high positions such as ministers, army commanders, senior officers, ambassadors, and high offices in ministries and establishments. Do you know that the Egyptian Jews live almost in isolation? The majority of them were grouped in Beersheba, which is located in the south. Such a phenomenon is not accidental. It reveals the sectarian divisions within the Zionist society despite superficial appearances to the contrary.

On the whole these factors, and others which we do not want to reveal, guide us in our complicated plan to confront the enemy objectively. In other words we must know the enemy as it is in reality and not-as we imagine it to be. You may be sure that we calculate the enemy's strong and weak points accurately and

149

do not overlook the dynamic relationship that exists between them.

Khouli: I would like to thank you for the opportunity of having this dialogue with you and for the frankness of your discussion in it, and to con du d e I would like to ask you a question that is often asked by some foreign friends: What is your attitude if any Jew in the world is subjected to persecution? I always replied that I would stand by him against persecution. What is Al-Fatehs answer to such a question about the persecution of a Jew inside or outside Palestine?

Abu Eyad: Our answer is clear and there are two aspects to it. If we welcome living with the Jews after the liquidation of the Zionist entity and the establishment of the Palestinian democratic state, we will stand by any persecuted Jew, and we are ready to give him a gun and fight on his side.

Al-Fateh ANSWERS QUESTIONS

Q : What do we mean if we say that Al-Fateh is a movement?

A : Al-Fateh is a movement. It is not a party or a front. A party has a constant social ideology. A front is composed of revolutionary organizations based on a specific work program . Al-Fateh is a movement because it believes in the necessity of subjecting its thought to practice and experience. It is dynamic. Through practice and experience it can enrich the necessary contents of its thought. It does not believe in the logic of static theory. It is a movement which has specific aims and acts in accordance with basic principles. It has incontestable principles, yet the contents of Al-Fatehs thought cannot be determined except through actual practice because a theory is the result of experience, and practice is the test of thought and attitudes. In this sense Al-Fateh is a movement which is continuously subjecting the totality of its concepts and policies to practice. It continues to change these concepts and policies in order to build the final thought of the movement Thus as long as Al-Fateh is a movement it rejects the logic of static theory and cannot define the man of the future, because in doing so it will be following a metaphysical line of thinking which determines the form of man. This is an ideal understanding which cannot be applied to reality.

Al-Fateh and the Left

Leftism as defined by many of leftist ideologues is, in short, "The will to abolish the exploitation of man by man. The leftist movement always speaks in the negative form. The left resists so and so, revolts against so and so and fights so and so. The left does not have a positive content except when exemplified in the form of a party or movement, and then this content becomes the tool for continuous change. The element of time in the leftist movement is not continuous. When we fight against a specific society because it is corrupt, and we are able to change it radically, then, with the passage of time, all the changes attained become positive connotations. These, in their turn, are rejected because the movement of history is in a continuous state of revolution and rejection. The given society, after a period of time, becomes rightist, and the creation of a leftist movement is inevitable in order to reject this society.

Al-Fateh and the Bourgeoisie

Many people claim that the classes of peasants and workers are the classes on which the Palestinian revolution depends. This statement is contrary to reality because the new class of refugees, which has not been taken into consideration by many thinkers, is the class on which the Palestinian revolution depends. Workers, especially in the under-developed countries, form a simple and ineffective class which cannot be easily relied on. Palestinians were evacuated from their homes, the implication being that a class of refugees has been formed and not one of workers and peasants. If the Palestinian revolution represented by Al-Fateh is said to be bourgeois, this implies that there should be factories, capitalists and workers, in other words specific classes. We cannot say that there is a bourgeois class if there is no working class. What is this class? Because of the evacuation of the Palestinians, Al- Fateh represents the refugees. It is the only revolutionary movement which has transcended the Arab movements, Arab parties and the Palestinian regional movements, and it has done this because it has depended on the refugee class. The bourgeois concept, on the other hand, is one of attributes. For example there have been socialist thinkers who have come from the bourgeoisie, yet they have lived under the same material conditions as those of the toiling people and have become truly revolutionary and not bourgeois. 'Bourgeois is a material condition under which a human being lives and which makes him tend towards bourgeois intellectualism. Then where are the bourgeois tendencies in Al-Fateh?

Yet there is an infantile leftism among those who propagate socialist thought by applying the experiences of others. On this basis such movements can be described as idealistic and infantile, because any movement must study the given reality. These movements have not studied the given reality but described it according to descriptions of other societies. As a result their understanding and description is abstract. Our description is nearer to reality Thus Al-Fateh is the only actual revolutionary movement in the Palestinian field.

Social Ideology

The act of being committed to a specific social ideology implies a commitment to a specific social principle. As long as the revolution is fighting against the present situation, it rejects the leftist connotation of general rejection. For we have made our intellectual revolution against the existing situation, rejected it and undertaken armed resistance. In other words, we have undertaken, in a practical way, to change the tin g situation. The thought and action of the left is directed towards the rejection of the existing situation and actually changing it This is the leftist trend. Evidently, then, Al-Fateh movement, if it is given the proper name, is further to the left than any movement in the Arab world.

The Arab parties wanted to find a historical justification for their existence, so they created guerrilla organizations to prove that they should exist. These organizations, which are affiliated to parties, are a justification for the parties historical existence. Their task is not easy. For every movement that has lost its dynamic ability to awaken the masses through its political organizations has, by implication, lost its historical values. But, through the existence of guerrilla branches, it wanted to create an historical justification. This is a temporary thing which is bound to come to an end. However, the historical revolutionary movement in the Arab world, which has quite different political, military and theoretical dimensions, is Al-Fateh. It is more of a leftist movement because, intellectually and practically, it is committed to the act of changing the existing situation in which the Palestinian people are living. All those who say that Al-Fateh is a bourgeois movement are -using an abstract terminology because they want to apply theories that have resulted from the experience of specific people and do not fit our present experience.

Why Has Al-Fateh Not Put Forward a Specific Social Ideology?

It is not easy to put forward a specific social ideology at a time when the struggle is against the occupying power. In the present phase, the struggle

should be a national one. This means that all the classes which are against Zionism and imperialism should form an alliance to destroy the Zionist imperialist occupation of Palestine. Thus, to put forward a social concept would have a direct effect on the alliance by sowing dissension among its members. Since, within the alliance, there are secondary conflicts, these should be frozen for the sake of the main conflict which is that of our existence or the Zionists. Calling for any social concept in this phase implies the adoption of a specific error, namely, the destruction of the popular alliance, or the forces of the Palestinian people. This is the phase of national struggle. If one studies the history of the Chinese people, one finds that Mao Tse Tung formed an alliance with Chang

Kai Chek, who was extremely reactionary, because it was a phase of national struggle.

Remark from the Audience:

Q : Can we say that Zionism and imperialism in Palestine represent the Japanese colonialism of China and the Chinese bourgeoisie, and that we are fighting Zionism and after solving the question of Zionist colonialism we start to solve the secondary conflicts?

A : It does not matter whether the forces against us are imperialism, the bourgeoisie or capitalism. It will be inevitable that new conflicts will emerge during the act of development of struggle between the people and the enemy, and at the phase of liberation. For example, a conflict with the bureaucrats in the revolution may appear. A bureaucratic class in the revolution may emerge which should be resisted. There may develop differences in the ideas of the revolution because we aim at social justice and abolishing the exploitation of man by man.

Remark: Then we are leftists.

A : Leftism does not mean that. A leftist is the one who rejects a specific reality and works to change this reality. Leftism has many trends. The com m unist movement in Jordan is a reactionary movement because it lags behind the national movement which has carried arms and started to change the reality. The Jordanian communist movement wants to maintain this reality while it raises the slogan of national rule and we want to blow up the basis of this reality. Thus as far as we are concerned it is a rightist movement. As for the social content, any such content requires certain bases before it can be realized.

1. There must be land a regional unity.

2. There must be people living on this land a social unity and not a divided people like ours.

3. There must be a political unity, namely a state, in order to achieve the social content.

We have not yet built these bases. We must have land on which our people will be grouped, and a state in order to put forward the social content.

Remark from the Audience: If we compare the Palestinian revolution with the Algerian revolution, we find that the latter did not put forward any social content. It started as a national liberation movement struggling against French colonialism. After the liberation it became a national bourgeois movement because it did not have any social content. Thus, when the revolution was on the verge of attaining victory, the contradictions within the movement exploded into the open.

A : Firstly, in the Arab homeland there has not actually been any experiment with social content that has proved itself a guiding experience. Secondly, world socialist experiments differ from one country to the other, such as Yugoslavia, Poland, the Soviet Union and China. In the Soviet Union the concept of state capitalism has emerged which the Chinese call socialist imperialism. If we believe that evolution is inevitable, then, as long as there are differences in the social content of the different experiences of the socialist revolutions, it will be difficult to judge the future in the light of a specific social content. We should, however, adopt the following general principles:

1. **The abolition of the exploitation of man by man.**
2. **The question of social justice.**

These general goals are the backbone of the Palestinian revolution. We have started to apply the question of social justice by establishing social institutes such as: The School of the Martyrs' Sons, the Martyrs' Institute, the Cubs Institute.

The idea behind the establishment of such institutes is that we should become responsible for all our people. This experiment will inevitably mature and become enriched, achieving the social content we desire. It is not permissible to put forward a specific social content Whoever does that works in the abstract and is an infantile leftist. There are many infantile leftists in the Palestinian and Arab fields. They are called, if this expression is correct, revolutionary missionaries.

Remark from the Audience: We always say that the peak of ideology is armed struggle. What does this mean?

A: To say that the highest form of struggle is armed struggle is more leftist than any other ideology; for it is an intellectual rejection followed by a practical rejection.

Q: What is Al-Fatehs attitude towards the progressive parties in Israel?

A: Progressiveness and progressive parties should have concepts of right, justice and the non-exploitation of man by man. However, the trends found in Israel are part and parcel of the Zionist existence. They believe in the existence and the consecration of this racist state, and their struggle is merely against the governing group. Consequently, they are part of that aggressive entity which is contrary to any teal progressive trend. There will be no progressive trends and parties in Israel as long as arms are not carried against the Israeli racist entity and an armed

160

struggle is not embarked upon for its elimination as a state, society, Zionist movement, and military establishment. If the members of these parties start fighting the Zionist presence or the Israeli political presence with arms to destroy the so-called Israeli state, if they fight and struggle against the Israeli army to eliminate the existence of this facist military establishment, if they fight against class discrimination between Eastern and Western Jews, Arabs and Zionists, if they struggle against Zionist ideas for the establishment of the Israeli state, then these parties become progressive. In reality these parties accept the political, military, intellectual and social situation, but they claim that the men in authority are deviationists. Thus these parties are part and parcel of the Israeli fascist aggressive entity and they are not progressive.

Remark from the Audience: The Israeli Communist Party's Secretary General, Meir Vilner, has drawn a plan recognizing the right of the Palestinian's to return anti be compensated for their land. The problem, according to Vilner, does not pertain to it. Existence or non-existence of the state of Israel, or to an Israeli and a Palestinian; but it is a problem of struggle between reactionary and progressive forces. The party considers Israel to be reactionary because it supports imperialism and it is a base for the US, and it claims that it is against the Zionist movement which is militarily controlling Israel. But if Isra e l. ruled by a progressive party, it will recognize the right of the Palestinians, for as long as Palestine can take in seven million Jews "according to Ben Gurion," it can take in the Palestinian refugees who do not exceed two millions. The Palestinians will return but within the framework of the Israeli state.

Vilner claims that carrying arms against Israel strengthens the presence of Zionism and the military Zionist movement in Israel, because the man in the street fears arms being carried against him, and the only persons who can give him a feeling of security are the military Zionists. Israel is a reality and carrying arms against it will never solve the problem, on the contrary it will complicate it.

A: Actually this opinion is one of the contradictions found in Israel which may develop into struggle. Carrying arms is the way of the Palestinian armed struggle against this entity. The Israeli entity is an artificial one contrary to the logic of evolution. The existence of any state in the Arab area of Palestine which is not an Arab Palestinian state is contrary to the logic of history and evolution. If a non-Arab Palestinian state was created, it would face the same problems, but from a different angle, that the Israeli state is facing.

The international existence of Israel is what we are objecting to, and it is contrary to the nature of Arab existence in this area. Israel, as a state, contradicts the logic of evolution, for a state Must have its civilization, economic, political and historical roots in the area in which it exists. This means that the people who live there and want to form a state should be in

162

harmony, with regard to civilization, with the peoples of the Arab area. On the other hand if they want to secede and form a new civilization or way of life, the logic of history will inevitably condemn them to death. What we are objecting to is the existence of the state of Israel because we cannot separate its substance from its form. I f you strike at the substance, you also strike the form. The claim of the Israeli Communist Party contradicts the facts and is an attempt on the part of these deviationist forces in the Zionist entity to paralyze progressive forces in their work by malting them adopt ideas which are far

from reality. For these reasons the existence of Israel contradicts the logic and evolution of history, and it also contradicts the way of life of the peoples in the Middle East, namely the Arab people. Any state created, whether Israel or any other that was not civilizationally, politically and linguistically harmonious with the peoples of this area, would inevitably wither away. Thus the Zionist or Israeli entity is what is objected to, the termination of this entity will put an end to all these contradictions.

Remark from tbe Audience: Some people say that if we allow the Jews to remain, the problem will be solved. For the Jewish state will be founded on the basis of a Jewish nation which will result in the establishment of a socialist society.

A : A progressive socialist society cannot be established in Israel because there are basic principles for building such a society/forever in the Arab world, the establishment of socialism cannot be achieved if each state attempts it separately. This experiment in socialism has failed in Egypt, Syria and Iraq. A basic requirement for creating a socialist state is regional unity. Israel, as a state, does not have the natural and social forces to enable it to be a progressive state. The reason is that this artificial state urgently and continuously needs foreign aid and support. Israel's support is given by capitalism and world imperialism. Thus Israel will depend on colonial forces as long as it remains a state. It will also remain a tool in the hands of world imperialism to hinder the Arab progressive movement in the Arab East and W est. Thus the Israeli state cannot become a progressive state, nor be a basis of socialism. Israel does not possess the natural resources to enable it to survive as a progressive state. It will remain a colonial state via which technical aid is passed to the Arab, Asian and African states. Moreover, the economy of Israel cannot help in establishing a socialist or progressive state. There will always remain in Israel the class of middlemen, or the compradoric class, which monopolizes foreign capital and then sends it to other areas in the form of technical aid. Israel is a means of hindering the Arab progressive movement. It must be term inated as a state in order to put an end to these contradictions and have peace in the Arab Middle Eastern area.

Remark from the Audience: Some people say that Israel is the only socialist state in the Middle East. The example given is the Kibbutz.

Israel is not a socialist state. The evidence is found in its class structure.

A : There is discrimination between Eastern and Western Jews which means that there is a class struggle. If that statement means that Israel is nearer in time to socialism because it has reached the stage of capitalism, whereas the Arab states are still at the stage of feudalism according to Marxist interpretation, this is correct. Israel is coming dose to the peak of the conflict which can result in a struggle between the poor classes and the exploiting classes. More over, the nature of Israeli society is artificial. It has not evolved through long historical interaction; it is 20 years old. The act of social homogeneity cannot be created in such a short period; mans struggle needs a long time. The leftist societies are hundreds or thousands of years old. How could these people who came from the west, others from the east, north, and the south, who spoke different languages and bad different habits and nationalities, form a homogeneous society in such a short period? Such a society needs a long time for there to be an interaction between it and its objective economic and material conditions. Moreover, the Israelis are living under circumstances of continuous struggle with the Arab people, whose land they have stolen. Thus the question of being more progressive and nearer to socialism is a great deception, and those who propagate it are deceived by Zionist propaganda.

Remark from the Audience: Don't you think that Al-Fatehs aim of having Muslims, Jews and Christians live together with equal rights in Palestine, after a struggle has taken place between them is utopian and idealistic?

A : No, our aim is neither utopian nor idealistic. On the contrary it is realistic because past experience has proved that the Arabs do not have any anti- Semitic tendencies since they are Semites. The Arabs civilizational structure is such that, if we admit that the Islamic civilization has created a tolerant mentality toward other religions, the Jews can live in peace with the Arabs. Judaism in our view is a religion and not a nationality. There are Arabs whose religion was Judaism, thus there are Arab Jews. There are also non-Arab Jews such as French Jews, etc.

We do not view Judaism as a nationality but as a religion. We can live peacefully with the Jews and we were doing so until foreign colonial and imperial forces and the Zionist movement, the offspring of colonialism and its ally, filled Jewish society with such poisonous views and made them move in another direction. Nazism produced the same alienation from human society in the Germans. When Nazism was finished, the Germans started to live peacefully with the peoples of the world.

Remark from the Audience : After attaining victory what will be the attitude of Al-Fateh to the Jews who wish to remain in Palestine, taking into consideration that numerically they may be greater than the Palestinians?

If the revolution attains victory it will apply its humane and practical A. principles. It is not a question of numbers and a defeat (1967). It is not a numerical but a potential, practical and revolutionary question. The victory of the revolution implies the implementation of the humanitarian principles of the Palestinian revolution. The fate of the Jewish group will be decided according to the principles of the revolution, which are humanitarian.

Since the establishment of the state of Israel in May 1948, the Palestinian and Arab people have hoped that the Arab regimes and their regular armies would liberate Palestine. As the attitudes of the individual Arab states towards the adoption of the Palestine question have varied greatly, the hopes for liberation, at different times, have been concentrated on different Arab states to lead the rest in the war of liberation. Following the establishment of the state of Israel there were a number of coups de tat in Arab states. These coups were an expression of the Arab peoples resentment of their governments. At the same time they were an assertion of their belief in a regular war for the liberation of Palestine. In the different Arab countries the Palestinian people have taken leading roles in bringing about these changes. Thus the Palestinians have focused their attentions on the internal problems of the Arab states in order to establish regimes which would build up strong armies, equipped with modem heavy armaments and capable of defeating the enemy's army.

In the light of this analysis two facts should be pointed out:

1. The war of liberation against the Zionist conquest is a war against great forces in alliance with Zionism and capable, in every circumstance, of maintaining the military superiority of Israel. The Arab nation, including the Palestinian people, cannot wage a successful regular war against Israel and its allies. The Arab nation is composed of a great number of underdeveloped states. These ate, by themselves, incapable, at least in the near future, of industrialization and unifying their forces to be able to wage a regular war against the enemy. Imperialism and the forces which are in alliance with it are able to hamper the desired change in Arab society until Israel can consolidate its existence and attain its objectives. Past experience has proved to the Arab nation that it should a special weekly bulletin published by the Central Information Bureau of the Palestine National Liberation Movement (Al-Fateh), Nos. 12 (7 July 1969). 13. 14. 13, 16, 17 and 18. Will be aware of the role of all of the enemy forces, and at the same time it should distinguish, isolate and fight the enemies most harmful to its

168

development in order to be able to concentrate on the principal enemy. Thus in the war of liberation it is necessary to use weapons which the enemy is unable to defeat. Furthermore, it is necessary to eliminate the enemies one after the other.

The Zionist enemy in its struggle to attain its objectives in our homeland was able to mobilize material and human forces to a far greater extent than it was able to mobilize regular armies. The Zionists were able to mobilize world Jewry to fight a war by diverse methods. The role of the regular army was the spearhead for the attainment of the enemy's objectives. Thus it has become not only difficult for the Arab forces to attain victory by a simple preparation of superior armies which are capable of inflicting a military defeat but, due to reasons already mentioned, it is impossible.

These two facts, in addition to other less important facts, caused the Arab struggle for the liberation of Palestine to reach a dead end. The Arab nation should have been aware of its experience and should have devised a method which would fit the reality of the Palestinian and Arab people. At the same time these methods should have been an expression of the will of the people with regard to total liberation.

This is the revolutionary way which expresses historical necessities as exemplified in the reality of the Arab nation. Their will has been the historical justification for the creation of Al-Fateh with its actions and methods that express its belief in the people as the main force capable of attaining victory, and call for the peoples participation in a revolutionary war in order to attain their objectives.

The revolutionary war, which Al-Fateh calls for, aims at liberating the people of Palestine, giving them back their country, and establishing a legal political power emanating from the will of the Palestinian people and serving their interests. The method is that of waging a popular war of liberation in which the people will participate on a large scale. This war of liberation will be exemplified by political struggle and armed struggle which go hand in hand and in which the people participate. Thus it should be made clear that both the political and the armed struggles are inherent means for attaining the aims of the revolutionary war. Whereas, differentiating between political struggle and armed struggle, or being satisfied with only one of them, will deprive the popular war of its ability to attain victory.

If we only adopt armed struggle and undertake to mobilize the people in armed units, and if we consider that this alone will serve our purpose, then we will condemn ourselves to failure. The military forces which we can mobilize will not be able, in every circumstance, to face a regular military force. At the same time if the military forces are separate from the people, one cannot evaluate them except from the point of view of their number, equipment and technical capabilities. Such revolutionary forces cannot face the existing challenge.

On the other hand if we only understand political struggle to mean the mobilization of the people, their education, organization and leadership, then such a struggle is going to run against a self-evident reality, namely that the enemy will not desist from following his policy of aggression unless his military forces are crushed. The unarm ed organized people cannot fulfill this role. The enemy will maintain his positions by force of arms and be is capable of striking against the people without the latter being able to h it back or even defend themselves. Thus political struggle without armed struggle cannot hurt the aim of the revolution.

In the light of the above-mentioned, the method of armed struggle and that of political struggle are complementary. Adopting one m ethod at the expense of the other will lead the revolution to failure. The attempt to differentiate between the two methods in this study has been done to explain the method of political struggle and it is not considered as the seed method necessary to accomplish the tasks of our struggle.

The first question to be answered is: Why is political struggle a necessity?

Political struggle is one of the important methods of our revolutionary war for the following reasons:

1. The revolutionary war that we are waging is not based on the belief that regular war alone can achieve the aims of the revolution. Revolutionary war is based on the rejection of the traditional concept which considers parity with the enemy in military strength a basic condition for victory. Our understanding of the revolutionary war is that it should be waged by the peoples armed forces and the ordinary people who believe in the aims of such a war. The participation of the people on the side of their armed forces will hamper the effectiveness of a great number of the enemys armaments; it will make it lose its ability to use the methods of modem warfare and will force the enemy to face different weapons, some of which are modem and others primitive. This will prohibit the enemy from setting up stationary front lines at which it can assemble and mobilize its military forces in a manner that best serves its interests.

2. The ability of political struggle to enlighten, educate and organize the masses will guarantee the revolutionary program and ensure that the military struggle will not deviate from its aim. Furthermore it will create the forces necessary to direct the armed struggle in a way that accords with the tactics and strategy of armed revolution and avoids falling into the

logic of regular warfare which the enemy is always trying to draw us into.

3. The effectiveness of armed struggle among the people will make them capable of supplying the armed forces with the required fighters who are aware of the aims of the struggle and capable of bearing all the difficulties which they will encounter in it. I f the elements who join the struggle have revolutionary awareness and experience their solidarity and ability to resist become greater.

The mobilized people will offer the armed forces their experience and capabilities and will provide them with the necessary armaments and other material aid. The masses have proved, through a great number of revolutions which have taken place in different parts of the world, that they are capable of discovering and inventing effective methods, for encountering the enemy and inflicting heavy losses on it, despite their apparent priorities.

The revolutionary war which we are waging spreads over a wide area which our military forces cannot defend. The enemy is capable of striking in different places, thus we cannot consider that we have front lines. Moreover, the enemy occupies a large area inhabited by a great number of our people. These, through their struggle, can prevent the enemy from setting up front lines which it can protect. As far as the enemy is concerned, the absence of front lines is a very important matter, since it paralyzes its ability to carry out its military operations in a manner which suits the structure of its army and the training of its soldiers.

Our enemy, in addition to its military campaigns, has been waging a political campaign for a long time. It has solid political bases all over the world, including the Arab homeland. It is capable of moving these political bases in a coordinated and effective manner to support its military aggression. We cannot confront the political bases, which the enemy has established, with military weapons. We must carry out an arduous political struggle to isolate and paralyze the political bases of the enemy and hinder their ability to support the aggression against us.

The second question to be answered is: What are the aims of political struggle?

The aims of political struggle are numerous, but the most important are the following:

- Political struggle will mobilize the people for the purpose of their participation in the struggle. Such a mobilization should pass through different stages. Moreover, one should take into account that there are differences in peoples readiness and ability to participate in the revolution.

The phases of the mobilization of the masses are as follows:

- o To enlighten the people about the aims of the revolution, its bask program and its political and social outlook. This enlightenment does not necessarily imply the adoption of a definite political ideology, nor is it subject to development as the landmarks of the revolution become clearer. The people should get acquainted with the new society which the revolution is planning to establish. They should also understand, to a great extent, the compelling reasons for carrying out the revolution and the necessities for which the people have to sacrifice.

- To educate the masses politically by defining the stand of the revolution and the role of the different external and internal forces. There are a great number of forces in the world which are natural allies of the enemy and are ready to participate in its aggression, protect it and defend i t At the same time there are other forces and nations which are ready to stand by the revolution, participate in it to varying degrees, and support the peoples struggle; knowing the role of the international forces of liberation is a basic factor in evaluating the future of the revolution. It is necessary that the people should know their allies and their enemy. Palestinian society and Arab society are tom by internal factions and are made of different classes. In every society there are revolutionary forces which are capable of carrying arms and of sacrifice. However, there are also other forces whose readiness is less than the above-mentioned, and still others who do not feel the necessity of making any sacrifices. While in complete contrast, there are yet other forces who are against the revolution. Some of them have expressed their antagonism from the very beginning of the revolution and others have kept it hidden for as long as they can. The people should be educated in all these matters in order to know their true course and in order to be able to act in a manner which serves the interest of the revolution. In addition to that, the people should be educated in all the activities of any section in order not to follow a course which does not serve the interest of the revolution. At present there are a number of proposals and solutions which are accompanied by attempts to terrorize or persuade people into accepting them. The people, who are politically educated, are in a position to choose the appropriate position. They are also capable of uncovering the plots aiming at the destruction of the revolution, and thus at all our hopes of liberation.

- The people should be organized to enable them, through their different organizations, to move at the appropriate time and in the tight direction. The organized people are the only ones who are capable of offering sacrifices and of acting in harmony with the program of the revolution. Otherwise, the people's affection for the revolution will be lost. We, at the moment, enjoy wide support and we are proud of it. But, if this support does not stem from organized people, we cannot consider it as a constant force on the side of the revolution on which we can depend in every circumstance.

- The peoples organizations cannot be led through a pyramid-style system. They need cadres which are politically aware at all levels. Such cadres require training and experience in order to provide the effective link between the people and the leaders of the revolution.

The second aim of political struggle is the establishment of a unified command. This will lead the people and the armed struggle by ensuring complete coordination between the different forces in such a manner that will best serve the interest of the revolution. This leadership, which bears the main responsibility, has to transfer its determination and will to the armed forces and the people.

The third aim of political struggle is to carry out continuous uprisings which aim at:

Enlightening the people and increasing their adherence to the revolution. Through these uprisings the peoples sense of responsibility and enthusiasm will be sharpened. The people will become gradually aware of the slogans and aims of the revolution.

Mass uprisings constitute a determining factor in protecting the armed forces. The people, more than once, were able to protect armed action from destruction and from plots planned and carried out by certain Arab regimes. The experiences of the revolution in Jordan and Lebanon are a clear manifestation of the people's physical ability to protect the revolution more successfully than weapons. This in an is especially so since we are Arab land, and any armed confrontation with the Arab armies will cause great difficulties for the development of the revolution. As for the people who are residing in the occupied territories, they are capable of protecting armed action and paralyzing the enemy's ability to strike such action and to ensure its lines of communication and supply routes. There is no doubt that the people will be living and able to provide armed action with assistance and protection at the time when they become highly mobilized.

In addition to maintaining legal rights, mass uprisings aim at achieving new benefits. However minute these benefits may be, they increase the link of the masses to the revolution and their conviction of the necessity of supporting it. The revolution cannot achieve all of its aims at one time. The people, through these uprisings, should take by force their rights, one after the other, so as to be able to take up a position from which they will be more capable of action.

The people will be in a stronger position to exploit the conflicts within the enemy when they are mobilized through political struggle.

Our enemy's affiliations differ, thus the methods of exploiting the conflict is among its members differ. The army of the enemy is composed of members of the Jewish sect who do not belong to one nationality and who are not directed by the same motives. The masses, by interacting with the forces of the enemy, will be in a position to recognize and feed these conflicts, and even win over certain elements to work for our interest. Moreover, there are non-Jewish forces in the enemy's army some of whom are Arabs and it is not difficult to handle them. These forces, whether they agree, or not, cannot forget about their origin and relatives, one hopes to revive the spirit of nationalism among them. As for the Arab armies, which in their entirety are composed of national elements, the mobilized people can easily establish relations with members and officers of these armies to form a protective shield for the revolution whatever the plans and intentions of the Arab regimes maybe with regard to it.

- Political struggle aims, through the mobilization of the people, at choosing the effective elements for the formation of the peoples militia. This militia will be responsible for protecting the people from oppressive acts directed against them by the enemies of the revolution. The ability of the people to resist will be affected, to a great extent, by their ability to protect themselves and prohibit the acts of annihilation carried out by the forces of counter-revolution. The militia is a defensive organization whose task is to defend the people. Unless it is not a part of the armed forces but of the people who undertake political struggle.
- Political struggle through mobilizing the people aims at crushing the arguments of the psychological warfare waged by the enemy.
- Psychological warfare is a great force which the enemy has skillfully used. This kind of warfare has left the marks of its handiwork on our struggle. It has led to the disruption of the unity of the Palestinian forces and the weakening of their morale. In addition, the mobilized people will be able, through their resistance, to wage a counter-psychological war and accomplish the goals which such a war is supposed to achieve.

- The people who actively participate in political struggle will be able to defeat the espionage plans, uncover the agents, and prohibit the acts of sabotage which the enemy carries out among their ranks. At the same time they will be able to protect the lines of supply and the armed bases and prevent the enemy from inflicting any harm on them. Moreover, the people will be able to communicate to the armed forces and the revolutionary leadership, information about the enemy forces, movements and military equipment so that the revolution will be in a better position to confront the enemy. Furthermore, the people will become the eye of the armed forces in order not to fall into the traps and ambushes of the enemy.

- Political struggle ensures the ability of the revolution to continue the struggle. Our revolution depends on the participation of the people through their contributions. We cannot depend on such a situation for a long time, because such overt contributions might be discontinued when any political changes occur. The revolution needs a great amount of money, arms and supplies. Its dependence on contributions which are threatened with disruption endangers the destiny of the revolution. The aim of political struggle is to mobilize the organized people and to make them the pillar of revolutionary resistance in every way possible. If the people are aware of their responsibilities, they can provide the revolution with its requirements and thus enable it to resist all pressures exerted on it and plots planned by certain Arab governments to curtail it. The people should distribute the responsibilities among themselves, so that while the peasant is in his field, the worker in his factory, and every other producer in his proper place, they will still be in a position to participate in supporting the revolution through production, in addition to supporting it by struggle. The peoples participation in securing the material needs of the revolution will increase its solidarity and the peoples adherence to it.

• Political struggle will ensure the support and participation of the Arab forces and progressive forces of the world. The political struggle of the Palestinian people residing in the Arab states should be directed towards the Arab people to increase their solidarity with the revolution. The Arab people are involved in the war of liberation and capable of participating in it. The Palestinian people who are involved in the political struggle should focus their attention on the Arab people to make them participate in the battle and play their role in protecting the revolution against the plots of certain Arab governments. The world progressive forces, led by the countries of the socialist camp, and the rest of the nations who support justice, love and peace could play a role in sup porting and protecting the revolution. This requires an organized political struggle to be carried out by the Palestinian people to contact the mentioned forces and win over their support for the revolution. Our view of the war of liberation should not be limited to the Palestinian level, recruiting supporters requites political struggle on the international and Arab levels. Different forces outside the Palestinian arena are capable of giving military and financial aid and experience. In addition they can support and exert pressure on their government or other governments to prevent them from joining the enemy camp and secure their support for the revolution.

- Political struggle makes the people feel the necessity of self-dependence. The principle of self-dependence is basic to securing the right direction of the revolution and its victory. All the forces of the world can play a role in supporting the revolution, yet the Palestinian people are the ones who have suffered from the aggression. Consequently, they should always be in the first line in fighting the enemy. We cannot depend on external support because it is always threatened with disruption as a result of political changes. There is no doubt that such support enflames the revolution and increases its effectiveness. In spite of all that, the Palestinian people should be able, always and under all circumstances, to keep the revolution going. This is a basic safety factor for the revolution. In its first phases the revolution expressed its belief in the principle of self- dependence. After the expansion of revolutionary action it has become necessary to translate this principle into a reality which the Palestinian people will live everywhere. The present interference of certain Arab regimes in the affairs of the revolution could be traced back to the fact that the Palestinian people have not been self-dependent. They have limited their activities with regard to the revolution to contribution campaigns and contacting money holders in a disorganized manner. Thus the revenues of the revolution have become unstable.

- Political struggle increases the attachment of the people to the homeland through reviving its heritage, culture, local habits, and historical struggle, so that the people will be totally linked to the homeland. Such an act will revive among the people the need to go back to their homeland, in addition to their feeling of pride and dignity.

The Arab regimes, during the past years, have put into effect the international plot to cancel the identity of the Palestinian people, and allow the factor of time the opportunity to weaken the will of the Palestinian people and their attachment to the homeland. Reviving the national heritage will unite the people and make them feel the irreplaceable loss. National heritage cannot be separated from national feelings and love of the homeland.

The ability and qualifications of the people to use all means to defend the homeland will be increased by political struggle. The mobilized masses have played an important role in the progressive world revolutions through the application of the methods of primitive warfare. The people can set up traps and ambushes and exploit all natural means such as irrigation and tillage in fighting. Furthermore, they can, through their long experience, exploit animals for their purposes. The people, in their struggle, can find a role for bees, camels, doves and other animals.

Following this presentation of the necessity for political struggle and its aims, we should answer the third question which gives these aims their factual picture and points out the means for their achievement. Political struggle is a practical stand which requires the people to participate in the revolution. Keeping political struggle within its theoretical framework makes it lose its basic value and gives armed struggle the opportunity to be the only practical expression of the revolution with the resultant dangers that that would involve. A detailed study concerning the method of undertaking political struggle does not aim at putting forward definite formulas for it inasmuch as it puts forward means which do not necessarily imply that they are the sole possible means available.

Our knowledge of the aims of political struggle will suffice to put us in a position in which we can apply different means to enable our people to express their ability to invent new means. In this way our peoples experience will participate in enriching the revolutions of other people.

Yet we must base our political struggle on the rich revolutionary experience fought by different people. Our revolution is a humane one which often resembles the revolutions of other people from the point of view of aims. Thus it was necessary for us to adopt the following methods which they have applied:

1.   Establishment of popular organizations. This is the basis of political struggle. Generally speaking the masses political awareness and readiness to bear the burdens of the struggle differ. Thus it is necessary to take into consideration these differences and establish popular organizations on different levels. It can be summarized as follow s:

2.   Broadly-based popular organizations which may act lawfully, such as the workers, students, peasants' and merchants federations; religious, sports, social and women's organizations; and any other kind of organizations whether they be based on a trade or anything else.

The distinguishing feature of such organizations is their ability to encompass all the elements of the people irrespective of their readiness to be committed to the program of the revolution. Thus the revolution can work through these organizations and influence tb d r members. Moreover, through these organizations, the revolution can get in touch with the leadership and direct them on an individual basis in order to induce them to enlighten the people with regard to the aims of the revolution. Furthermore, these organizations are capable of transforming the masses from being diversified, ineffective and helpless, even with regard to matters which concern their interests, into pressure groups capable of taking by force their rights and taking up attitudes that accord with their will. These organizations open the door for organized revolutionary action. Yet this does not imply that the above-mentioned organizations are capable of undertaking effective actions unless the revolution completes its work in this field. This is especially so since the enemies of the people's cause have established vague popular organizations whose aim is to distract the people from their revolutionary program and prevent them from practicing their role.

1. Establishment of groupings and organizations with political affiliations. These differ from the above-mentioned popular organizations since they represent a phase of action which is more developed. These organizations have

different forms, but, generally speaking, they can be limited to two:

2. The groupings which are created by the revolution within the popular organizations. For example, the revolution, through its action among members of the worker's federations, can recruit workers who believe in the aims and slogans of the revolution and attempt to gather the largest possible number of workers in one grouping which represents the revolutionary workers. Through this grouping, which calls for the implementation of the aims of the revolution, the revolutionary workers can get in touch with and recruit different elements of the workers. In addition they will recruit an avant-garde of politically aware workers to strengthen their commitment through revolutionary organizations. The distinguishing feature of these groupings is their ability to operate law fully, and, at the same time, work among organizations with the largest membership. Moreover, through their struggle, these groupings can achieve social and economic benefits for the workers. Thus, these groupings improve the workers conditions and increase their ability to resist, and, at the same time, they recruit the mass of workers for the revolution.

3. Organizations with definite
political aims. These organizations are
not based on popular organizations but
encompass elements recruited from
different organizations who agree to
pursue an objective which is in harmony
with the aims of the revolution. There are
many such organizations; for example
youth organizations whose aim is
grouping different elements of the youth
for the support of the revolution and who
undertake exploration and light training.
Moreover, one can set up organizations
to resist Zionist occupation. These will
be responsible for holding discussions
and rallies, undertaking financial projects
and publishing pamphlets, etc.

Committees for the support of the revolution
can be established with the aim of contacting the
Arab peoples to make them aware of and
participate in the revolution in one way or
another. More over, committees of solidarity
with friendly people can be established such as
the Afro-Asian committees of solidarity. Further
more, organizations for combatting anti-
Semitism, or organizations of friendship
between the Arab people and the non-Zionist
Jews can be established. Along these lines the
following organizations can be cited: The
Committee for Reviving the Camp, Friends of
Jerusalem Society, The National Enlightenment
Society against the Dangers of Zionism, The

Fighters Sweater Committee, The Committee for the Care of the Martyrs Families, The Fifth of June Society, etc. These different organizations should be organized in such a way that they direct their efforts according to a revolutionary orientation.

The revolutionary organizations of the cadres. These are the back bone of the revolution, its security and moving force. The weakness of the cadres or their absence will cause the disintegration of the relationship between the will of the revolutionary leadership and the masses, thus depriving political struggle of one of its most important links. As a result, the subject of the cadres should be given great attention and effort. The cadres are the connecting link between the revolution and the masses, and they constitute the true leadership of the people. In the absence of the cadres the revolution will be exposed to a profound split between itself and the people. The building of the cadres will be achieved naturally through the application of (A) and (B). Through the struggle of the organizations which have political affiliations, the revolution becomes better acquainted with the avant-garde elements among the people and can recruit the leading elements who are in harmony with the revolutions political program. The cadres should be disciplined, politically aware, able to move easily and ready to sacrifice. When it becomes capable of leading all kinds of popular organizations, thus any popular movement becomes complementary to the political struggle of the revolution. The revolution cannot afford to commit many errors in building up its cadres because these will be directly reflected in its ability and destiny. the revolution is equipped with such cadres, sing legal methods to carry out political action which aims at protecting and acquiring the legal rights of the people. Every regime which is against the people is bound to allow certain legal forms of mass agitation and has to give the people some of their rights, however few these may be. As far as our people under Zionist occupation are concerned, the Zionist terrorist measures, cannot deprive them of the right of movement in every circumstance. For example, our people in the occupied territories can gather in mosques and churches, can visit the tombs of the dead, and can pay family visits. In addition, the Arabs in the territories occupied prior to 3 June participated in one or other of the political aspects of the political life of the country. They had the right to vote and belong to political parties. Moreover, there are social, religious, sports and charity organizations and establish elements. Through these rights, despite their paucity, the revolution can carry out different activities such as making people politically aware, developing organizations and getting to know different elements who have never been organized or contacted.

As for the Palestinian masses in the Arab countries their situation, although it differs from one state to the other, is, generally speaking, very different from those in the occupied territories. They have legal rights which we are not going to enumerate here. The revolution must benefit from these rights to the fullest extent, because, as it is able to work through legality, it is easier for the revolution to contact the people for the purpose of enlightenment and participation. As a general rule, the masses, before undertaking serious political struggle, will not be ready to carry responsibility or offer sacrifices. A great number will only participate in the official authorities, in order to avoid any acts of revenge on the part of the authorities. The absence of contact between the people and the revolution makes the former weak and incapable of resistance. Thus it is necessary that revolutionary action should reach the hearts and minds of the people through lawful activity, after which the relationship will develop.

The development we are talking about in the relationship between the masses and the revolution should happen in stages. At first the revolution should push the masses to struggle to get more lawful rights. Thus, the revolution will make the masses feel that it aspires to acquire more benefits for them, and at the same time it will create more favorable conditions to increase the peoples ability to struggle. In April 1968, when the crisis broke out in Lebanon, there was a great disparity between the level of armed struggle in establishing bases on Lebanese territory and the Palestinian people who had been deprived for more than 20 years. This disparity disabled the masses from protecting armed action in a serious and definite manner.

The masses who possess more rights will be more capable of supporting, protecting and escalating armed action. The relationship between armed action and the lawful rights of the Palestinians will become stronger as long as the revolution is aware of its importance.

1.   Political struggle and armed struggle should go hand in hand. Our revolution, at present, suffers from the disparity between the level of political action and that of armed action. Such a disparity poses a threat since it proposes the adoption of armed struggle as the only method of struggle. Thus it was necessary to depend on armed struggle to protect and develop political struggle, at a time when the latter was preparing itself to become the nucleus of revolutionary action. Political struggle, at present, can carry out activities to support armed struggle as a means of developing itself. In this context political action must accomplish the following:

2.   To create the necessary atmosphere for armed action by adopting it, calling for its support and expressing the desire of the people to strengthen it. The slogan calling for the support of armed struggle is an easy one to work through and the revolution can mobilize the people to carry it out. The enemies of

the revolution will find that it is difficult to fight the idea of armed action and its implications, since it represents readiness to the, sacrifice, altruism, heroism and idealism. Those elements who do not hide that they are against the content of the revolution, do not dare to attack or severely criticize armed action. One of the methods of undertaking political struggle was adherence to armed struggle: not to use it and be protected by it, but to give political action a dimension equivalent to that of armed struggle as far as heroism, idealism, commitment to the revolution and the resulting sacrifices are concerned.

3.   To choose the right elements to participate in armed action. Our masses, as a result of their eagerness to struggle, and their long endured deprivation, are ready to participate in armed struggle to retrieve their lost pride and dignity. Political struggle, if it aims at achieving closer association between the revolution and the masses, should be the road to secure contact between the right elements and the armed struggle. When the people feel that their political organization is the only link between them and armed struggle; and when they are assured that participation in political struggle will open the road for armed struggle and martyrdom, they will respond more to that struggle.

4. To build the political groups as a centre for armed bases. The people, especially in the first stages of their political awareness, feel that their political struggle aims at transform ing the places where they are grouped into bases in which to live and protect the members of the armed forces. Political struggle must respond to this aim so that places of mass groupings will become a primary source for armed bases. This matter is obvious with regard to the Arabs in the occupied territories and the people residing in places near the armed bases.

5. To create a popular militia. The creation of the militia in the political bases and places of mass groupings achieves, in addition to defending the people, a suitable atmosphere for political struggle.

Political struggle, in which broad sections of the masses participate, needs to offer them a degree of self-confidence. For example, the presence of the militia in the camps is, no doubt, an incentive to participate in the political struggle, and, at the same time, it is a factor which will protect the people against being crushed.

Establishment of a wide national front from among the different national forces. The revolution struggles to recover the homeland and liberate it and its people.

This slogan answers the needs and wishes of many of the groups and national forces.

Every nation which is passing through the phase of national struggle needs to find a common formula to unify its efforts. Thus the creation of a national front is a fundamental determining factor in preparing the basic conditions for the continuation of the revolution, and its victory. The fragmentation of our society through the dispersion of our people has contributed to their weakness vis–vis their enemies. There are many forces and groups who are loyal to our nation, but because of their political beliefs and social status cannot join the revolutionary organizations. There are other forces and groups who can, at one stage, participate, in one form or other, alongside the revolution. Thus the revolution, in its different phases, should establish a national front which will fulfill the aims of each phase. The structure of the national front is not meant to be a perm anent one which organizes relations among the national forces and groups. On the contrary, it is a temporary frame work which develops in accordance with the changes that occur in each phase. The revolution, as it progresses, attempts to group all the forces which serve a certain phase. In case the revolution is faced with difficulties which require it to retreat to less developed positions, it should establish relations with different forces and groups to be in a better position to protect itself while preparing for a counter-attack. The national fronts slogans and aims will differ at every phase. In the first stages of its development, the front's aim will be fighting Zionism, later fighting Zionism and its allies, etc ..

In its first stages the national front can include all the popular groupings, but in its more developed stages the front becomes clearer and more revolutionary so that it expresses all the political aims of the revolution. A large number of the allies of yesterday become the enemies of today, many of the allies of today will become the enemies of tomorrow, and many of the allies of tomorrow will abandon the revolution all together. We cannot build the national front on the basis of achieving all the aims of the revolution. However, under no circumstances, should this imply that we should avoid knowing our temporary and perm anent political aims during the process of establishing the national front. These aims should be always remembered so that the national front will be a step forward instead of being a step backward which would result in diluting the revolution and blurring its aims.

1.   A continuous process of clarification of the policy of the revolution in its broadest aspect. Such a clarification will provide the revolution with people who believe in it, and will help to discover the elements who are qualified to join the revolution. If the political program of the revolution is clear, the atmosphere of political struggle becomes dear and attractive. The revolution does not struggle

for the sake of revenge, or to inflict harm on the Jews, or to bring to an end economic competition between our people and the aggressors. The revolution struggles to recover the homeland for its people and for the sake of the coming generations of our people ~who must live on their land, practice their rights, enjoy their freedom and the fruits of their land. It is a revolution against all forms of exploitation. It is a revolution which believes in the right to self-determination for all peoples. It is a revolution which is linked with all the progressive forces of the world. It fulfills its humane role of enriching the experience of the people struggling for liberation. It also endeavors to place our people in their natural place so that they may carry out their obligations and commitments towards humanity. The Palestinian people cannot join the revolution unless it is positive and aims at building before demolishing. In terms of the revolution, the acts of demolishing is a step in the direction of the creation of reliable individuals. This clarity in the policy of the revolution is a basic factor in strengthening the political struggle and clarifying its details. The means of such clarification are numerous, but the most effective is the direct verbal explanation at both the individual and collective levels, in addition to other educational means, such as books, pamphlets, newspapers, broadcasting, posters, communiques, etc .

2.   Political education of the people. The aims of such education ate: to point out to the people who are the enemies and who are the

allies of the revolution ; and to acquaint them with the political situation of the revolution in order to increase their ability to react favorably to its slogan, and know the true program for which we are struggling. The enemies of the revolution are numerous, but we have to know the main enemy, to isolate it and destroy it. U ten the revolution will choose the second enemy to concentrate on and confront. Thus political struggle, by educating the people, can lead them in the direction which serves the policy of the revolution, and will not allow temporary commotions against secondary enemies to create pockets which will distract the revolution from its basic program. There can be no doubt that political education, which aims at making the people know their enemies and capable of evaluating them, will help to clarify and strengthen political struggle. Political struggle which does not educate the people along these lines will find itself hesitating before different courses; this will be reflected by the people and will weaken the struggle.

3.   Knowledge of the enemies of the revolution and the ability to evaluate them are basic factors in the political struggle; yet there is another, and no less important factor, and that is knowing the friends of the revolution. The friends of the revolution vary. There are temporary friends who may become enemies in the future. There are other long term friends who may lag behind the revolution in its development. There are also perm anent friends who will be able to support the revolution under

199

all circumstances. A discussion concerning the friends of the revolution should be based on a political and sociological study which is not the subject of this paper. Yet educating the people along these lines is very important; because, in this way, the revolution will maintain its leadership of the people, and will prevent the people, in the future, from adopting stands which will put them under a non-revolutionary leader ship and make their ability to side with the revolution temporary.

4.   Leading the people gradually according to the way in which they have been prepared from a lower to a higher level of struggle. The people who have never struggled and home hardships and dangers are usually in no position to participate in the highest level of revolutionary struggle. Unless one of the obligations of political struggle is to undertake such preparation of the people. Raising the standards of the people with regard to struggle requires their gradual participation in it. We can encourage individuals to voice their support of the revolution verbally, or to support certain primary demands pertaining to the revolution. Then we proceed to allow the people to sign petitions, form delegations to contact those who are responsible, and submit demands however simple. After that we can call for closed or open meetings in houses and dubs, and then proceed to call for licensed rallies to celebrate a memory, an occasion, or in support of a demand of the people. Following that we can call on the people to participate in licensed demonstrations, then

unlicensed ones which usually lead to a confrontation with the authorities.

5. Such a confrontation will require the people to strengthen their ability to defend themselves and carry arms. These steps give only an idea of the methods that should be followed in advancing the mobilization of the people to the point at which they will be able to participate in the revolution. The experiences of each particular camp or state will help to give a clearer guideline on the methods of helping people participate in the political struggle. At times we can exchange one of these methods and use another, and at others we can dispense with certain steps if the people prove their readiness to surpass them. The danger of pushing the people to a high level of struggle without preparation will lead to the revolution's separation from the people and a discontinuation of the sacrifices that they give. The above-mentioned steps cannot all be applied at once but should be applied gradually to different groups so that the experience of one group will be more advanced than another.

6. To exchange services. Political struggle aims at recruiting the masses to participate in revolutionary action. Yet the people do not have the same degree of political awareness, and many of them have personal problems concerning education, work, health, residence, production, etc. The revolution cannot mobilize the people and put them in their proper place without offering them something in return. Interaction between the revolution and the

people requires continuous exchange in services. The masses offer sacrifices for the revolution in addition to assistance and support; the revolution offers the masses what it can achieve in the form of benefits and protection with regard to the requirements of daily life.

7.   This sort of exchange in services increases the masses adherence to and belief in the revolution. Our revolution has attempted many times to achieve this. There is no doubt that it has not yet been able to offer the required assurances which express its belief in the necessity of ex changing services. What the revolution offers at present in the fields of medical and educational services does not suffice the needs of the people. But the revolution, in addition to the services it does offer, can revive among the people the spirit of cooperation so that they can serve each other and lighten the burdens of others. The revolution should assist all those whose houses are blown up by the enemy authorities so that they will not be exposed to emigration. The sons of the locality in which a house is blown up can cooperate to rebuild it in a short period in order to give confidence to every citizen that the loss of his house will not be final. Another example is that many people suffer from arbitrary dismissal by their employers. The revolution can, through different means at its disposal, strive for the re-employment of the dismissed worker or provide him with another job. In this way people will feel that the revolution gives as much as it takes, and that they should give it as

much as they can. This cooperative spirit among the people themselves and between them and the revolution must truly exemplify itself in the cadres. Members of the cadres should set an example by being the first ones to offer their services.

8.   To purge the ranks of the revolution from the bad elements. In order to undertake political struggle, we should give the masses a good image of the elements participating in the revolution. In the eyes of the masses revolutionary elements should set an example in morality, discipline, good behavior, altruism, and humility. Thus the revolution has to purge its ranks of all the bad elements in order to preserve its translucence vis–vis the masses who do not accept being led by elements whom they do not trust or admire.

9.   To destroy agents. Political struggle needs an atmosphere of mutual trust among the people so that the individual will not feel that he is surrounded by agents who will report him to the official authorities. In many incidents people have desisted from continuing their resistance for fear of being reported agents. An atmosphere of confidence among the people will protect their movement, and at the same time will increase their self-confidence and belief in their ability to participate in the revolution. Our revolution has carried out some of these activities and threatened a number of agents in the occupied territories and executed others. In spite of this there are many agents who are still safe from the power of the revolution. As for the agents

operating outside the occupied territories, their role in aborting the revolutionary trend is known, and using different means to nullify the harm they inflict on the _ people will be another of the factors which will promote political struggle among the people.

10. To raise slogans and honor heroes and martyrs. The masses are not expected to be aware at one stroke of all the means that will lead to their participation in the political struggle. The revolution must raise different slogans to help in enlightening and educating the people, prompting them to work in different fields that, in the final analysis, will serve the trend of the revolution. General slogans can be raised among the masses which express our political aims and methods, such as, "Guns . . . all guns against the enemy." This slogan is an emotional call for the creation of the national front and the rejection of internal struggles. Another slogan is, "Let us carry the hammer and plow in one hand and the gun in the other." This slogan urges the people to pay attention to pro duction and at the same time to prepare themselves for sacrifice so that the worker will not be in a position to choose between productive work and revolutionary work. Other slogans can be raised, such as, "The land for those who liberate it," expressing the belief of the revolution in the masses and its determination to prohibit exploitation. In this context we can mention slogans calling for the improvement of health and a strengthening of the economic situation thus manifesting the

ability to confront the enemy at any place or time. Moreover there can be slogans directed to students, teachers, women, youth or any other group.

As for the martyrs, fighters, heroes, by announcing their heroism and reminding the people of their sacrifices, the people will, no doubt, be led to sense the high spirit of the revolution, and to increase their adherence to it. A readiness and desire to act in a similar way may be awakened in them.

These are the means for carrying out political struggle. They are general guidelines which portray forces that show that political struggle is a difficult and long term work, but that, at the same time, it deserves every effort and sacrifice. The means of political struggle are numerous. The revolution can fill each day with struggle and make the masses participate in every step it takes without separating the daily reality of the masses from their inevitable role in the war of liberation.

As has been pointed out in this study, political struggle is the sound base for revolutionary action. The movement of armed struggle should pass through an act of continuous escalation of political struggle. The reality of the present situation forces us to exert every effort in order to fill the vacuum created by the emergence of armed struggle before the natural development of political struggle. The circumstances which forced the revolution to undertake armed struggle make it our duty not to leave this struggle without its basic pillar, which is, political struggle.

PLO National Charter
(Palestine Liberation Organization)

- Article 1: Palestine is the homeland of the Arab Palestinian people; it is an indivisible part of the Arab homeland, and the Palestinian people are an integral part of the Arab nation.
- Article 2: Palestine, with the boundaries it had during the British mandate, is an indivisible territorial unit.

- Article 3: The Palestinian Arab people possess the legal right to their homeland and have the right to determine their destiny after achieving the liberation of their country in accordance with their wishes and entirely of their own accord and will.
- Article 4: The Palestinian identity is a genuine, essential and inherent characteristic; it is transmitted from parents to children. The Zionist occupation and the dispersal of the Palestinian Arab people, through the disasters which befell them, do not make them lose their Palestinian identity and their membership of the Palestinian community, nor do they negate them.
- Article 5: The Palestinians are those Arab nationals who, until 1947, normally resided in Palestine regardless of whether they were evicted from it or have stayed there. Anyone born, after that date, of a Palestinian father whether inside Palestine or outside itis also a Palestinian.
- Article 6: The Jews who had normally resided in Palestine until the beginning of the Zionist invasion will be considered Palestinians.
- Article 7: That there is a Palestinian immunity and that it has material, spiritual and historical connection with Palestine are

indisputable facts. It is a national duty to bring up individual Palestinians in an Arab revolutionary manner. All means of information and education must be adopted in order to acquaint the Palestinian with his country in the most profound manner, both spiritual and material, that is possible. He must be prepared for the armed struggle and ready to sacrifice his wealth and his life in order to win back his homeland and bring about its liberation.

• Article 8: The phase in their history, through which the Palestinian people are now living, is that of national struggle for the liberation of Pales tine. Thus the conflicts among the Palestinian national forces are secondary, and should be ended for the sake of the basic conflict that exists between the forces of Zionism and of imperialism on the one hand, and the Palestinian Arab people on the other. On this basis the Palestinian masses, regardless of whether they are residing in the national homeland or in diaspora, constitute both their organizations and the individuals one national front working for the retrieval of Palestine and its liberation through armed struggle.

• Article 9: Armed struggle is the only way to liberate Palestine. Thus it is the overall strategy, not merely a tactical phase. The Palestinian Arab people assert their absolute determination and firm resolution to continue their armed struggle and to work for an armed popular revolution for the liberation of their country and their return to it. They also assert their right to normal life in Palestine and to exercise their right to self-determination and sovereignty over it.

• Article 10: Commando action constitutes the nucleus of the Palestinian popular liberation war. This requires its escalation, comprehensiveness and the mobilization of all the Palestinian popular and educational efforts and their organization and involvement in the armed Palestinian revolution. It also requires the achieving of unity for the national struggle among the different groupings of the Palestinian people, and between the Palestinian people and the Arab masses so as to secure the continuation of the revolution, its escalation and victory.

• Article 11: The Palestinians will have three mottoes: national unity national mobilization and liberation.

• Article 12: The Palestinian people believe in Arab unify. In order to contribute their share towards the attainment of that objective, however, they must, at the present stage of their struggle, safeguard their Palestinian identify and develop their consciousness of that identify, and oppose any plan that may dissolve or impair it.

• Article 13: Arab unify and the liberation of Palestine are two complementary objectives, the attainment of either of which facilitates the attainment of the other. Thus, Arab unify leads to the liberation of Palestine; the liberation of Palestine leads to Arab unify; and work towards the realization of one objective proceeds side by side with work towards the realization of the other.

• Article 14: The destiny of the Arab nation, and indeed Arab existence itself, depends upon the destiny of the Palestine cause. From this inter dependence springs the Arab nations pursuit of, and striving for, the liberation of Palestine. The people of Palestine play the role of the vanguard in the realization of this sacred national goal.

• Article 15: The liberation of Palestine, from an Arab viewpoint, is a national duty and it attempts to repel the Zionist and imperialist aggression against the Arab homeland and aims at the elimination of Zionism in Palestine. Absolute responsibility for this falls upon the Arab nation peoples and governments with the Arab people of Palestine in the vanguard. Accordingly, the Arab nation must mobilize all its military, human, moral and spiritual capabilities to participate actively with the Palestinian people in the liberation of Palestine. It must, particularly in the phase of the armed Palestinian revolution, offer and furnish the Palestinian people with all possible help, and material and human support, and make available to them the means and opportunities that will enable them to continue to carry out their leading role in the armed revolution, until they liberate their homeland.

• Article 16: The liberation of Palestine, from a spiritual point of view, will provide the Holy Land with an atmosphere of safety and tranquility, which in turn will safeguard the country's religious sanctuaries and guarantee freedom of worship and of visit to all, without discrimination of race, color, language, or religion. Accordingly, the people of Palestine look to all spiritual forces in the world for support.

• Article 17: The liberation of Palestine, from a human point of view, will restore to the Palestinian individual his dignity, pride and freedom. Accordingly the Palestinian Arab people look forward to the support of all those who believe in the dignity of man and his freedom in the world.

- Article 18: The liberation of Palestine, from an international point of view, is a defensive action necessitated by the demands of self-defense. Accordingly, the Palestinian people, desirous as they are of the friendship of all people, look to freedom-loving, justice-loving and peace-loving states for support in order to restore their legitim are rights in Palestine, to re-establish peace and security in the country, and to enable its people to exercise national sovereignty and freedom.

- Article 19: The partition of Palestine in 1947 and the establishment of the state of Israel are entirely illegal, regardless of the passage of time, because they were contrary to the will of the Palestinian people and to their natural right in their homeland, and inconsistent with the principles emboldened in the Charter of the United Nations, particularly the right to self-determination.

- Article 20: The Balfour Declaration, the mandate for Palestine and everything that has been based upon them, are deemed null and void. Claims of historical or religious ties of Jews with Palestine are incompatible with the facts of history and the true conception of what constitutes statehood. Judaism, being a religion, is not an independent nationality. Nor do Jews constitute a single nation with an identity of its ow n; they are citizens of the states to which they belong.

• Article 21: The Arab Palestinian people, expressing themselves by the armed Palestinian revolution, reject all solutions which are substitutes for the total liberation of Palestine and reject all proposals aiming at the liquidation of the Palestinian problem, or its internationalization.

• Article 22: Zionism is a political movement organically associated with international imperialism and antagonistic to all action for liberation and to progressive movements in the world. It is racist and fanatic in its nature, aggressive, expansionist and colonial in its aims, and fascist in its methods.

(Israel is the instrument of the Zionist movement, and a geographical base for world imperialism placed strategically in the midst of the Arab homeland to combat the hopes of the Arab nation for liberation, unity and progress. Israel is a constant source of threat vis–vis peace in the Middle East and the whole world. Since the liberation of Palestine will destroy the Zionist and imperialist presence and will contribute to the establishment of peace in the Middle East, the Palestinian people look for the support of all the progressive and peaceful forces and urge them all, irrespective of their affiliations and beliefs, to offer the Palestinian people all aid and support in their just struggle for the liberation of their homeland.)

• Article 23: The demands of security and peace, as well as the demands of right and justice, require all states to consider Zionism an illegitimate movement, to outlaw its existence, and to ban its operations, in order that friendly relations among peoples may be preserved, and the loyalty of citizens to their respective homelands safeguarded.

• Article 24: The Palestinian people believe in the principles of justice, freedom, sovereignty, self-determination, human dignity, and in the right of all peoples to exercise them.

• Article 25: For the realization of the goals of this Charter and its principles, the Palestine Liberation Organization will perform its role in the liberation of Palestine in accordance with the Constitution of this Organization.

• Article 26: The Palestine Liberation Organization, representative of tira Palestinian revolutionary forces, is responsible for the Palestinian Arab peoples movement in its struggle to retrieve its homeland, liberate and return to it and exercise the right to self-determination in it in all military, political and financial fields and also for whatever may be required by the Palestine case on the inter-Arab and international levels.

- Article 27: The Palestine Liberation Organization shall cooperate with all
- Arab states, each according to its potentialities; and will adopt a neutral policy among them in the light of the requirements of the war of liberation; and on this basis it shall not interfere in the internal affairs of any Arab state.
- Article 28: The Palestinian Arab people assert the genuineness and independence of their national revolution and reject all forms of intervention, trusteeship and subordination.
- Article 29: The Palestinian people possess the fundamental and genuine legal right to liberate and retrieve their homeland. The Palestinian people determine their attitude towards all states and forces on the basis of the stands they adopt vis–vis the Palestinian case and the extent of the support they offer to the Palestinian revolution to fulfill the aims of the Palestinian people.

• Article 30: Fighters and carriers of arms in the war of liberation are the nucleus of the popular army which will be the protective force for the gains of the Palestinian Arab people.

• Article 31: The Organization shall have a flag, an oath of allegiance and an anthem. All this shall be decided upon in accordance with a special regulation.

• Article 32: Regulations, which shall be known as the Constitution of the Palestine Liberation Organization, shall be annexed to this Charter. It shall lay down the manner in which the Organization, and its organs and institutions, shall be constituted; the respective competence of each; and the requirements of its obligations under the Charter.

• Article 33: This Charter shall not be amended save by (vote of) a majority of two-thirds of the total membership of the National Congress of the Palestine Liberation Organization (taken) at a special session convened for that purpose.

THE POPULAR DEMOCRATIC FRONT FOR THE LIBERATION OF PALESTINE

The national Palestinian question cannot be separated, all through history, from the circumstances which involve Palestine and international struggles. A scientific historical review of the Middle East situation reveals that there is a dialectical relationship between the development of the Palestine situation and that of the Middle East in general and the immediate area surrounding Palestine in particular. The totality of these developments has decided, and is still deciding, the future of Palestine and its struggling people.

The modern history of Palestine ultimately proves the validity of this historical truth. The weakness of the Ottoman regime, which was based on religious feudalism, in the face of European capitalism, prompted imperialism to covet the inheritance of the Ottoman Empire and to divide the 'sick man of Europe.' At the same time Zionism, led by Jewish capitalism, began to envisage the seizure of Palestine under the pretext of religion, in order to establish a Zionist racist movement encompassing Jewish groupings in different countries of the world. As a result of their common interests, the colonial-imperial powers and Zionism, which opposed the liberation movement of the Palestinians and the Arabs, formed one bloc in the face of the Ottoman Empire.

Following World War I, two of the imperialist countries Britain and France annexed the Arab East. (In 1917 Britain had published the Balfour Declaration which gave Zionism a national right for the Jews in Palestine.) The British attitude was not accidental, or an error on the part of its foreign minister, but was an objective result of its imperialist policy in the Arab East. The aim was to implant in the Arab world an armed human stronghold of the Popular Front for the Liberation of Palestine, August 1968.

For imperialism which would resist the Arab nationalist liberation movement whose success would threaten imperialist bases and interests in their entirety in this strategic area of the world. In addition, the attitude adopted by Britain was in compliance with Zionist aspirations to settlement, which agreed with colonial-imperial plans, and opposed Palestinian-Arab national liberation aspirations.

The Arab feudal regimes in Palestine and the other Arab states provided imperialism and Zionism with good opportunities to execute their plans for Palestine in particular, and for the other Arab states in general. Since their establishment the Arab feudal regimes essentially bourgeois have associated themselves with the colonialist-imperialist powers, i.e., the counter-revolutionary bloc, against the Palestinian and Arab national liberation movements. The common interests of imperialism and the Arab feudal regimes have led to an alliance between them. Such an alliance is best exemplified in the protection accorded by imperialism to the Arab feudal regimes and the exploiting class, in addition to the protection it has given to its own imperialist exploiting interests. Furthermore, the Arab regimes protected the interests of imperialism since neither of them could exist in the area without the help of the other.

As a result of the dependence on imperialism of the Arab feudal, bourgeois regimes, they remained handicapped vis–vis Zionist aspirations, and the promises made by imperialism regarding the "Judaization" of Palestine. These regimes were satisfied by merely calling on the "ally" Britain to understand the rights of the people of Palestine.

It is natural that the reactionary Arab regimes took such a defeatist attitude towards the judaizing of Palestine because, as a result of their feudal- bourgeois set-up, they could not confront the plans of imperialism and Zionism with the force of arms and popular national revolutions. Reactionary regimes, at all times and places and this applies to the Arab states fear the masses more than they fear imperialism. The confrontation of imperialist and Zionist plans requires arming and organizing the people and this is specifically what the reactionary regimes refuse to do, as they oppose national liberation in the Arab states and in the under-developed countries of Asia, Africa and Latin America. Furthermore, the interests and existence of these regimes, by the very nature of their feudal bourgeois structure, are intertwined with imperialism and neo imperialism connected with the interests of traditional imperialism in the Arab world.

Thus since the beginning of the modem history of Palestine, it has become clear that the destiny of Palestine will be decided by the struggle of a national movement. This will be essentially a class struggle between the national liberation bloc on the Palestinian and Arab land and the enemies of the liberation movement, such as imperialism, Arab reactionary regimes in alliance with imperialism, and world Zionism.

Since the comprador, feudal-bourgeois classes, by their control over the suppressive, police-like agencies of the government, were able to dominate the leadership of the national movement, the destiny of Palestine was predictable. In spite of all the slogans put out by the governing classes, they adopted a cooperative and defeatist stand vis–vis the judaizing of Palestine. Instead of defying imperialism and opening a national front against itbut this is not in the nature of the reactionary ruling classes these classes undertook, throughout the history of the Palestinian and Arab liberation movement, a policy of suppression and siege vis–vis revolutionary national forces. At the same time the ruling classes continued to cooperate with imperialism and protect their interests in the Arab world, foremost among which is the exploitation of Arab oil.

If one analyzes the history of Palestine, it becomes clear that the history and destiny of Palestine is decided by the totality of the circumstances involving Palestine and international policies and struggles. The modem history of Palestine is a proof of the truth of such an argument. The 1948 defeat came at the hands of religious feudal Palestinian leaders such as Hajj Amin al-Husseini, the bourgeoisie, such as the Independence Party and the Defense Party, etc., and the Arab feudal regimes exemplified in the Arab kings and presidents. This defeat gave direct evidence of the dialectic connection between the actual state existing in Palestine, the Arab world, and the international set-up. The disaster of Palestine and the creation of the "state of Israel" is the result of the Palestine-Arab dialectic.

This condensed introduction is necessary in the present decisive circumstances through which the Palestine question is passing in order to point out the inevitable connection between the developments in the Arab world and the destiny of the Palestine question. The developments which took place, and are still taking place, in the Arab world and throughout the history of Palestine, touch, in one way or another, on the situation and destiny of Palestine. Any attempt to ignore such a question is suspicious; it is a reactionary, imperialist or Zionist attempt.

At the present stage the national Palestinian question is passing through its most difficult phase. To be more specific, since the June 1967 defeat, proposals have been made, and are still being made, by some Palestinian and Arab rightists calling for the isolation of the Palestine struggle movement from all the happenings and developments in the Arab area under the slogan of "noninterference in the internal affairs of the Arab countries." In the final analysis this slogan, at the hands of the Palestine resistance movement, has been transformed into "non-interference in Palestinian affairs," since what happened, and is happening, in the Arab land is dialectically connected with the Palestine question, and the lessons of 1996, 1948 and the 1967 defeat are still fresh and before our eyes. After June 1967 the Arab regimes did not isolate themselves from the Palestine question and whatever happens inside their countries touches on the Palestine question.

The reactionary Palestinian, who is partnered by the Arab reactionary rightist in his call for a separation between the Palestinian question and the Arab regimes, implants the beginning of a new political or military defeat. This defeat will lead to the liquidation of the Palestine question in accordance with the political settlement proposed by the Security Council on 22 November 1967. Such a call on the part of the reactionary Palestinian rightists aims at ignoring historical facts and obliterating the contradiction between the existing Arab regimes, which were responsible for the 1948 disaster and the 1967 defeat, and the question of liberating Palestine. With regard to the imperialist-colonialist-Zionist attack of June 1967, the Arab reactionary and defeatist regimes have issued suspicious statements concerning the dimensions of the national liberation movement within their countries. Similar statements have been made about the lessons and results of the 1948 disaster and the 1967 defeat, the responsibility for which falls on the existing regimes. At the same time these regimes continue to handle the Palestine problem on the basis of the Security Council resolution. Thus, the Palestine resistance movement should judge the Arab regimes on the basis of their actual stand vis–vis the Palestinian national problem. Otherwise, the Palestinian resistance movement will lose its Palestinian identity and will be transformed into a quantitative addition to the present circumstances and to the existing Arab regimes responsible for the failure of the 1936 revolution, the 1948 disaster, and the 1967 defeat. Any public examination of the Palestinian national question cannot be isolated from the examination and criticism of the circumstances of the Arabs responsible for the "historical dilemma which now faces the Palestine problem after the June defeat The existing Arab regimes, and the Palestinian and Arab liberation movements, are faced with two basic alternatives vis–vis the Palestine problem. The destiny of Palestine depends on one of these alternatives: the liquidation of the problem, or the adoption of a popular liberation plan. Any judgement to be passed on these alternatives is not isolated from the work plans of the existing Arab regimes and the national Palestinian and Arab liberation movements. The formulated plans, manifested in daily interpretations from the June 1967 defeat until the present day, will decide which alternative will be adopted, liquidation, or national liberation. The question of choice does not depend on the w ill, or intentions, or emotional and demagogic slogans, but on the daily work programs which the existing Arab regimes and the national Palestinian and Arab liberation movements adopt and practice. To make claims contrary to the actual facts and adopt demagogic slogans is an expression of rightist reactionary behavior whose result will be another political defeat, or a

military defeat which will be crowned by a
political defeat.

Lessons from the June 1967 Defeat

The June defeat was not only a military one,
but also a defeat for the totality of the class,
economic, military and ideological set-up of the
national Palestinian and Arab liberation
movements (official and popular). The feudal-
bourgeois Arab regimes were not responsible for
the June war and defeat because those regimes
had already revealed, in 1948, the utter
bankruptcy of their policies. However, the June
defeat was not only a military defeat. In 1948
the disaster had been a defeat to the feudal-

bourgeois regimes and all the class, political and reactionary practices that they represented. These regimes were responsible for the under-developed economy of Palestine and the Arab world, which was at the mercy of international capitalism. Furthermore, those regimes, because of their feudal-bourgeois structure, failed to solve the dilemmas of the national Palestinian and Arab liberation movements, by achieving their countries economic and political independence from international capitalism, colonialism and imperialism. On the contrary they collaborated with the colonial powers to protect their class privileges in the economic and political fields. It was these regimes who sided with colonialism against the national Palestinian and Arab liberation movements. Throughout their modem history they have followed a policy of encirclement and sup pression towards the national Palestinian and Arab liberation movements, (e.g., the 19 19 revolution in Egypt, the 1939 revolution in Palestine, and the 1941 revolution in Iraq).

As a result of the nature of those regimes which are under-developed, feudal, bourgeois, weak and in alliance with colonialism and imperialism, they could not form modem national armies capable of protecting their countries and confronting the imperialist and Zionist policies in Palestine and the other Arab countries. Thus, those regimes entered the 1948 war with weak armies and only attempted military and political action within the geographical limit of the partition resolution.

The disaster and the creation of the "State of Israel" came as a result of Palestinian and Arab conditions which were dominated by feudal, bourgeois and under-developed regimes, in alliance with colonialism. Such results also indicate that the elimination of the state of Israel and the "liberation of Palestine" depend on the rejection of feudalism, colonialism and the bourgeoisie, the basic causes of the disaster. This is what the lessons of 1948 offered to the national Palestinian and Arab liberation movement. President Nasser was right when he said to his comrades that "the defeat was not decided in the battlefield, but here in Cairo," and "the liberation of Cairo from the feudal-bourgeois regime of King Farouq, in alliance with colonialism and Arab reaction, constitutes the basic requirement in the national work plan for the liberation of Palestine."

Thus, the basic point in the program of the national Palestinian and Arab liberation movement became the liquidation of the feudal-bourgeois regimes responsible for the 1948 disaster. The liquidation of these regimes has paved the way for the national liberation movement to overcome the dilemmas of the national Palestinian and Arab liberation movements. Such liberation required the destruction of the under-developed feudal-bourgeois economy, linked as it' was, with international capitalism, and the setting-up of a modern national economy (through industrialization and agrarian reform) independent of international capitalism. It is impossible to build regular or popular armies capable of taking part in a long term war against counterrevolutionary forces on the soil of Palestine and the Arab countries (Israel plus colonialism plus reactionary Arab regimes in alliance with colonialism) without building a solid economic base free of pressures exerted on it by international capitalism and colonialism.

Since the 1948 disaster the national Palestinian and Arab revolutionary movement has entered a new phase with regard to class, ideology and politics. In the light of the bankruptcy of the feudal-bourgeois regimes and leadership, which wholly allied themselves 'with the counter-revolutionary forces after the disaster, the national resistance movement began to adopt new class, ideological and political definitions. The basic features of such definitions could be traced back to World War II. The emerging petit bourgeois class, which perceived the bankruptcy of the feudal-bourgeois class with regard to the solution of national liberation dilemmas, adopted an active nationalist policy hostile to colonialism, imperialism and Zionism.

The new leadership proposed the establishment of an alliance between workers, peasants, the poor and the military. Thus, the petit bourgeoisie began to play the role of the leading class as their ideology became dominant.

This national struggle, which is basically a class national struggle, was expressed in the changing class, economic and political programs officially represented in the United Arab Republic, Syria, Algeria and to an extent in Iraq which aimed at disrupting the alliance between feudalism, capitalism and imperialism. This leadership also attempted to solve the dilemmas of national liberation and the democratic national revolution. It broke up the feudal economy, which was bourgeois and compradoric in nature, and established an economy which depends in the first place on light industrialization. It attempted to solve the problems of the agricultural sector of the economy in favor of the wage-earning peasants and the poor. All this was done to establish an economic base, independent of world capitalism; and a national political and social base, hostile to colonialism, imperialism and Zionism; and to build modem, organized, national armies with which to protect the home- land and liberate Palestine. In face of the fierce national-class struggle, the forces of counter-revolution did not wait long. They began to plan the 1956 Anglo-French-Zionist aggression to liquidate the regime which was hostile to imperialism, reaction and Zionism, and which threatened the interests and basis of the counter-revolutionary forces in Palestine and the Arab world. After the 1936 aggression, neocolonialism headed by the United States of America attempted to patronize the Arab national liberation movement. But the national regimes resisted this encirclement and continued to fight their national battle against traditional colonialism and neo-imperialism. This continued in accordance with their hesitant petit bourgeois class nature. Eventually the Americans were convinced of the failure of their policy of peaceful encirclement to break the Arab national liberation movement, to liquidate the Palestine problem in the interest of Israel, and to re-arrange the class and political map of the Arab world for the benefit of the bourgeois-feudal regimes, which act as the material and political base for imperialism in the area and guarantee the security of the state of Israel.

Thus it was not the Arab reactionary regimes, but the nationalist regimes and the whole Palestinian and Arab national liberation movements who were responsible for the June war. Why did they fail? And with what work program did they face the June defeat?

Theoreticians of the Palestinian and Arab petit bourgeoisie, reaction and the bourgeoisie proper, gave explanations and analyses of the defeat which were limited to the educational, technical and cultural superiority of Israel and American imperialism which protects it. The Arab countries are underdeveloped, small and cannot "confront and fight" American imperialism which is far superior technically to any under-developed country in Asia, Africa and Latin America. This group of analysts concluded that to be able to defeat Israel we should become superior to it in education and technology.

Another group of petit bourgeois and feudal intellectuals attempted to explain the defeat in terms of technical military faults committed by this army or that, such as their unpreparedness in the face of the devastating surprise attack on the Arab air forces.

The Palestinian and Arab petit bourgeois and reactionary theoreticians and analysts deliberately neglect the facts of modem history in their analysis of the Arab defeat in June. They ignore the basic reasons for the acceptance of the six-day defeat, in spite of the heated slogans prior to 3 June, such as "inch by inch," "popular liberation war," "the policy of the scorched earth." These slogans formed the material objective antecedents to the following result: the June defeat. If the educational and technical superiority of Israel and imperialism is the main cause of the defeat, what is the explanation for the ability of the North Vietnamese people to confront half a million Ameri can soldiers in addition to half a million soldiers of the Saigon Government? If we did not have the ability as a weak and under-developed country to resist and fight the United States, how can the ability of the Vietnamese and Cubans to fight against American imperialism be explained? And if the defeat was a result of a vast number of technical military faults, how can one explain the acceptance of this defeat and the disappearance of the above-mentioned slogans, particularly at a time when Vietnam is conducting its popular revolutionary war "'inch by inch, both in word and deed, and its war is not devoid of set-backs and defeats?

If the people of Palestine and the peoples of the Arab world accept the analyses of the reactionary and petit bourgeois theoreticians, it will need more than a century to catch up with the Zionist-imperialist educational and technical superiority, and overcome the wide cultural gap between the under developed agrarian countries of the Arabs and modem industrialized Israel, supported by American imperialism.

The facts of the modem revolutionary history of the under-developed nations expose and falsify the claims of reactionary and petit bourgeois theoreticians. They also disclose the basic cause for the Arab defeat in June, as well as the resistance of the small Vietnamese nation (30 millions), and of the Cuban nation (7 millions) in the face of American imperialism.

There are in Vietnam and Cuba national regimes composed of the proletariat and poor peasants, which use the material, cultural and moral potentialities of their countries to solve the dilemmas of national liberation, and the democratic national revolution. This is achieved by liquidating all the material and m oral class concessions (feudal and bourgeois) and by the establishment of the solid material base for economic and political independence through heavy industrialization and agrarian reform. In society, the revolutionary classes head the alliance of classes and political forces which oppose feudalism, capitalism and imperialism.

232

Such a national economic and political program can mobilize and arm all the revolutionary classes to solve the dilemmas of national liberation and foster the struggle against imperialism and neocolonialism. Under such circumstances the slogan of popular liberation acquires its practical connotations where the working and poor masses are organized into a popular militia force, partisan phalanges, and the regular national army in order to defeat imperialism and the local forces in alliance with it.

In the Arab world the problem is different: the circumstances and composition of the Palestinian Arab national liberation movement were responsible for the June war, and it is that movement which must be responsible for the reversal of the June defeat. The petit bourgeois class occupies the leading role in the Palestinian and Arab national liberation movements and this class has led the entire range of the class, political, economic and m ili tary changes within the ideological, class and political structure of the petit bourgeoisie. In June 1967, this program was the one which was defeated. The economy that was set up by the petit bourgeoisie could not resist the Zionist-imperialist attack because it was a consumer economy based on light industrialization and agrarian reform s (the redistribution of land to raise self-sufficient production). Such an economy following the closure of the Suez Canal was forced to retreat and ask for assistance from the reactionary oil-producing countries, to be able to sustain itself.

As for the political and ideological relationship, this class remained at the head of the social-political pyramid and translated the alliance of the popular working forces into an alliance which put it at the top of this pyramid and the masses workers, peasants, the poor, soldiers at its base. Therefore the petit bourgeoisie remains in control of the totality of changes that are taking place in the Arab homeland and in the Palestinian and Arab national liberation movements.

Because of the nature of the petit bourgeois class which fears the popular masses as much as it fears the feudal-capital concentration it could not through its ideological, political and class program "build a national war economy independent of world capitalism. As a result the petit bourgeoisie could not break all its connections with neo-colonialism and world imperialism in general, and American imperialism in particular.

The petit bourgeoisie has gambled with the necessity of protecting the country and preparing it (economically, politically and militarily) for the liberation of Palestine. It gambled on the regular armies, refusing to arm the people and train and organize them into popular militia forces, thereby putting the slogan of "popular liberation war," which they had superficially adopted, into practice.

Under such circumstances, and with this national program, the petit bourgeois regimes entered the June war, only to prove that such a program cannot resist neo-imperialism and Zionism. The moment the defeat of the regular armies became known, these regimes asked for (or accepted) a cease fire, and all their revolutionary slogans "fighting inch by inch," "the popular liberation war," and "the policy of the scorched earth" evaporated.

The petit bourgeois regimes had to choose between two alternatives. The first alternative was to follow the Vietnamese and Cuban experience by drastically changing the national work program of their countries. This could be accomplished by mobilizing the material, human and moral capabilities of society and the national Palestinian and Arab liberation movements, and by arming the masses and waging a revolutionary popular liberation war. This war should be directed against all the interests and bases of colonialism, Zionism and reaction in alliance with colonialism; and should apply the slogan "fighting Israel and those supporting Israel" by resisting all the counter revolutionary forces which support Israel or which interact with those who support Israel. By doing so the balance of power would start to shift to the side of the national Palestinian and Arab liberation movements, and the possibility of antagonizing the United States would become practical. Moreover, Arab human superiority waves of fighting people would overcome the Israeli-

American technical superiority as happens daily in Vietnam and Cuba.

The second alternative was to stick to the positions and programs which prevailed before June 1967 and which resulted in the June defeat. This would mean that the national Palestinian and Arab liberation movements would be forced to retreat continuously in the interest of Israel, imperialism, and Arab reactionary forces in alliance with both neo- and traditional colonialism. This is what actually took place and it was not by accident. The feudal-bourgeois regimes cannot wage a war on colonialism and imperialism since they have formed alliances with imperialism against their people and the national liberation movements.

Since 1948 they have proved that they cannot protect the homeland and liberate Palestine and they have allied themselves wholly to the counter-revolutionary camp. Moreover, the national regimes which are hostile to colonialism and Zionism are incapable because of the nature of their petit bourgeois ideological class structure of drawing up and executing programs for a "popular liberation war since this would necessarily re quire them to give up all of their material, political and moral concessions in favored the economic, political and military program of the popular revolution against Israel and neo-imperialism. In the course of history, no class has worked in a manner harmful to its interests, and given up voluntarily its interests and concessions to save its country from disintegration.

The Vietnamese-Cuban course of action is the only course leading to victory for underdeveloped countries against the educational and technical superiority of imperialism and neo-colonialism. The rejection of this course necessarily means the adoption of a policy of retreat in the face of Zionism and neo-colonialism, led by the United States of America, enemy number one of the under-developed countries throughout Asia, Africa and Latin America.

The progressive and reactionary Arab regimes, for the last fifteen months, have adopted the same positions and programs which were adopted prior to June and which resulted in the defeat. They have adopted the policy of continuous retreat. First they declared that the Security Council resolution was rejected, then they considered it insufficient, then ambiguous and demanded that certain clauses (especially passage through the Suez Canal) should be linked to the whole Palestine problem , and lastly they accepted the Security Council resolution as a whole without any conditions coupled with statements of re-assurance to Israel considering it one of the facts of the Middle East.

Any objective look at the Security Council resolution of 22 November 1967, proves that its acceptance and execution means the beginning of the liquidation of the Palestine problem. The

Security Council resolution is in itself an imperialist plot for the liquidation of the Palestine problem. The resolution stipulates:

- The right of each state in the Middle East to live within secure boundaries to live.
- The right of "innocent passage through waterways for all the states of the area without exception.
- Finding a "just solution for the refugees."

Thus the Security Council resolution places the Palestine problem in a critical historical situation which necessarily and ultimately leads to the liquidation of the Palestine problem.

The demand put forward to the present Arab regimes and the national Palestinian and Arab liberation movements is not to embark on a discourse on the Security Council resolution and what it offers the Arabs and Israel. N or is it a discussion of the nature of the stand to be adopted by the Arabs. The question we put concerns the nature of the economic, political, military and ideological program which the Arab regimes and the national Palestinian and Arab liberation movements will adopt. Will this program lead to the liquidation of the consequences of the June aggression, namely the liberation of Sinai, the West Bank and the Golan Heights, as a step in the direction of a long-term war for the liberation of Palestine and the liquidation of the Israeli-racist-aggressive entity?

The presentation of the question in its proper context is a national need. It must be done in order to circumvent the Palestinian reactionary rightist intellectuals who call for the isolation of the Palestinian resistance movement from the development of the Arab region.

These same reactionary intellectuals, together with those of the petit bourgeois class, at times present their attitude towards the Security Council resolution as a tactical step. At other times they assert that it is an unavoidable necessity because Arabs cannot fight the United States with its educational and technical superiority. What applies to the United States also applies to Israel. Thus they argue that the acceptance of the Security Council resolution is a necessity.

Even those who reject the resolution, are requested to link this rejection with the need to establish a war economy and a military program of a different calibre from that which existed prior to the defeat. If not, their attitude of rejection becomes a demagogic false attitude of no value whatsoever; similar to the demagogic revolutionary slogans which were put forward before the June war and not applied.

Tbe Arab Situation and the Palestine Problem

Fifteen months have elapsed since the June defeat and it has become clear, through direct analysis, that the Arab regimes and the national Palestinian and Arab liberation movements have been incapable of judging critically the events which led to, and the results which came from, the June defeat. Further, they have been incapable of the crystallization of this judgement in a national revolutionary work program , which would be able to effect a series of changes in the Arab situation and capacities to prepare the area for a "popular liberation war" against counter-revolution (Israel plus Arab reactionary forces in alliance with neo- und traditional imperialism). It is natural that this should be so because the Arab regimes and the national Palestinian and Arab liberation movements are not prepared under their present conditions (class, ideological and political) to put into practice deep-rooted policies which would prepare the Palestinian and Arab masses to resist the forces of counter-revolution. Instead, the Arab and Palestinian masses have remained, and are forced to remain, observers awaiting a miracle in an age when miracles do not happen. Furthermore, asking the present regimes to adopt a policy of "popular liberation war is basically a fallacious request. These regimes will not harbor their antithesis, which could only ultimately clash with their nature, interests, and local and international relationships.

Instead of adopting a "popular liberation war" program, such as the Vietnamese Cuban one, and resisting and struggling against the imperialist- Zionist attack, the Arab regimes have maintained the same program and pre mises which prevailed until June 1967 and resulted in the defeat.

This is what has made these regimes, whatever their class and whatever their policies, retreat continuously since June to the advantage of Israel and imperialism. The Arab regimes have not waged an ideological, political, revolutionary campaign throughout the Arab lands to start an armed and unarmed popular action to destroy the interests and strategic bases of imperialism, beaded by the United States, which has outrageously supported and protected Israel since 1948. Instead the regimes retreated and started courting the United States by protecting all of its imperialist interests. It is a well-known fact that breaking Israel will come about by breaking American imperialism throughout the Arab Land.

Instead of rejecting the liquidationist Security Council resolution, the Arab regimes ended up by accepting it and calling on the four Great Powers to guarantee it internationally and to force Israel to accept it.

Instead of immediately, without any hesitation, adopting plans for a ' long term war" by drawing up plans for a war economy, arming the people, organizing people's militia units in addition to the arming of the regular armies, the Arab regimes adopted the policy of depending on the regular armies which had collapsed in the face of Israeli-imperialist educational and

technological superiority in the June war.
(Regular war is not to the advantage of the
Arabs nor of any under-developed country
involved in a national liberation struggle against
forces superior in the field of education and
technology.) This at a time when it has become
clear that national liberation wars in under-
developed countries require numerical
superiority to overcome imperialist technical
superiority.

Tie Palestinian Resistance Movement and the National Palestinian Question

Following the June defeat the Palestinian
and Arab masses put their faith in the Palestinian
resistance movement to pave the way for a new
course of action to promote the liberation of

Palestine, in particular, and the Arab liberation movement, in general.

Has the resistance movement paved this way?

A critical analysis of the development and activities of the Palestinian resistance movement during the last 15 months will give the answer to such a question.

Within the Sphere of Arab Relations: All groups of the resistance movement put forward the slogan "non-interference in the internal affairs of the Arab countries. How did the movement translate this slogan? It is clear that the Palestinian resistance movement is not required to take the place of the national liberation movement of each Arab state in its struggle to solve the dilemmas of national liberation and national democratic revolution. But it is also clear that the slogan non-interference in the internal affairs of the Arab countries is a double-edged weapon. In addition to meaning that the

Palestinian resistance movement should not take the place of the Arab liberation movement, it should also mean that the former should interfere with whatever affects the Palestine problem in the policies adopted by the Arab regimes. Otherwise the slogan, in the final analysis, will mean "non-interference" on the part of the Palestinian resistance movement in Palestine affairs. The Palestinian problem cannot be separated from the developments taking place in the world. Such a step is a suspicious attempt to overlook ancient, medieval and modem historical facts. Following June 1967 the Arab regimes in an attempt to face the imperialist-Zionist aggression adopted the policy of finding a political solution to the Palestine problem through the liquidationist Security Council resolution. Thus a new relationship between Arab affairs and the Palestine problem has been established.

Reactionary Palestinians who, following the June defeat, put forward the slogan "non-interference in the internal affairs of the Arab countries arbitrarily separated Arab affairs from developments in the Palestine problem. When it attempts to imitate the Algerian experience, the slogan forgets, or pretends to have forgotten, that the subjective and objective characteristics that connect the Palestine problem with developments in the Arab world and the policies of imperialism in the Middle East, radically differ from those of Algeria. Moreover, these reactionaries have previously determined to neglect the particularities of Israel and its difference from all other kinds of neo- and traditional imperialism.

Israel represents the spearhead and base for neo and traditional imperial ism in the Arab countries and the Middle East. Israel is supported by imperialism which gives it the freedom according to imperialist plans to participate in quelling the national Arab liberation movement which threatens the interests of imperialism in the Arab world. An observer should notice the link between the "promise to Judaize Palestine" and the imperialist invasion of Palestine and the Arab countries. Furthermore, he should watch the role Israel and Zionism have played since the defeat in responding to the imperialist plans drawn up for the Middle East to liquidate the nationalist regimes and the nationalist liberation movements in the area for the benefit of counter revolutionary forces.

Israel represents a dynamic society which has expansionist aims in the area in addition to Palestine. As a society it is superior to the under-developed Arab countries in the educational and technical fields. This makes its expansionist policy easier. The relationship between Israel and American imperialism necessitates the amalgamation of the national Palestinian and Arab liberation movements. In addition, Palestine is a part of the Arab world and its future is related to that of the Arab countries.

In spite of all this reactionary Palestinians neglect the facts of history and put forward the slogan "non-interference in the internal affairs of the Arab countries. This has quietly overlooked defeatist Arab stands with regard to the problem of Palestine. All groups of the resistance movement, including the Popular Front for the Liberation of Palestine, went along with this reactionary demagogic slogan which was interpreted as "non-interference" in the Arab stand vis–vis the Palestine problem. Not one of the resistance groups has passed a critical judgement on the June defeat or on Arab responsibility for this defeat after 20 years of preparation for the liberation of Palestine. Because of the principle of "non-interference in the internal affairs of the Arab countries, not one group has openly condemned the stands taken vis–vis the Palestine problem and the Security Council resolution. It is ridiculous to find H ajj Amin al-Husseini, who sold the 1936 revolution, openly criticize certain Arab leaders' statements regarding the Security Councils resolution in Le Monde, in May 1968, While all the groups in the resistance movement, including the Popular Front, kept quiet about these developments in the Palestine problem .

The Popular Front openly condemns this slogan in the context in which it has been practiced for the last fifteen months. The resistance movement is not expected to substitute for the national liberation movements in the Arab countries, but it is expected openly to criticize the stands adopted by the Arab governments towards the Palestine problem and put the blame on those responsible for the defeat. If the resistance movement keeps quiet about the Arab governments with regard to derisions pertaining to the Palestine problem, then it will be plotting against Palestine.

The Question of Palestinian National Unity: All groups of the resistance movement, including the Popular Front, have committed a basic error towards the question of Palestinian national unity, both on the theoretical and the practical level. This has come about through the leadership of the Palestinian right and its ideology and theories.

The resistance movement has neglected the modem history of Palestine in its understanding and application of the problems of "'national unity.' The policies adopted towards the question of national unity were reactionary and wrong. This has led to placing the reactionary classes at the head of the resistance movement This leadership is the same one which has led the national Palestinian liberation movement and the national revolution to its failure throughout the modem history of Palestine. At a time when the sons of the revolutionary classes of poor workers and peasants and revolutionary intellectuals fight for the liberation of the homeland and rejection of the Zionist occupation, the military leadership of the resistance movement has placed political leadership in the hands of rich feudal capitalist groups which have had nothing to do with the armed struggle throughout the modem history of Palestine. The resistance movement has understood the slogan of "national unity" in an inverted manner. Thus the concept of national unity was formulated under the leadership of feudal elements, bankers, big mer chants and reactionary Palestinians. The starting point was participation in the "Jordanian national front," which was composed of Palestinian and Jordanian reactionary elements under whose hands the people have suffered many hardships.

The final point was the creation of the National Palestinian Congress which is composed of reactionary Palestinian elements headed by bankers and big contractors whose condition for joining the Congress was that they should be given its leadership, while the Popular Front and Al- Fateh should form its left and right arms.

The problem before us is not how to choose between acceptance or refusal of the slogan "national unity. The problem is putting this thesis in its proper perspective, nationally and politically.

We have already pointed out the treachery and failure of the feudal and bourgeois classes. This review also brings out one of the basic laws of national liberation movements, namely, that the anti-imperialist and anti-Zionist classes which are capable of leading the national liberation movement and of carrying arms in the period following June 1967, are the same classes which fought against British imperialism and the plots to judaize Palestine. These are the revolutionary classes in Palestinian society. They will lose nothing if they carry arms and fight until death, on the contrary they will gain everything their land and their homes. This has been re-asserted after June 1967 Those who carried arms were the sons of the poor workers and wage naming peasants, while the sons of the feudal landowners and capitalists disappeared from the scene of armed struggle. In spite of all the experience of the national Palestinian movement and its basic lessons, the Palestinian right has been able to penetrate the leadership of the resistance movement and take over its political leadership for fifteen months since 3 June, under the slogan "Palestinian national unity and the pretense that the liberation question concerns everybody, at a time when historical facts, both before and after 1948, disprove these claims.

Palestinian national unity is a political necessity. But what sort of national unity? The sort of national unity which accomplishes liberation. It leads the resistance movement on the road to victory by mobilizing and arming the Arab masses. It awakens their basic and collective capabilities in the long struggle of resistance. This resistance will depend upon violence in the face of an enemy whose strategy is to deliver rapid blows and accomplish swift victories.

This unity is the unity of all classes and political forces under the leadership of the revolutionary patriotic classes which have carried arms throughout the modem history of Palestine. It is the sons of these classes who have answered the call to arms since June 1967. The modem history of the people of Palestine, and that of popular liberation wars in all under-developed countries, proves that the workers and peasant classes are the ones who are pre pared to carry arms and fight a long term war against the enemies of national liberation, namely, imperialism and its agents.

National Palestinian unity should be based on the unity of the revolutionary fighting forces, under whose leadership all the class and political forces will be organized in an all-embracing national liberation front, committed to a national political and military work program for solving the dilemmas of national liberation and democratic national revolution.

Thus the Popular Front openly declares its condemnation of the slogan "national unity in its present context and application. Furthermore, it condemns and openly criticizes its previous practices starting with its participation in the Jordanian national front and finally in the National Palestinian Congress.

The Popular Front puts the slogan national unity" in its proper perspective, namely, as a unity whose vanguard and leadership are the revolutionary fighting forces. This slogan has to be exemplified in a radical national work program , the aim of which is the organization of a national liberation front to include all the class and political forces hostile to Zionism and world imperialism in general, and American imperialism in particular, and all the forces which collaborate with and are agents of imperialism.

The Palestinian Resistance Movement at the Present Stage

The nature of the practices of the resistance movement (Palestinian and Arab) during the period following the June defeat, have led to political results which in their totality form a relapse as far as the ideological, class and political lessons of 5 June 1967 are concerned. These results also form a relapse as far as the modem history of the national Palestinian popular liberation movement is concerned. The resistance movement has come to the following basic conclusions:

On the theoretical and practical level all groups of the resistance movement (including the Popular Front) have become captives of the ideology of the reactionary Palestinian and Arab right. They have actively participated in obliterating Palestinian and Arab class ideological and political contradictions. This has led to the defeat of the Palestinian and Arab peoples at the hands of the ruling regimes. These regimes have kept the masses, and the more radical and revolutionary classes, away from any responsibility for, or even participation in, the war. They have allowed the revolutionary forces to play the role of observers by limiting the concept of liberation to mean combat between the armies.

Consequently, the resistance movement has fallen victim to a series of demagogic slogans (such as "non-interference in the internal affairs of the Arab countries," "Palestinian national unity," "no right and left in the national liberation stage"). These slogans are used as a cover for the reactionary forces of the right and the Arab regimes, which have led to the defeat of the Arabs. Moreover, the resistance movement has applied these slogans within a context which has served the interests of the forces and regimes of defeat and not those of the Palestinian and Arab liberation forces. By doing this it has completely failed to expose and condemn the seasons, intellectual, class and political, which led to the 1948 disaster and the 1967 defeat in fact the resistance movement has assisted in hiding the existing contradictions which have resulted in the defeat. It has also defended the Arab regimes that caused the defeat and those Arab countries which are in alliance with imperialism and therefore against the liberation and progress of their people. This will ultimately lead to the failure of the Palestinian and Arab liberation movements.

Through its dependence for arms on the Arab regimes, the resistance movement has allowed itself to be transformed into a tactical weapon of pressure in the hands of the regimes pressure to be used to keep the Arab masses as observers awaiting relief from afar. All this is taking place in the name of the Palestinian resistance movement. This alternative has been put forward instead of arming and organizing the people in popular militia units, and preparing them ideologically, politically and economically for a long-term war of popular liberation against Israel, and those who are behind Israel, throughout the Palestinian and Arab homeland.

In addition, the resistance movement is being used as a tactical means of bringing pressure on imperialism and Israel in order to attain a political settlement of the Palestine problem. It is hoped that the concessions demanded by Israel and imperialism as a price for the application of the Security Council resolution concerning withdrawal from the occupied territories will be minimized as a result of this pressure.

In the light of such wrong policies and demagogic slogans of the resistance movement, the Palestinian and Arab masses have remained ideologically, politically and materially disarmed. They cannot protect and develop the resistance movement in the face of the possibilities of a 'political solution,' the basis of which would be "liquidating the resistance movement

The resistance movement, by keeping quiet about the lessons of 1948 and 1967 and by its refusal to take a critical national stand towards the Palestinian and Arab situation (both subjective and objective) which resulted in the defeat, have disarmed the masses of the intellectual and political weapons through which the resistance movement could be protected. Furthermore, the resistance movement, by keeping quiet and not putting forward to the masses a program for a war of popular liberation, has assisted in opening the way for demagogic slogans. Thus, when the possibilities of a "political settlement" are put forward, the resistance movement will only find superficial and limited support from the masses. This will be so because the masses are not armed and are not equipped with an ideological, political and national consciousness.

The Dilemma of Existing Resistance Movements

All groups of the Palestinian resistance movement are a part of the Arab national liberation movement because of their subjective constitution (ideological, class and political) and because of the objective circumstances which find their expression in the daily dialectical relationship between the dilemmas of national liberation and the responsibilities of the democratic revolution Palestinian and Arab.

The dilemma of the Palestinian and Arab liberation movements is specifically the dilemma of the petit bourgeois class which has occupied the position of leadership since the Second World W ar. This class, because of its education and interests, which are anti-feudal and anti-imperialist, has recognized the failure of feudalism and the bourgeois class to solve the problems of national liberation and of attaining economic and political independence. It has also understood the dependence of the feudalist-bourgeois regimes on colonialism and imperialism.

Since the 1948 disaster the role and ideology of the petit bourgeois class has dominated the scene, thus enabling this class to lead the Palestinian and Arab national movements. The petit bourgeoisie put forward a work program, based on its class and ideological structure, to solve the dilemmas of national liberation as a step on the road to mobilizing the material and human capabilities of the masses to liberate Palestine. The main part of the program was based on the need to foil the alliance between feudalism, capitalism and colonialism (in other words, the counter-revolutionary camp) and to establish an alliance between the petit bourgeoisie, workers and poor peasants.

The June defeat put the programs of the petit bourgeois class and its leadership to the test. As was pointed out in the course of this report, the defeat proved their failure to withstand the imperialist-Zionist attack, and to solve the dilemmas of national liberation in an underdeveloped country in this age the age of colonialism and imperialism.

Thus the petit bourgeois class was confronted with two alternatives: either to adopt the Vietnamese-Cuban course of action to face the consequences of the June w ar; or to retreat continuously before the forces of counter revolution and accept the liquidationist UN Security Council resolution of 22 November. The petit bourgeois class has chosen what best serves its interests and its class-ideological and political considerations, i.e., the Security Council resolution; the Vietnamese course of action has its own price, namely the totality of its class and political concessions. Of course, the regimes of the 1948 disaster, the regimes of feudalism and the bourgeois class, blessed this choice and cooperated with it.

The Palestinian national liberation movement is of the same ideological, class and political structure as that of the Arab national liberation movement led by the petit bourgeois class. At the same time it represents one of the weakest groups in the national liberation movements in the area. This is the case because of a number of subjective and objective characteristics, headed by the contradictions of the Palestine problem and the large number of non-productive human beings among the dispersed Palestinian people.

From here we can touch on a basic characteristic of the Palestinian liberation movement. The petit bourgeois class, the leader of the Arab libera tion movement, was able to eliminate the forces of feudalism and the bourgeois class from a leading position within the national movement, and was able to expose the alliance of these forces with colonialism and imperialism. Yet the Palestinian petit bourgeois class failed to remove this incapacitated bourgeois class from playing a national role. Thus the petit bourgeois class was able continuously to infiltrate the leadership of the national liberation movement and make it serve its ideological, political and class interests. Consequently, and following June 1967 the Palestinian right supported by the Arab right was able to dominate the resistance movement through demagogic slogans and lead it within the scope of its theoretical and political beliefs. These beliefs serve the interests of the bourgeoisie and those of Arab reaction and destroy the means by which the Palestinian and Arab national movements can save themselves from imperialist-Israeli occupation. In the final analysis, these policies do not serve the resistance movement. They tend to transform it into a tactical means of bringing pressure to bear. This pressure aims, first, at containing the national revolutionary uprising of the Arab masses. Secondly, it aims at minimizing the concessions to be made by Arabs in order to ensure the implementation of the Security Council resolution, which threatens the Palestine question, in its entirety, with liquidation. The leadership of the petit bourgeois class has failed to salvage itself and the leaders of the resistance movement. The reasons for this failure are: its adoption of hesitant ideological and political policies; its failure to comprehend the basis of a nationalist policy; and the domination of the ideology of the reactionary right over important sectors of it.

In spite of the belief that a popular war of liberation is the course of action to be adopted in order to achieve the liberation of Palestine and in spite of the high morale among the Palestinian people in the Arab nation, the leadership of the resistance movement, namely, the bourgeoisie and petit bourgeoisie, has put the resistance movement in a critical historical situation which has transformed it into a means of pressure.

The Course of National Salvation

The concept of armed struggle will necessarily result in an ideological and political dialectic among the members of the resistance movement and those outside it. Through this dialectic the more revolutionary and progressive elements will stress the necessity to overcome the present critical period by looking forward to the development of a more radical resistance movement. This will interact openly and responsibly with the masses, and refrain from the adoption of demagogic slogans.

The resistance movement will critically examine the experiment of the Palestinian and Arab national liberation movements in order to point out the basic laws of failure and success. It will also draw up a program for national salvation. This will reject all proposals that aim at re-instating the pre-5 June programs "reliance on regular armed forces and a swift regular war; a consumer economy dependent on capitalism ; holding back the struggle against those who are behind Israel; and limitation of the war to the areas occupied after 1 June, 1967." The resistance movement considers the acceptance of the Security Council resolution of 22 November to be the logical conclusion of the programs which resulted in the June 1967 defeat.

The experience of the national liberation movement in our countries (Palestine and the Arab countries) is similar to that of the under-developed countries of Asia, Africa and Latin America. It clearly shows that the road to national salvation and liberation of the homeland, together with the solution of the problems of national liberation, requires forces armed with revolutionary arms. These will be capable, in under-developed countries, of defeating the advanced imperialist powers in the fields of military effort and skill.

These experiences teach us especially the experience of fifty years of failure of the Palestinian national liberation movement and the successful experience of Vietnam and Cuba that the course of national salvation starts with, and depends on, the following:

The adoption of a revolutionary scientific ideology (the ideology of the proletariat) which is anti-imperialist, anti-Zionist, anti-reactionary and anti-under-development. The masses will be armed with this ideology, which will depend mainly on the more revolutionary and radical classes in society. Such classes do not have any interest in concluding a truce with imperialism, reaction and Zionism. They also do not have any interest in adopting a policy of retreat. The interests of these classes will be served by waging a bloody struggle by which they will lose nothing but will gain everything, i.e., nation hood, the homeland and true political and economic independence.

The experience of our countries and that of the national liberation movements in Asia, Africa and Latin America have proved the failure and incapacity of the feudalist ideology to lead the national liberation struggle. They have also proved the futility of the ideology of the bourgeoisie which leads its country to depend on and ally itself with colonialism and imperialism.

Furthermore, the ideology of the petit bourgeoisie has proved incapable of solving, and unprepared to solve, the dilemmas of national liberation or to adopt a policy of long-term struggle against imperialism and the forces allied with it.

The national salvation course starts with arming the people with revolutionary ideas. These ideas are those of the revolutionary classes in any society, namely, the workers and poor peasants, whose sons are now taking part in armed resistance in the land of Palestine.

The basic national political consciousness of the masses should be failed beyond the level of demagogic slogans. Our people are facing a modern enemy, supported by the strongest imperialist country, the United States of America. A scientific national consciousness, depending on direct analysis of our situation and that of the enemy should be the main basis in the relationship of the resistance movement with the masses and the man in the street. National political consciousness starts by unfolding the reasons and causes for the failure of the Palestinian and Arab national resistance movements and then putting forward a program for national salvation and liberation.

Defeatist proposals and the Security Council resolution of 22 November 1967 should be rejected. Furthermore, the resistance should insist on drawing up plans for a war of popular liberation by arming and organizing the people in popular militia troops. In this way the war will become that of the people as a whole and it will be waged against Israel and those who are behind Israel. (These include the interests and bases of imperialism plus Israel plus the Arab forces which are in alliance with imperialism and the protector of its interests in our homeland.)

A long term war is the course of salvation and victory. For this way we must depend only upon ourselves. Everything must be mobilized for it our economy and our lives and to fight it we will be armed by the consciousness of the political ideology of the proletariat. It is also the only course to supersede the educational and technical superiority of Israel and imperialism, which depends on the strategy of a short-range war, the war of administering rapid blows and accomplishing swift victories.

The destruction of the counter-revolutionary forces and the breaking down of their morale and economy will not be accomplished unless a long term war is waged.

A program of national salvation will reject all forms of retreat and embark on operations on a wide front. Our aspiration to achieve such a program will not be accomplished unless the dialectical argument going on between members of the Arab national resistance movement is reinforced. For this reinforcement of the dialectical argument will distinguish the leadership of the vanguard of the movement, armed with a scientific revolutionary ideology is the ideology of the proletariat. This rejects the Security Council resolution and will lead the organized masses in a long term war, depending entirely without this dialectic, the resistance movement will remain captive of the wrong policies, which have been persistently followed and have made it a mere tactical pawn, to be used to apply pressure in the hands of the Arab regimes.

The road to national salvation requires strong w ills from the members of the resistance movement. National salvation rejects whatever is existing and pushes forward on a new course the course of transforming the resistance movement into an organized mass movement. It is armed with political, material and radical national ideologies under the leadership of the vanguard fighting forces which are equipped with political consciousness and the ideology of the proletariat, hostile to Israel and imperialism and its allies throughout the Arab land.

The vanguard of the proletariat will bring about the national unity of all classes and political forces which are hostile to counter-revolution. These must be committed to a program of arming the people for a long term war under the leadership of the revolutionary fighting forces in a wide national liberation front.

The spirit of resistance will spread among the Palestinian people; it needs the vanguard which will lead it on the road of national salvation. Such a vanguard, through analysis and criticism of the Palestinian liberation movement, has not yet been born.

The young elements among the members of the resistance movement and the Palestinian people who are armed with a consciousness of scientific ideology should lead the dialectical movement to bring forth such a vanguard, which will lead the people with all its classes and national political forces on the toad of victory, the toad of a long term war.

1.   Rejection of the chauvinistic and reactionary Zionist-colonial solutions which are based on recognizing the state of Israel as one of the facts of the Middle East area; because these solutions, besides contradicting the right of the Palestinian people to self-determination in their land, consecrate the Zionist expansionist entity in liaison with colonialism, and are hostile to the Palestinian and Arab national liberation movements and all the progressive and socialist forces in the world.

2.   Rejection of the chauvinistic solutions of some Palestinians and Arabs, which were put forward before and after June 1967 and are based on slaughtering the Jews and throwing them into the sea. It also rejects the reactionary solutions which

are based on accepting the state of Israel within secure and recognized boundaries, as exemplified in the November Security Council resolution. The afore-mentioned solutions are put forward at the expense of the right of the Palestinians to self-determination in their land; and because the solutions implant in the Middle East area a racist, capitalist, expansionist state dialectically in liaison with world capitalism which is hostile to the Palestinian and Arab national liberation movements, and all the progressive and socialist forces in the world.

3. The struggle for a popular democratic solution for the Palestinian and Israeli questions, to be based on the liquidation of the Zionist entity exemplified in all the government establishments (arm y, administration, police) and all the chauvinistic Zionist political and labor organizations. The establishment of a people's democratic Palestinian state in which the Arabs and (Israeli) Jews will live without any discrimination whatsoever. A state which is against all forms of class and national subjugation, and which gives both Arabs and (Israeli) Jews the right to develop their national culture.

Resistance Movement: A Critical Study, Dar al-Tali'ah, Beirut, 1969, PP- 163-167.

In accordance with the link of both history and destiny that exists between Palestine and the Arab nation, the peoples democratic state of Palestine will be an integral part of an Arab federal state in this area. The Palestinian state will have a democratic content hostile to colonialism, imperialism and Arab and Palestinian reaction.

1. The democratic solution put forward is capable of liberating the Arab and the Jew from all forms of chauvinistic (racist) culture; liberating the Arab from reactionary culture, and the Jew from Zionist culture.

2. The democratic solution, being hostile to class and national subjugation, is capable of disassociating Palestine from imperialism, and converting it into a progressive revolutionary fortress on the side of all the forces struggling against imperialism and counter-revolution in this earthly world.

3. The national liberation movement will only be able to realize the people's democratic state of Palestine, by armed struggle and a popular war of liberation against Zionism, imperialism and reaction and by eliminating the Israeli state and liberating the Jews from the Zionist movement. Only

by continuous armed struggle against all chauvinistic, reactionary and colonial solutions, can we achieve the total and complete liberation of Palestine and the establishment of the democratic state which will encompass Arabs and (Israeli) Jews enjoying equal national rights and obligations; a state in the service of all the forces struggling for national liberation and progress in this world.

The Popular Democratic Front for the Liberation of Palestine calls on all the Israeli and Jewish elements and groupings who are hostile to Zionism and imperialism to support the above-mentioned solution and participate in the common Palestinian and peoples armed struggle for the implementation of this democratic revolutionary solution.

The Middle East crisis is becoming more and more complicated as a result of the attitudes of Israeli reaction and of American imperialism. Both of them are insisting on reaping the harvest of the consequences of the 1967 war. Their demands include recognition of Israel within secure frontiers which, far from corresponding to the pre-June 1967 frontiers, imply further territorial expansion at the expense of. the people of Palestine and the neigh boring Arab peoples. They also demand that a crushing defeat be inflicted on the Arab national liberation movement; and the class and political map of the Middle East be re-drawn in accordance with the interests of American imperialism in particular, and those of Zionism and Arab reaction in general. This was why the wars of 1948, 1936 and 1967 were fought.

In spite of the fact that the ruling class forces in Israel rejected the 22 November Security Council resolution, an objective observer cannot but remade that this rejection was not absolute; acceptance of the resolution was made conditional on new expansionist gains and negotiations with the Arab regimes (The rhodes formula, for example). Even though the US approved the Security Council resolution, the American attitude is, practically and objectively, the same as the Israeli attitude, not to mention US ambitions to liquidate the petit bourgeois nationalist regimes in the area as a step towards the eventual repression and liquidation of the Arab national liberation movement.

Because the Security Council resolution stands on two legs, not one only (the withdrawal of Israeli forces to the 3 June frontiers, and, in return for this, recognition of both, the fait accompli which confronts the people of Palestine, and the secure frontiers for the state of Israel), the Palestinian resistance movement immediately rejected it, though naturally the reasons for this rejection were different from those of the Zionists. For acceptance of the resolution directly implies:

- Endorsement of the conquest and loss of territory that befell the people of Palestine in 1948.
- The liquidation of the Palestinian resistance movement to safeguard the frontiers of the state of Israel.
- The continued existence of an expansionist state closely linked with American imperialism by virtue of the common interest of the two parties that Israel should continue to exist as an instrument for expansion and for the repression of the national liberation movement in the Middle East.

The Palestinian resistance movement therefore sees the Security Council resolution as a reactionary and imperialist solution of both the Palestinian and the Israeli questions, a view which is incompatible with that of most of the Arab regimes, which either accept the resolution or reject it in theory but in practice work along with it Saudi Arabia is a case in point. What then is the solution?

The resistance proposes a democratic solution of the problem that calls for long term political, ideological and armed struggle, for only if the struggle is carried on in all three fields can it assume its truly practical and objective significance. The democratic solution proposed rejects all the chauvinistic solutions, whether Arab or Israeli, which were in existence until 3 June 1967 Israeli expansion, or massacring the Jews and throwing them into the sea, etc. It also rejects the reactionary solution offered by the Security Council resolution. What it is striving for is the right of the Palestinian people to decide their own future in their own territory, which-was seized from , them by a nationalist, Zionist and imperialist act of usurpation in 1948, and the construction of a democratic popular state in the whole of the territory of Palestine, in which Arabs and Jews will enjoy equal rights and obligations, .every one being entitled to develop his national culture in a democratic, progressive spirit. The constitutional form assumed by this state is not important it may be a unitary state, or a federal one, on the model of Yugoslavia or Czechoslovakia, or anything else.

With this end in view PDFLP submitted to the Sixth National Palestinian Congress, which met in Cairo in early September 1969, and at the same time, to the Palestinian and Arab masses, a "proposed democratic solution of the Palestinian and Israeli problem s." Obviously, this solution can only be achieved through long term progressive popular armed struggle, and it must be supported by the common struggle of all progressive and democratic forces in the are, especially in the ranks of the Palestinian resistance movement, Israeli society and progressive Jews. This proposed democratic solution, in fact, calls on all progressive Israelis and Jews to organize themselves into an armed popular Palestinian front to ensure the day by day objective implementation of this solution. For as progressive and democratic trends grow stronger' in the ranks of all the Palestinian resistance organizations, this solution will impose itself all the more forcefully on the citizens of Israel. Israeli reaction cannot always be watching Israeli society, and reactionary Zionist culture must inevitably disappear as progressive trends grow stronger in the Palestinian and Arab national liberation movement.

With this progressive aim in view, PDFLP has called for a dialogue to be initiated with Israeli organizations which follow an anti-Zionist and anti-imperialist line, although they have not yet arrived at a decisively progressive attitude^ in their understanding of the Palestine problem and the nature of the composition of the state of Israel. Such Israeli organizations are Eakab and Matxpen. PDFLP has published in this book several analyses of Matxpen, and in its pamphlets has clearly drawn the distinction between the attitude of this organization and that of the Zionist left Matxpen and the Israeli reactionary forces.

The radical democratic solution of the Palestine problem is a long and complicated question in an area thick with reactionary regimes that are allied with colonialism and imperialism and steeped in a rightist reactionary culture. To use a Marxist expression the prevailing culture is the culture of the predominant classes. It is an area, too, in which an essentially Zionist state has been established, a state with a double character, with chauvinist and expansionist ambitions. It has organic links with colonialism and imperialism, and, with its reactionary Zionist culture, plays a double role in the area, in addition to the fact that it is a state established on the conquest and the national usurpation of the people, of Palestine. "A people that persecutes another people cannot be a free people, as M a n said, and his saying has ~been borne out by the course of ancient, medieval and contemporary history.

In the Arab world, as is the case with the peoples of all backward countries, the only way to rout the counter-revolutionary forces and to defeat them by imposing solutions which will ensure that the people can choose their own future by themselves and in their own territory, is by adopting the Vietnamese method, the method of a popular war of liberation to overcome the technical superiority of imperialism, Zionism and reaction. This is the course being followed by the Palestinian resistance movement, in preference to traditional wars, in which victory must go to the triple counter alliance. In spite of the crisis which is now besetting the Palestinian resistance movement as a result of the composition of a number of its petit bourgeois leadership cadres, the left wing of the resistance, in bearing arms against imperialism, Zionism and reaction, is also fighting ideologically and politically for the development of the resistance movement along progressive and democratic lines. The daily growing victory of Vietnam is the result of a popular war led by a united liberation front in which the revolutionary communist party plays the central role in leading the operation of national liberation and the democratic revolution.

However complicated the Palestinian and Israeli questions, it is only through the insistence of the resistance movement, and its left wing in particular, on breaking the reactionary regimes and its rejection of reactionary solutions, that a new trail can be blazed towards the liberation of the peoples of the Middle East. Even if, for local and international reasons which cannot be discussed in the present context, the ruling and dominating regimes in the area succeed in imposing reactionary solutions and repressing the Palestinian resistance movement which rejects such solutions, the resistance movement will have achieved an important revolutionary advance if it sows the seeds of a violent democratic revolution in the Middle East in the near future. For the course of history is forward; adverse forces may sometimes compel it to take a step backwards, but this is only a preparation for two steps forward.

THE POPULAR FRONT FOR THE
LIBERATION OF PALESTINE

THE POPULAR FRONT FOR THE LIBERATION OF PALESTINE

February 1969

PART I

Introduction

The Popular Front for the Liberation of Palestine (PFLP), in spite of the short period that has lapsed since it has come of age its political age is one and a half years has formed objectively a politico-military phenomenon which attracts the interests of large sectors of the Palestinian people. In addition the scope of the interest in PFLP is daily widening on both Arab and international levels.

In so that this phenomenon embodies elements of revolutionary development by which it tries to rise to the level of historical revolution, it faces, at the same time, a series of dangers, both subjective and objective, which threaten its future and impede its development and progress.

In this light, that is in term s of a general evaluation of the present situation of the front, PFLP held a conference in February 1969 in which it discussed the strategy of Palestinian revolutionary action, and drew up the general lines political, organizational and military which would ensure the progress and growth of the front at a level necessary for liberation. The aim of this report is to put forward to the members of the front an account of the conference's discussions and plans.

The Political Report
Importance of Political Thought

A basic condition for success is a clear vision of the circumstances, the enemy and the forces of revolution. In the light of this vision, the strategy of the battle can be defined, and without its national action becomes hap hazard and improvised, ultimately leading to failure. It has become necessary for the Palestinian people, after decades of fighting and sacrifice, to ensure for their armed struggle the bask conditions for success. The Palestinian people have been engaged in a long struggle against the Zionist and imperialist plans. Since 1917 (The year of the Balfour Declaration), the Palestinian masses have been struggling to keep their land, attain their freedom, evict the colonialists from their country, apply the principle of self-determination and exploit the land for the benefit of their people. In spite of all this, the people of Palestine have not yet succeeded. Thus, it is not enough to take up arms in order to be sure of the struggle's success. There have been armed revolutions in history that have been successful and others that have failed. It is necessary to face facts frankly, courageously with a revolutionary, scientific mentality. What determines success is clear vision of the circumstances and objective forces that are involved in the struggle; and what determines failure is ill-planned and impromptu action. This explains the necessity for scientific political thought to direct the revolution and determine its strategy. Scientific revolutionary thought can lead the masses to understand their enemy, its pointe of weakness and strength, and the forces which support it and are in alliance with i t Moreover, scientific revolutionary thought leads the masses to understand their own strength, how to mobilize the forces of the revolution, how to overcome the enemy and take advantage of its weak points, and the organizational-military-political programs which should be adopted to defeat the enemy and ensure victory.

Revolutionary political drought explains to the masses of the Palestinian people the reasons for their failure in their confrontation with the enemy up till now, such as their armed revolution in 1936 and all their attempts prior to 193d, and the June 1967 set-back.

As far as we are concerned, the understanding of political thought implies that the battle we are fighting becomes clear. What does it mean to fight without political thought? It means fighting in an improvised manner and committing errors without realizing their dangers and the ways to solve them. Furthermore, political attitudes will be determined haphazardly and not on the basis of clear vision. When political attitudes are determined without proper consideration the result is a multiplicity of policies and this in turn implies a dispersion of forces. The ultimate result would be the dispersion of the revolutionary forces of the

Palestinian people instead of their acting as one unified force.

It is necessary to warn against taking such a matter lightly. Here exists among the Palestinian fighters and in their bases a trend which confuses revolutionary political thought and" politic rust which was represented by certain "political forces" and "political leaders". In addition, this trend confuses revolutionary political thought with the obsolete political methods which were adopted by the Palestinian national movement prior to the strategy of armed struggle. Furthermore, this trend confuses political thought and the act of" verbal philosophizing, as represented by certain intellectuals in their discussion of the revolution. As a result this trend tries to under-estimate political thought. Thus it is necessary to undertake radical action to correct this situation. Revolutionary political thought uncovers political rut and deepens the conviction in armed struggle. It also reveals to the masses the triviality of "verbal philosophizing" which complicates revolutionary causes instead of allowing revolutionary thought to be a weapon in their hands.

Political thought can fulfill this role if it is (1) scientific; (2) clear, so that the masses can comprehend it; and (3) surmounts generalities and is deeply rooted in a strategical and tactical vision of the battle to guide the fighters in facing their problems.

Who Are Our Enemies?

Mao Tse Tsung says in his Analysis of the Classes of Chinese Society (March 1926): "Who are our enemies? Who are our friends? This is a question of the first importance for the revolution. The basic reason why all previous revolutionary struggles in China achieved so little was their failure to unite with real friends in order to attack teal enemies. A revolutionary party is the guide of the masses, and no revolution ever succeeds when the revolutionary party leads them astray. To ensure we will definitely achieve success in our revolution and will not lead the masses astray, we must pay attention to uniting with our real friends in order to attack our real enemies, we must make a general analysis of the economic status of the various classes in Chinese society, and their respective attitudes towards the revolution.

Then . . . who are our enemies?

Political thought behind any revolution starts by putting forward and answering this question. It is necessary to confess that the masses of the Palestinian people have not yet given a dear, specific and definite answer to this question. Without a dear definition of the enemy dear vision of the struggle becomes impossible.

Up till now the masses' evaluation of the enemy has been an emotional one. When partial successes are achieved the masses start to minimize the strength of the enemy and visualize the struggle as an easy and a quick one which will result in success in a short period. When the enemy directs heavy blows at the masses, they go to the other extreme and consider it a force which can never be defeated.

It is clear that such emotional vacillation prohibits a scientific vision of the battle and continuous planning for its victory.

The time has come for the masses to understand the reality of the enemy it is confronting, since, through this understanding, the vision of the battle becomes clear.

(1) Israel

The battle of liberation is directed firstly against Israel as a political, military and economic entity trying to mobilize approximately 2.5 million people to defend its racist-aggressive-expansionist entity and prevent the Palestinians from regaining their land, freedom and rights.

The enemy enjoys technological superiority which is dearly reflected in the level of its armament, training and dynamic movement. It also enjoys a high degree of mobilization as a result of its feeling that it is taking part in a battle of life or death and thus has no choice but to defend itself until the last moment.

The enemy's high level of mobilization and technology should always be remembered. It is not by accident that the Arabs have lost all their battles with this enemy, and it is a great mistake to explain these defeats by referring to particular accidents. Knowing the enemy is the first step in drawing up the strategy of success.

But is Israel the only enemy we are fighting against? The Arabs will commit a great error if their vision of the enemy is limited to the state of Israel.

(2) The World Zionist Movement

Israel is an indivisible part of the world Zionist movement; in reality it is its offspring. Thus the Arabs are not fighting Israel alone but Israel which is objectively dependent on the strength of the Zionist movement. The Zionist movement as a racist religious movement endeavors to organize and recruit 14 million Jews living in different parts of the world to support Israel, protect its aggressive existence, establish it firmly and expand it. This support is not limited to providing Israel with m oral support, but, in fact, it provides Israel with material aid which includes people, money, arms, technological and scientific knowledge, alliances and propaganda. In other words, when the Arabs declare that their enemy is Israel plus the Zionist movement, they do not add to their enemy another descriptive word but material strength of a certain size which should be taken into consideration when the details of the battle are discussed.

Here it should be pointed out that this report does not aim at studying Israel and the Zionist movement in detail. Yet such a study should be carried out in order to get rid of any superficial view of this enemy

During the last few years, studies covering Israel and the Zionist movement have been made. Such studies point out the facts about the enemy from different angles: political, military, economic and sociological. The political and military leadership should read these studies irrespective of the political line which governs the writers, since through figures, facts and detailed information the image of the enemy is clarified.

It is necessary to point out that the enemy, exemplified in Israel and the Zionist movement, is full of conflicts. Conflicts inside Israel, similar to any other society, and conflicts between Israel and the Zionist movement.

These conflicts should be closely studied by the Arabs. There is no doubt that the development of the resistance movement is going to accentuate these conflicts to the advantage of the Arabs in their war of liberation. Yet, it should be remembered, that these conflicts have not yet reached a level which could hamper the mobilization and solidarity of the Israeli state and the Zionist movement.

Is this the dear picture of our enemy? The Arabs will commit a great error if their image of the enemy is limited to such an analysis. The war of liberation of Palestine faces a third force, namely, world imperialism led by the United States of America.

(3) World Imperialism

World imperialism has its own interests which it furiously defends in order to and protect them. These interests consist of exploiting and buying at cheap prices the raw materials of the under-developed countries and then processing them and re-selling them, for high prices, to the under developed countries. Through this transaction imperialism accrues its exorb itant profits, thus increasing its capital at the expense of the poverty and misery of other people. The Arab homeland has valuable raw materials, the most important of which is oil. It also forms a large market for manufactured goods. Imperialism aims at maintaining the status quo in the Arab world so as to continue the accumulation of its wealth, on the one hand, and maintain and increase the poverty of the Arabs on the other. In order to attain this end the imperialist forces are particularly interested in crushing any revolutionary movement which aims at liberating the Arabs land and people from such exploitation.

Mass revolutionary movements in the Arab world aim at destroying Israel, which is considered to be a force that has illegally seized part of the Arab homeland and presents a great threat to other parts of it. Thus Israel has to fight every Palestinian or Arab revolutionary movement. This provides imperialism with the best of situations. Through Israel, imperialism can fight the Arab revolutionary movement which aims at exterminating the imperialist presence in the Arab homeland. Thus Israel becomes a base and a power through which imperialism defends its presence and interests. Such a situation generates an organic unity between Israel and the Zionist movement on the one hand, and world imperialism on the other, since the interests of both meet over the question of subduing the Arab and Palestinian national movements. Thus, protecting and strengthening Israel becomes a basic necessity as far as the interests of world imperialism are concerned. The vision of the enemy becomes more unified; it clearly includes Israel plus the world Zionist movement plus world imperialism.

In this context imperialism means more weapons, support and financial aid to Israel. It means the Phantom fighters, secrets of the atomic bomb and the building of an economy which can resist the economic blockade and perm anent state of war, which the Arabs are trying to impose. Millions upon millions of German marks and US dollars are adding to the strength of Israel, and should be taken into account by the Arabs.

Therefore, the Arabs' enemy is not Israel alone. It is Israel, Zionism and world imperialism. If the Arabs' knowledge of their enemy is not clear and scientific, they will never be able to conquer it. The opinion which calls for "neutralizing the question of the liberation of Palestine on the international level by asking why the Arabs do not win the US over to their side in the battle is mistaken and dangerous. Such thinking is unscientific, unrealistic and lacking in objectivity. Its danger lies in falsifying the truth of the enemy and thus causing failure through miscalculating the strength of the enemy.

Are these the only forces whom the Arabs are fighting against in the Palestinian war of liberation?

(4) Arab Reaction Represented in Feudalism and Capitalism

Arab capitalism whose interests are represented and are protected by the reactionary regimes in the Arab homeland is not an independent form of capitalism and thus, cannot take independent political positions. In fact this capitalism is a weak branch of world capitalism, intermingled with it and forming an integral part of it. The millionaires in the Arab homeland are merchants, bankers, feudal lords, big landowners, kings, princes and sheikhs; their wealth is accumulated through cooperation with world capital ism. They are either agents of foreign companies or secondary shareholders in foreign banks and insurance companies, or ruling sheikhs, princes and kings who defend and protect the interests of imperialism and put down any mass movement which aims at liberating the Arab economy from this exploiting influence. These millionaires cannot preserve their wealth except by maintaining the Arab homeland as a market for foreign goods and capital and by allowing imperialism to exploit Arab oil and other raw materials.

This means that Arab reaction in a true war of liberation waged by the people to uproot the influence of imperialism in the Arab world cannot but stand by its interests which depend on the continuation of imperialism. In other words it cannot side with the people.

These reactionary Arab forces especially the intelligent ones can on the surface support superficial national movements and use these movements to settle a number of their partial conflicts with Israel or world imperialism for their own benefit. But in the end, the reactionary forces stand against any national revolutionary movement which aims at uprooting imperialism in the Arab world and building an independent economy which serves the interests of the people.

The development of a revolutionary mass movement implies for these forces the growth of the peoples sovereign power. And the peoples sovereign ty means the destruction of the authority of the reactionary forces. Thus, however great are their conflicts with Israel and imperialism, the reactionary forces will always realize that their basic conflict is with the Arab people who aim at destroying their interests and power.

Defining Arab reaction as a part of the enemy's force is a matter of paramount importance. The absence of this fact implies an unclear vision of the enemy and of forces which support it among us. These forces can play an important role in distorting the facts about the struggle for liberation as far as the people are concerned, and, at the appropriate time, attack the revolution unexpectedly and lead to another defeat.

This is then, the camp of the enemy which the Arabs are objectively facing in their war for the liberation of Palestine. The Arabs cannot win the war without a dear vision of the different branches of this camp. By defining these branches and seeing their connections it becomes dear that the Arabs real, basic and strongest enemy is world imperialism and that

Arab reaction is simply one of its branches. Furthermore, the hub of lands strength is the fact that it is one of the bases of world imperialism, which provides it with all the requirements of strength and turns it into a great military force with technological superiority and an economy that makes it possible for it to survive in spite of the conditions it is living under.

Thus the war to liberate Palestine becomes, like any other war of liberation, a struggle against world imperialism, which insists on exploiting the wealth of the under-developed world and maintaining it in a market for its goods. Naturally Israel and the Zionist movement have their own subjective particularities, but these particularities should be seen in the light of the organic link of Israel with world imperialism.

After World War I, Palestinian reactionary and bourgeois forces attempted to present the enemy in the war of liberation u the Zionist movement and the Jews in Palestine. British imperialism was portrayed u a neutral force in this struggle.

But the people and their progressive nationalist sections realized that their basic enemy was British imperialism, which wanted to strengthen and support the Zionist movement in Palestine In order to use it u a means of destroying the progressive ambitions of the people.

The Arab people have no further need for new experiences and unprepared actions.

The Arabs, in their Palestinian war of liberation, are facing, in the first place, world imperialism, and basically their war is against it and its base, Israel, and Arab reaction which is linked to it. The Arabs will never win the war if they do not know their enemy so that their assessment of the struggle may be correct.

Any under-estimation or faulty understanding of the enemy's camp in all its branches, sectors and alliances means an under-estimation and faulty understanding of the level of revolutionary mobilization which the Arabs should carry out in order to be able to confront this camp and overcome it. On the basis of the above-mentioned the main features of the enemy which the Arabs are confronting are as follows:

(1) The Arabs' enemy in the war of liberation: Israel, Zionism, world imperialism and Arab reaction

This enemy has definite technological superiority which naturally is converted to military superiority and a great fighting force. The enemy has long experience in opposing the peoples development towards economic and political liberation. It has the ability to abort this movement if the people's political awareness is not of a sufficiently high level to overcome the tactics of neo-colonialism in its efforts to abort revolutions.

The nature of the war of liberation, as far as the main military base of this enemy Israel is concerned, is a war of life or death which the political and military leadership inside Israel will attempt to fight until the last breath.

The above-mentioned factors will determine the duration and place of the battle and the nature of the fight, which are the following:

The importance of the revolutionary concept and revolutionary political thought capable of mobilizing all the revolutionary forces in order to confront the enemy, resist it, and repel its attempts at aborting and sabotaging revolutionary action.

A solid political organization which will lead the revolutionary forces in the war of liberation to a determination onto defend their existence to the last man, a determination which supersedes that of the enemy.

The nature and size of the revolutionary forces which should be mobilized to confront the enemy's camp.

The method of armed struggle has taken, in the beginning, the form of guerrilla warfare and is developing towards a long-range popular war of liberation which, in the final analysis, guarantees success over the technological and military superiority of the enemy.

The nature of the enemy determines the nature of the confrontation. And here lies the danger of any superficial or unscientific view of the enemy's camp and its characteristics.

Who Are the Arab's Friends?
"The forces of revolution."

What are the forces of revolution on the Palestinian level?

It is necessary to define the forces of revolution on the Palestinian level from the point of view of class. To say that the Palestinian people, in all their classes, are in the same revolutionary situation vis–vis Israel, and that all classes of the Palestinian people have the same revolutionary capacity in the light of their being landless and outside their country is an unrealistic and unscientific statement. This statement could be valid if the totality of the Palestinian people lived under the same material conditions. Since the totality of the Palestinian people are not living under the same conditions, scientifically it is impossible to ignore this fact, and these different conditions and resultant differences in the adopted attitudes must be discussed.

It is true that a great majority of the Palestinian people were driven from their country in 1948 and found themselves in almost similar vagrant conditions. It is also true that those who remained in Palestine were constantly threatened with the same fate. Yet during the last 20 years the conditions of the Palestinians have been settled and have taken definite class dimensions. Thus, to claim that the whole of the Palestinian people are landless and revolutionary is erroneous. During the last 20 years definite class interests have become the determining factors in the attitudes adopted by the Palestinians. The Palestinian bourgeois class has its own land and interests. These interests have made it important for that class to look for stability and security.

In determining the revolutionary forces on the Palestinian level it is necessary to start from a class point of view. Arab and Palestinian rightist thought tries to nullify or dilute the class concept and invalidate all attempts to explain the present circumstances with reference to this concept. For example, they claim that the class concept cannot be applied to the Palestinians and the under-developed countries because it is not as well-defined as in the developed capitalist countries. It is wrong, they say, to treat the class concept in the under-developed countries as one treats it in the developed ones

Other rightist elements claim that in the phase of national liberation the struggle between the totality of the people and the forces of imperialism.

The phase of national liberation is not a phase of class struggle. Class struggle is justified during social revolution; While at the time of national liberation, the conflict between classes should be made subordinate to that between the totality of the people and the foreign imperialist. Furthermore, rightist thought declares that Israel represents a special kind of imperialism which threatens the Palestinian people in all its classes.

Thus, the problem is not a class problem but that of a struggle between the Zionist existence and the Arab Palestinian existence.

To allow this kind of thought to go unchallenged would mean total loss and the inability to identify the true revolutionary forces which form the core of the revolution. It would, also, mean that the revolution would be led by a certain class which cannot carry the revolution to its conclusion and draw up radical revolutionary programs which can ensure victory in the battle.

The class structure in an under-developed society differs from that of industrial societies. In industrial societies, there is a strong class of capitalists and a very large class of workers, and the struggle between these classes is violent. This situation does not obtain in the under-developed societies. However, the latter are also class societies, in which there are exploiting super classes represented by imperialism, feudalism and the bourgeoisie, and exploited classes represented by the workers and peasants. Thus each class has its own attitude with regard to the movement of history and the revolution. The super classes are conservative and are pro the status quo and resist historical changes. The sub-classes are revolutionary, w ant to change and contribute to the movement of history. In other words, discussing the characteristics of under-developed societies is scientific as long as it objectively analyzes the differences between the characteristics of the class structure of the underdeveloped societies and those of the developed ones. I f the discussion abrogates the question of masses or if it lessens the differences of attitude to be adopted by these masses with reference to the question of revolution, the discussion becomes biased and unscientific.

It is correct to say that the Arabs live in a phase of national liberation and not one of socialist revolution. But national liberation, also, involves class struggle. Which classes are with the national revolution and which are against it in each phase? The national revolution does not abrogate the class question or the class struggle.

Wars of national liberation are also class wars. They are wars between imperialism and the feudal and capitalist classes, whose interests are interconnected, on the one hand, and the other classes of the people who form the majority, on the other. If the statement that wars of national liberation are nationalist wars means that they are fought by the great majority of the people, then it is true; but if it means that such wars deviate from the concept of class struggle between the exploiting and exploited, it is false.

One should also view, from this angle, the saying that the Israeli-Zionist danger threatens the Palestinian and Arab existence and that the struggle is between the Zionist presence and that of the Arabs. I f the meaning behind this declaration is that the Zionist presence threatens the majority of the Palestinian and Arab people, this is true and definite. But if its meaning Is to deny the meeting of interests between Israel and

Arab reaction (in spite of its numerical minority when compared to the m asses), or to deny the disparity in the revolutionary roles of the remaining classes by considering the revolutionary impetus of the urban petit bourgeoisie on the same level as that of the peasants or the camp dwellers, it is false.

One can summarize What has been stated above by saying that the class concept of the Palestinian revolutionary forces should take into consideration the characteristics of the class structure and the fact that the Palestinian war is a national war of liberation. It should, also, take into consideration the special nature of the Zionist danger. This implies that there must be a scientific definition of the classes of the revolution and their role in the light of these characteristics, and it is not permitted to abrogate the class concept in determining the forces of revolution.

Rightist thought aims at abrogating the class concept in defining the forces of revolution in order to allow the bourgeoisie the possibility of infiltrating to positions of leadership and aborting the revolution at the limits which are dictated by its interests.

The Arabs should face forcefully all theories which attempt to conceal the objective facts of the classes. A re the sons of all classes represented on the battlefield? Or are the great majority of the fighters the sons of workers and peasants? If this is the case, then why does not the political thought of the revolution conform to the actual objective facts?

In the light of the scientific socialist method, the experiences of revolutions in the world, and the actual facts on the Palestinian battlefield, one should clearly determine the classes of the revolution which are capable of carrying its burden.

The classes of the revolution on the Palestinian battlefield are the workers and the peasants. These classes daily suffer from the oppressive exploitation practiced by world imperialism and its allies in the Arab homeland.

Workers and peasants are the ones who fill the camps of misery in which the great majority of the Palestinians live. When one talks about the camps, this means, in fact, talking about a class structure which represents the workers, peasants and destitute petit bourgeois Palestinians. The Palestinian bourgeois class does not live in the camps.

There must be a d ear view of matters and clear political thought which conforms with the above-mentioned view. It is necessary to determine the forces of the revolution, its classes, and the masses which shall lead the revolution at this new phase of national Palestinian action. One should work according to this determination, otherwise one would be repeating the ill- planned fighting which the people have carried out in the last SO years without any positive results.

The material and basis of Palestinian revolution are the workers and peasants. These classes form the majority of the Palestinian people and fill the camps and poor quartets of cities and villages. H ere lies the revolution, the force of change and true readiness to carry on the fight for many years to come. H ere one finds conditions of daily living under which people are prepared to fight and the, because the difference between life and death cannot be appreciated in such circumstances.

With this objectivity it is possible to determine the demarcation line between the haphazard struggle of the Palestinian people during the last 30 years and the new phase of struggle. It is also possible, then, to distinguish between clarity and ambiguity, and comprehend the vast difference between a revolutionary journey culminating in success and a hesitant journey ending in failure.

When one appeals to the workers and peasants inhabitants of camps, villages and city slums and makes them politically aware, provides them with the organization and means of fighting, then one will find the material and the solid base for an historical revolution of liberation. The setting up of this solid backbone to the revolution will make it possible for class alliance to be made which will serve the revolutions purpose without exposing it to vacillation, deviation or abortion.

The Petit Bourgeois

Who is this class? What is its size? What is its stand with regard to the revolution? What are the relations that exist between the petit bourgeoisie and the workers and peasants the very stuff of revolution?

The petit bourgeoisie includes craftsmen and manual industrial workers, small intellectuals such as students, elementary and high school teachers, small officials, small shop owners, lawyers, engineers and physicians.

The petit bourgeoisie in the under-developed countries is numerous and can form a high percentage of the people. Thus it is necessary to realize that any discussion of this class will center around a great number of the people. Therefore, it is necessary to define the position of this class on a clear scientific basis. Otherwise a great error which will affect the progress of the revolution will be committed through giving note credit to the role of this class in carrying out the revolution than It deserves.

In any discussion of the petit bourgeoisie, It Is difficult to define its class features. For one part of this class lives comfortably with all its basic requirements taken cate of and it attempts to rise to the level of the bourgeois class. While another part cannot attain subsistence level, thus they are nearer to the revolution and more inclined to change. It is necessary to study in detail the class structure of the petit bourgeoisie and the stand of each of its sections towards each stage of the revolution.

It can be said that the petit bourgeoisie could be an ally of the revolution and its basic class, the workers and peasants, during the stage of democratic national liberation. But such an alliance should be on an enlightened basis to avoid it infiltrating into positions of leadership and subjecting the revolution to vacillation, deviation and stagnation.

Generally, the revolutionary stand with regard to the petit bourgeoisie is determined by the following.

- This class is an ally of the revolution.
- This ally is not the basic material of the revolution.
- The revolution could not be led by members of the petit bourgeoisie, its programs or its strategy.

The application of these rules is very delicate and difficult. The petit bourgeoisie, in addition to its numerical size, has two important qualifications: awareness and education. If the workers and peasants are not aware, organized and capable of leading the revolution, the petit bourgeoisie will use this alliance to infiltrate into the leadership of the revolution.

To defeat the petit bourgeoisie in its attempt to lead the revolution without undermining the basic conflict with the enemy, the other classes namely, the peasants and workers should know when to ally themselves with it and when to struggle against it. Otherwise the struggle will lead to the following:

- The struggle between the petit bourgeoisie and the workers peasants will be at the expense of the struggle against the enemy.
- The petit bourgeoisie will succeed and take over the leadership of the revolution.

The criterion, according to which we determine the soundness of our stand in this connection, is to ally ourselves with the petit bourgeoisie when the interests of the revolution and people require it, and to struggle against it when the people can sense and understand the reasons for this struggle. The most important thing is that we should be on the side of the people, and the people on our side when we struggle against the petit bourgeoisie and when we ally ourselves with it. During the periods when guerrilla action confronts teal dangers which threaten its existence, and the forces of counter-revolution attempt to liquidate the Palestinian problem, we should raise the slogan of alliance and call for it and represent to the people the force which calls for this alliance. The struggle against the petit bourgeoisie should be limited to a definite stand or a problem which the people sense. As a result of its class structure, the petit bourgeoisie will adopt attitudes which are sometimes vague, compromising and vacillatory. The meaning of this analysis is that occasions will arise when the organizations of the petit bourgeoisie will adopt such attitudes. Here the people can justify the struggle against the petit bourgeoisie, call for it and be on our side. A s an example we can cite the incident which occurred on 4 November 1969, when the reactionary Jordanian Government attempted, intelligently, to attack guerrilla action by striking against one of the guerrilla organizations. PFLP took a definite stand, led the battle and uncovered the vacillatory stand of compromising organizations. The masses sided with PFLP and, in spite of shortcomings, it succeeded in foiling the reactionary plan.

Settling the question of class leadership among the Palestinians is not an easy task. It will not be accomplished in a short period, and it should not take the form of a permanent struggle. It is wrong to think of this matter in unrealistic terms. Settling the problem of class leadership among Palestinians in favor of the workers, peasants and the poor class will take a long time, and ought to be accomplished without undermining our basic struggle and at a time when the people can justify and understand .the considerations and reasons for the struggle.

Whether it comes at a suitable occasion or not, a mere struggle of words of the kind that the people will be unable to justify, and conducted in a way that puts this struggle before the basic struggle, and makes us forget that the petit bourgeoisie is our ally in the revolution, will cause us to deviate from the battle and lose the position of leadership.

The basis of our vision of the revolutionary forces on the Palestinian level is that we realize that the workers and peasants are the basic material of the revolution. And that the strategy, attitudes, ideology, thought, nature and organization of the revolution should be those of the working class. When we realize that, with clarity and in depth, and when we work according to it, then capable political leadership is that which can in the period of national liberation win the petit bourgeoisie as its primary ally, on the basis of the programs of the working class and not those of the petit bourgeoisie.

The correct way, then, to settle the question of Palestinian leadership for the benefit of the people living in the camps is to ally, at a suitable time, with the petit bourgeoisie on the basis of a program and to oppose it, also at a suitable time, when its attitude to an issue can be sensed to be hostile. Furthermore, the settlement of this question should be accompanied by a realistic, dialectical and practical vision of the period and means required for such a settlement.

At this time the presence of the petit bourgeoisie at the head of the national Palestinian movement should be objectively understood. Without such an understanding it will become difficult for the working class to head this leadership successfully. The reason for the presence of the petit bourgeoisie at the head of the Palestinian national movement is firstly, that this class, during the stages of national liberation, is one of the classes of the revolution. Secondly, the petit bourgeois class is numerically large. Thirdly, because of its class structure, this class is educated and competent. Thus, in the light the working class structure concerning political of awareness and organization it is natural that the petit bourgeoisie should head the alliance of classes which are against Israel, imperialism and Arab reaction. To this should be added the special characteristics of the Palestinian petit bourgeoisie and the difference between it and the Arab petit bourgeoisie which heads the Arab national regimes.

If we take all these points into consideration the ascendency of the working class, its strategy and programs to head the alliance; the fact that this leadership is subject to development and crystallization in term s of political awareness and organization ; and th at it will be helped by the stimulus of armed revolt and the development of revolutionary stature then these will ensure that the Palestinian petit bourgeoisie will not be able to take over the leadership unless it is prepared to forego its own interests and its former position. In other words it must be prepared to oppose its own former attitudes of mind, programs and strategy.

How could the picture of the present stage of the Palestinian revolution forces be summarized?

The bask revolutionary forces are the workers and peasants. These alone, in the light of their living conditions, are able to lead the revolution to its final conclusion. The ultimate radical political thought and strategy of the workers are alone capable of confronting the camp of the enemy. Able leadership of the workers is the kind which could, by its scientific tactics, rally the petit bourgeois class to its side in this struggle without having the latter in the position of leadership and without diluting the thought of the revolution, its strategy and programs through the vacillatory thought and strategy of the petit bourgeoisie.

The Palestinian Bourgeoisie

The Palestinian bourgeoisie is in reality a commercial and banking bourgeoisie whose interests are interlinked and connected with the commercial and banking interests of imperialism. The wealth and riches of this class are the result of finding markets for foreign goods, insurance agencies and banks. Thus in the long-run it is against the revolution which aims at destroying the existence of imperialism and its interests in our homeland. The destruction of imperialism implies the destruction of the wealth of the bourgeoisie.

Since our battle against Israel is at the same time against imperialism, this class will stand by its interests, in other words, with imperialism and against the revolution.

It is natural that this strategic analysis will not be clear to all. It is also natural that tactical and temporary attitudes, and certain exceptions, will intervene.

What is the scientific basis for saying that all the classes of the Palestinian people are of the revolutionary forces? Our revolution is an armed revolution. Are all the classes of the Palestinian people part of the armed revolution?

Following the 5 June war, the young elements in the camps and villages carried arms, hid the fought Israelis and got hurt by the Israelis. At this time the traditional bourgeois leadership met Sassoon, Dayan and the Israeli rulers and discussed with them the Palestinian entity, while the Israelis were planning to liquidate the Palestinian problem and accomplish a political success after their military one. These attempts were on the verge of success, but the attempts failed through the escalation of guerrilla action which foiled the merchants on the West Bank of the Jordan River were seeking to link their interests anew with the Israeli state.

Is it justifiable, after all that, to allow the reiteration of such statements as 'We are all commandos', "All classes of the Palestinian people are waging the war of armed struggle", and "No rich and no poor as long as we are all landless without submitting these statements to close judgement, critical analysis, and preventing them from becoming widespread?

Revolution is a science. Scientific thought looks for actual sensible facts. We shall not be deceived by slogans and distorted statements, which are contradictory to the truth, uttered by certain class forces in defense of their position.

The Palestinian bourgeoisie which is living in Palestine under the Zionist occupation even if it has not overtly joined Israelis not a force of the revolution. It will objectively remain the class through which the enemy will try to abort the revolution and stop it in the Middle of its course.

As for the Palestinian bourgeoisie which is living now outside Palestine, its to guerrilla action interests at as long as the latter, at this stage, is performed within a limited theoretical, political and fighting field of vision. Thus, occasionally, it supports guerrilla action with part of its surplus wealth. But the revolutionary development of the Palestinian national movement, which will make it openly struggle against imperialism, will make the attitude which will this bourgeoisie adopt objectively conform with its class interests.

Actually we confess that certain sectors of this bourgeoisie will be an exception to the rule, and, because of the special nature of the Palestinian problem, they will remain on the side of the revolution and will not work against it.

But these exceptions should not over-ride the general rule which governs the stand of this class with regard to revolution.

The saying that it is necessary to benefit from any force which temporarily helps the revolution, and the capable leadership is the one which could mobilize the widest possible front to face the basic conflict, is a correct saying and should be adopted. However, there must be the condition that it should not be at the expense of the clarity of our political thought Clear political thought is the only means to mobilize and recruit true revolutionary forces. Such mobilization and recruitment are the basic condition for ensuring the success of the revolution. This success is more important than the financial aid if the aim behind this aid is the liquidation of dear vision of conditions.

In this light one can visualize the forces of revolution on the Palestinian level.

The forces of revolution are the workers and peasants the inhabitants of camps, villages and the slums of driesin alliance with the Palestinian petit bourgeoisie which also forms one of the forces of the revolution (in spite of the thought and strategic contradictions inherent in such an alliance which should be settled in favor of the workers leadership, thought and strategy). I t also benefits from any sector of the Palestinian bourgeoisie even if it is a temporary benefit without allowing this alliance and benefit to lead to any ambiguity in the identification of the true forces of revolution and the clarity of its strategy and programs.

The bourgeoisie, numerically, only forms a small percentage of society. Bourgeois society is merely half of one percent of the whole of society. Furthermore, this class is not the one which carries arm s or is ready to fight and the in defense of the freedom of the homeland and the people. In other words, any attempt to visualize this class analysis of the forces of revolution in term s which would squander and disrupt the forces of the nation and bring about an internal struggle within them is unscientific and false. The revolution in the light of this analysis does not lose an active fighting force. On the contrary, it gains clarity of vision and a correct definition of the positions of the forces of revolution; it puts the poor classes in a position where they can assume responsibility of leading the revolution and mobilizing their forces to the greatest extent. In the light of this analysis the vision of the war of liberation will be a nationalist one in which the great majority of the people will stand against Israel, imperialism and Arab reaction under the leadership of the poor, whose misery and poverty are caused by imperialism and reaction.

The Method of Organizing the Mobilization of Palestinian Revolutionary Forces

In the light of the above analysis what is the form of organizing the mobilization of the revolutionary forces? What is the form of relations that should exist between these forces in view of the present Palestinian situation? What is our understanding of the Palestinian national unity in all these circumstances?

The political organization armed with the ideology of scientific socialism is the highest form for the organization and mobilization of the forces of the working class. This truth has been clearly proved by all the revolutionary experiences witnessed in this century. The Chinese, Vietnamese and Cuban experiments, in addition to the October Revolution, assert this truth.

The ideology of scientific socialism, by explaining and clarifying the miserable conditions under which the working class lives, by pointing out the process of exploitation practiced by imperialism and capitalism against this class, by clarifying the nature of the basic contradiction which the societies of this age live at both international and local levels, by clarifying the dialectical development of history, by defining the role of the working class and the

311

this class; importance of by doing all this, the ideology of scientific socialism will make the working class aware of its existence, conditions and future. In other words, this ideology is capable of mobilizing the working class on a grand scale.

The ideology of scientific socialism and revolutionary world experiences have clearly pointed out that a revolutionary political organization armed with revolutionary ideology the ideology of the working class is the way for the working class to organize itself, mobilize its forces, unify its abilities, and define its strategy in its battle. The experiences of the Palestinian and Arab national movements have not yet succeeded in resisting and defeating imperialism, Zionism, Israeli and Arab reactionary forces because they have not adopted this ideology and form of organization. The failure of the political organizations in the Palestinian and Arab fields does not, generally speaking, imply the condemnation of the political party organization. It condemns a form of political organization which has not been based, from the ideological, class and organizational point of view, on the basis of the above-mentioned ideology and experience. Raising the revolutionary capacity of the Palestinian national movement cannot be accomplished by condemning the ideal of revolutionary political organization as a principle. The only way is by adopting the political organization whose nature has been determined in the light of the ideology of scientific socialism. This form is the organizational framework for mobilizing the basic force of the revolutionary forces, namely, the working class. Moreover, this form is the stages of national revolution as was proved by the great revolutionary experiments is also the one capable of mobilizing on a grand scale the forces of the peasants.

So, by adopting this form we would have determined the framework for the organization and mobilization of the bask classes of the revolution represented by the workers and peasants.

But... what of the petit bourgeoisie? The petit bourgeoisie according to our analysis is one of the forces of the revolution. Can we it within this framework? If the answer is negative then What is the organizational framework within which all the forces of revolution can be assembled and mobilized?

The majority of the Palestinian petit bourgeoisie will not be organized within the framework which is based on a political party organization armed with the ideology of scientific socialism. Revolutionary socialist thought is not the thought of this class. The petit bourgeoisie feels uncomfortable in front of a solid, committed and disciplined party organization. It prefers to commit itself to a general liberal thought which does not go beyond the general liberation slogans, and to vague political organizations which do not require of it more than it is capable of giving. In other words, the petit bourgeoisie will not be organized within this framework. It will join the other Palestinian organizations which do not clearly adopt the ideology of scientific socialism and the revolutionary political party organization. In the light of what has been said, the organizational form capable of comprehending all the forces of revolution is that of the political party committed to the ideology of scientific socialism. This ideology can mobilize the workers and peasants on a grand scale, and calls, at the same time, for the setting up of a national front through which an alliance can be established between the workers and peasants the basis of the revolutionary classes and the petit bourgeoisie, as one of the forces of the revolution.

With this, our vision of the Palestinian revolutionary forces and the organizational form which can be mobilized, will become complete.

In our opinion, this form is the one which fits the scientific analysis of the circumstances and objective interests of the revolution. Through this form, clear vision of the battle, mobilization of the basic forces of revolution and the widest front which can stand against the enemy camp will be attained.

In the light of this vision, the proposed wide national front, is, in our opinion, the realization of national revolutionary Palestinian unity. If the implication behind Palestinian national unity is the gathering together of all the forces of revolution in the phase of democratic national liberation to resist the basic enemy as represented by Israel, imperialism and Arab reaction, then this form will attain such an aim. The meeting of the three classes within the framework of the front even from the numerical point of view represents the great majority of the Palestinian people. As for national unity which is called for by certain elements, the aim of this is to ensure infiltration, by the traditional bourgeois and reactionary leadership, into the ranks of the revolution to destroy the idea of organizing a revolutionary political party, and to dilute the clarity of political revolutionary thought. Clearly this does not serve the revolution.

From what has been said the outstanding lines of our position with regard to the relations among the Palestinian forces and the problems at this level become clear:

1. We consider Palestinian national unity as essential in the mobilization of all the forces of the revolution to resist the enemy camp. On this basis we should adopt a definite stand in this direction.
2. The form of national unity is the creation of a front in which all the classes of the revolution workers, peasants and petit bourgeoisie should be represented.
3. We should attend actively to the mobilization of workers and peasants in one revolutionary political organization armed with the ideology of scientific socialism. On

this basis we should actively attempt to unify all the left-wing Palestinian organizations which, through dialogue between them and through their experience, can commit themselves to such an analysis.

4. The petit bourgeoisie will not join an organization committed to scientific socialism and strong political organization. Thus it will join those Palestinian organizations which raise general liberal slogans, avoid clarity in thinking and analyzing class structure, and exist in an organizational form that does not require of the petit bourgeoisie more than its capacity. In other words, our bourgeoisie will fill, in the first place, the tanks of Al-Fatch and the Palestine Liberation Organization (PLO).

5. On this basis, and on the basis of our understanding of the basic conflict, the nature of the present phase and the necessity of national unity to assemble all the forces of the revolution to resist Israel, we should work for the establishment of a national front with Al-Fateh and the PLO which can offer the war of liberation the necessary class alliance on the one hand, and protect the right of each class to view the war and plan for it in accordance with its class vision on the other.

This is our vision of the forces of the Palestinian revolution and the form of its mobilization.

If we recall the size and nature of the enemy camp, we will immediately realize that any form of strategic thinking for the Palestinian war of liberation should include the mobilization of all the forces of revolution, on the Arab and international levels. Through such a mobilization we can provide the force which is capable of resisting Israel, Zionism , world imperialism and Arab reaction. Only that Palestinian revolution, which is closely united with the Arab revolution and in alliance with world revolution, is capable of achieving success.

The mobilization of the forces of revolution on the Palestinian level even by way of a political organization committed to scientific socialism, which mobilizes on a grand scale the downtrodden classes, and forms one front with the petit bourgeoisie is not enough to create a revolutionary camp capable of defeating the camp of the enemy which is composed of a wide front that includes Israel, the Zionist movement, imperialism and Arab reaction.

The strategy of the Palestinian war of liberation requites, generally speaking, the mobilization of all the forces of revolution in the Arab states, and, more stresses the link between the Palestinian question and the Arab one, and the need for uniting the Palestinian liberation movement and the Arab liberation movement. PFLP further stresses the strategic necessity for an Arab "Hanoi" as a revolutionary base which can bring about such unity.

Although we do not say that the mobilization of the revolutionary forces on the Arab level is the direct responsibility of the Palestinian revolution, yet we can say that the destiny of the Palestinian revolution and armed resistance guerrilla action depends on the degree of its unity with the revolutionary strategy which aims at mobilizing the forces of revolution in Jordan, Lebanon, Syria, Egypt, Iraq and the remaining Arab states. The dilemma of the Palestinian resistance movement is not only due to the fact that it has not fulfilled the subjective conditions ideological, strategic and organizational which have been fulfilled by the successful national liberation movements in this age, but it is also due to the fact that the resistance is living under hindering conditions caused by the Arab states. These states threaten to liquidate the resistance movement by applying the Security Council resolution instead of being a revolutionary support giving the movement strength, widening its area of operation and doubling its force.

In the light of all this, the strategy of liberating Palestine, inasmuch as it is a battle against Israel, Zionism, imperialism and Arab reaction, requires a revolutionary Palestinian strategy closely united with a revolutionary Arab strategy.

The road which will lead to victory is: armed struggle against Israel and the imperialist interests in our homeland; extending the front of armed struggle which resists Arab reaction, the interests and military bases of imperialism in the Arab homeland; laying siege to Israel through a strategy of popular liberation warfare on all fronts Syria, Egypt, Lebanon, Jordan and inside the territories occupied before and after June 5. The important thing is not that the Palestinian people should register a heroic stand through guerrilla action, but that it should achieve liberation (victory). The road to liberation, in the light of our definition of the enemy camp, is that of a revolutionary Palestinian Arab front bringing guerrilla action to fruition, protecting this action and extending it until it encompasses Israel from all sides and confronts the enemy forces which give Israel aid and protection.

The strategy of revolutionary Arab action conforms in its broad outlines to the strategy of Palestinian revolutionary action. The basis of this conformity is the similarity of the conditions which have existed in the Arab states throughout the present period. In the light of Israels occupation of Sinai and the Golan H eights, its existence and presence as a stepping-stone for imperialism to strike at any Arab nation in spite of the class and economic transformations which have taken place in Egypt, Syria, Algeria, Iraq in the direction of socialism the Arab states are living in the stage of national liberation, namely, the stage of national democratic revolution.

The strategy of the national democratic revolution in this age has become dear as a result of the Vietnamese experiment and the Cuban and Chinese experiments prior to it.

The lines of this strategy are: the mobilization and concentration of the forces of workers and poor peasants on a grand scale; the leading of these class es to the revolution to scientific socialism; the alliance with the petit bourgeoisie whose interests are not in conflict with the nature of the democratic national revolution; the adoption of the method of armed struggle; the overcoming of the techno logical superiority of the enemy by a long-term war which starts with guerrilla warfare and then develops into a popular war having victory as its determined goal.

The national liberation movement in the Arab states has not yet crystallized according to these lines. But the development of the armed Palestinian resistance movement and its results, namely, pressure, mass popular awakening and the stimulus of the nature of struggle between Israel and the Arab states surrounding it, shall create the objective circumstances which will help in the development of the national liberation movement which will adopt this strategy under the leadership of the workers and peasants. Through this alliance and the dose union between the Palestinian national liberation movement and the Arab national liberation movement will emerge the Palestinian Arab force and Palestinian Arab strategy which can attain victory in a difficult and long-term war. The Palestinian national liberation movement should define its relations with the Arabs in the light of the present Arab circumstances.

Arab capitalists and feudalists are, even today, the ruling classes in certain Arab states. The rule of these class es is exemplified in the reactionary regimes of Jordan, Lebanon and other Arab states. These regimes are linked, as far as their interests are concerned, with world imperialism under the leadership of the US. In spite of the partial and outward conflicts between these regimes and Israel, it is nonetheless true that such partial conflicts are based on an objective meeting of interests with world imperialism. Thus these regimes realize that their basic conflict is with the movement of the people. From armed struggle with Palestinians at the moment and Arab people in the future is one.

As for the critical situation which confronts the Palestinian armed struggle and the Palestinian liberation movement, this is a result of its relations with the Arab nationalist regimes, and especially those nationalist regimes bordering Israel, namely, Egypt, Syria and Iraq.

Any daring revolutionary evaluation of these regimes should be based on the June defeat, its result and significance, in addition to what has followed this defeat in the form of strategy, programs and attitudes. Any attempt at mitigating the significance of this defeat, its meaning and lessons cannot but be an attempt at serving certain interests or an emotional unrealistic view of matters which is far from being scientific, objective and frank.

The June defeat has resulted in the total occupation of Palestine, in addition to the Golan H eights and Sinai. It has also resulted in the dispersal of hundreds of thousands of Palestinians and the degradation of a nation. A revolutionary position is the one which will not give false accounts of events, negotiate, or dilute a clear view of the matters, and by which we can understand and analyze the defeat, and be able to see the political and military strategy necessary to secure resistance and victory in the war.

The Palestinian and Arab people, and the Arab nationalist political parties and organizations, used to consider the Arab nationalist regimes as revolutionary and progressive, and capable of liberating Palestine and fulfilling the aims of the people. When the June war was declared the people and these forces did not expect a defeat similar to the June one. The June defeat has proved the great error in the way matters were viewed. There was error in our knowledge of the enemy and our determination of it and our evaluation of its plans and strength. In addition, there was an error in determining the phase, and a greater error in evaluating the totality of the revolutionary presence which was stifled by these national regimes and the Arab nationalist organizations and institutions.

What is the sound scientific evaluation of these regimes?

After World War I, France and England occupied Iraq, Syria, Lebanon, Jordan and

Palestine and consolidated their footholds on Egypt and other parts of the Arab world. The national liberation movement, waged by the Arab people against this colonialism, was led by the sons of feudal lords, aristocratic families and the bourgeoisie. H ajj Amin al-Husseini and the Arab Party in Palestine, and Shukri al-Quwatli and the Nationalist Party in Syria are examples of such leadership; there were similar leaders and parties in the other Arab countries. The bourgeoisie even headed the political leaderships of the armed revolutions which the people waged against the forces of occupation. However, it became clear to the people that, as far as the bourgeoisie was concerned, the aim behind the struggle with colonialism was the attainment of an outward form of independence which would give it the power to govern as a partner of the colonialist powers. In this way it could exploit the labor of the people and take its share of the profits resulting from capitalist investments in our homeland. It forgot about the slogans calling for liberation and union. Conflict became acute between this feudal-aristocratic-bourgeois leadership and its political organizations, on the one hand, and the mass movement, on the other. At this new stage of struggle, the people were led by groups of intellectuals, professionals and liberal officers, who, on the whole, belong to the petit bourgeois class. The petit bourgeoisie was a developing class, thus it was the one which led the people in their struggle against the bourgeoisie and feudal lords in alliance, directly or indirectly, with colonial capitalism. At the end of the thirties and the beginning of the forties these attempts took the form of parties and political and military organizations, on the Arab and regional levels. In 1948, the state of Israel was established, and the true nature of these outwardly independent regimes, set up by the bourgeoisie, their impotency in the face of Israel, and their radical contradiction with the aims of the people became known. The 1948 tragedy prepared for the fall of some of these regimes and the coming to power of the nationalist organizations military and political which were led by certain nationalist elements belonging to the petit bourgeoisie. These nationalist organizations depended for support on the petit bourgeois class and, in addition, on the masses of workers and peasants who rallied to these new organizations and conditions, because of their opposition to the reactionary alliance the alliance of colonialism, feudalism and capitalism.

There is no doubt that the international situation resulting from World War II, as exemplified in the victory of the USSR and the emergence of the bloc of East European Countries, was a basic element in the creation of these new Arab states and their ability to survive.

The basic conflict in the area took the following form: the alliance of workers, peasants and the petit bourgeoisie, under the leadership of the petit bourgeoisie, against colonialism, Arab reaction and Israel.

The first Arab nationalist regime to be created on this basis was that of Jamal Abed al-Nasser in Egypt. Other regimes then followed, namely that of Syria, Iraq, Algeria and the Peoples Democratic Republic of Southern Yemen. The regime of Nasser was, and still is, the clear example and manifestation of this trend.

Any historical evaluation of these regimes and what they represented in the Arab arena during the fifties and until June 1967, should not overlook the totality of great revolutionary accomplishments of these regimes, partial lady that of Nasser. The latter was able to get rid of the British forces of occupation in the area of the Suez C anal; fought against all the colonial proposals of alliances through which colonialism attempted to come back to the area using the argument of defense pacts against the communist threat; overthrew the reactionary colonial alliance which was dominating Egypt, its people and capabilities; broke the blockade which colonialism imposed on the area and established military, political and economic relations with the socialist bloc; put Egyptian national action in its sphere and its Arab nationalist scope; established the first union in the modem history of the Arabs; established a link between political and social progress by carrying out agricultural reforms, nationalizing the main industries and commercial enterprises, draw ing up public development plans and carrying out social reform s in Egypt Further more, it developed political thought by placing the revolutionary philosophy, which had formerly been merely expressed in terms of general slogans about progressiveness, unity and socialism, within the context of a class and socialist analysis of the progressive movement

These are the outstanding features of Nasser's regime and it is these which the other Arab nationalist regimes in Syria and Iraq have tried to follow.

These accomplishments prompted the enemy camp under the leadership of the US to fight against these regimes with every means at their disposal, including force. Such a response on the part of the enemy camp should have encouraged these regimes to introduce new revolutionary measures which would mobilize the political, military and economic forces of the people sufficiently to ensure resistance and victory. Instead, these regimes continued to maneuver within programs and plans imposed on them by their class nature. At this point the crisis of the formation of these regimes and their plans became dear. In the mid-sixties Nasser's regime began to live through this crisis without being able to overcome it. The June war revealed the crisis of this regime and its inability, within its class nature, to defeat the imperialist, reactionary, Zionist and Israeli camp.

The nature of these nationalist regimes was based on the organizations they had formed, their view of matters, the degree of sodalist transformation they had attained and the new class structures they had created. These regimes

have hit the interests of feudalism and capitalism
and their exploitation of the people, yet they
have preserved the petit bourgeoisie and its
interests in the industrial, agricultural and
commercial sectors of the economy. At the same
time these regimes created a new class of
military men, politicians and bureaucrats, whose
interests became interwoven with those of the
petit bourgeoisie and formed with the latter the
super-class in society. This super class became
interested in preserving the revolution within
such bounds that would ensure that it did not
clash with Its interests or contradict its thought
or view of the battle. This class is against
colonialism and reaction, but at the same time
wants to preserve its privileges. The political,
economic, military and ideological programs of
these regimes began to be defined along these
lines.

It was on this basis and through the military
establishment that the super-class put forward
its view of repelling colonialism and Israel,
because a war of popular liberation, as far as it
was concerned, would mean that the right of this
class to the position of leadership would depend
on sacrificing all its privileges and leading a life
similar to that of the guerrillas. On this basis the
super-class also put forward a diluted formula
for the political mobilization of the people,
because a true revolutionary mobilization of the
people through a political party organization for
the purpose of armed struggle would mean the
emergence of new leadership for the workers
and peasants, and also the ability of the people

to supervise and ask the super-class to account for its activities. On this basis also the super-class put forward its economic programs which limited socialist transformation to its present form. Moreover, it put forward a system of political thought which diluted its ability to view the reality of the struggle, its present phase, and the programs capable of resisting and attaining victory. Finally, it blurred the vision of exploitation, still practiced by these regimes, of the toiling workers and peasants.

Thus the June defeat is not only a military defeat, but also a defeat for these regimes and their program s, and demonstrates their inability to undertake the political, military, economic and ideological mobilization which can resist and defeat neo-colonialism and its alliances and plans in our homeland.

These regimes continued, even after the June defeat, to maneuver within the same programs. They put forward a number of proposals to confront the Israeli occupation. These proposals included the rebuilding of the military establishments, through their alliance with the USSR, so that they would be able to wage a tactical military war which would remove the traces of the aggression if it were impossible to implement the Security Council resolution in any other way than by war, knowing that the resolution aims at the recognition of the right of Israel to exist within new secure boundaries. These regimes support guerrilla action only as a revolutionary tactic to bring pressure on colonialism and Israel to implement the Security Council resolution within the terms of a settlement acceptable to those regimes.

The nationalist regimes continue to make proposals and maneuver within this strategy instead of adopting a radical revolutionary strategy aiming at long-term popular warfare waged by the masses under the leadership of the class of workers and peasants. This strategy should also include radical political, military and economic programs such as those adopted by the Vietnamese liberation movement, which has proved that with such a formula we can, confront imperialism and its technological, economic and military superiority.

When we put forward the Vietnamese liberation movement, which is waging a successful struggle against the US and Vietnamese reaction, as an example of a successful liberation movement in this age, we do not ignore the special difference in our war of liberation with regard to the nature of the presence of imperialism in our homeland as represented by Israel, or the special difference in the nature of the terrain. We always mean the basic strategic lines of the Vietnamese war exemplified in the strong political organization which is committed to scientific socialism, a high degree of mobilization of the forces of the people under the leadership of the workers, the slogan of a national front, the method of guerrilla warfare, popular liberation warfare and the resulting political, economic and military mobilization, a long-term war and a determination for the victory of the poor classes in society who cannot continue to live under the burden of exploitation practiced by imperialism and Vietnamese reaction. We also mean world revolutionary alliances which were established by the Vietnamese liberation movement in order to be able to confront imperialism with all its weight, strength and plans.

In the light of all this we can scientifically evaluate these regimes and their role in the Palestinian and Arab War of liberation, and the pattern of relations between the regimes and the revolutionary Palestinian national progressive movement:

- These regimes are against imperialism, Zionism, Israel and Arab reaction represented in feudalism and capitalism.
- These regimes have accomplished a number of revolutionary achievements on the road to national democratic revolution. These achievements have been linked, as is the case in Egypt, to the beginning of the transformation of society's economic structure towards socialism.
- These regimes are no longer capable because of the class structure which has resulted from their experiment to pursue their march on the road of revolution and raise the revolution to such a level that will enable it to face the state of mobilization which it has created in the camps of imperialism, Israel and Arab reaction.

- The programs of these regimes in facing the war of liberation are the programs of the petit bourgeois class that occupied the top of the pyramid and the position of leadership. The June war, and the developments that have occurred since that war, have proved these program s' impotence in bringing about ideological, political, military and economic mobilization capable of resistance, exhausting the enemy and attaining victory. These regimes still put forward the strategy of a conventional war and reform programs through which they attempt to fill the existing wide gaps in their structure without undertaking radical changes in their totality.

On the basis of the fact that these regimes oppose colonialism and Israel on the one hand, and the fact that they put forward compromising programs for confronting the enemy on the other, the relationship with these regimes should be one of alliance and conflict at the same time.

Alliance with them because they are opposed to imperialism and Israel, and conflict with them because of their strategy in confronting the enemy.

There will be two strategies to confront the Israeli occupation and to wage the Palestinian and Arab national progressive war. There is the strategy of the petit bourgeoisie which theoretically puts forward and practically tends towards the strategy of a conventional war by rebuilding the military establishment, as if it were impossible to achieve a peaceful settlement. On the other hand there is the strategy of the working class which theoretically puts forward and practically tends towards guerrilla warfare and a popular war of liberation to be waged by the people under the leadership of the working class and within the scope of the widest national front opposing imperialism. It advocates revolutionary programs which will mobilize the masses, on a vast scale, in the ideological, political, economic and military fields.

These two strategies and the forces which they represent will work together for a certain period of time. This will happen through their alliance and conflict, until the strategy of the working class succeeds in Palestine and in the Arab world. Its success will stem from confronting the enemy with a wide class alliance of workers, peasants and the petit bourgeoisie under the leadership of the working class, with its ideology and programs and in a progressive popular war.

The relations between the Palestinian national revolution and all the Arab forces shall be determined on this basis. The Palestinian revolution, strategically speaking, shall be in conflict with the forces of Arab reaction and the regimes they represent. The Palestinian revolution shall also be governed by relations of alliance and conflict with the nationalist regimes which are headed by the petit bourgeoisie. It shall also establish relations of close alliance with the Arab revolutionary forces workers and peasant sand their political expressions which shall evolve in the Arab field, in general, and the states surrounding Israel, in particular.

World imperialism, at this stage, has its own conditions and circumstances which differentiate it from previous phases. Moreover, it has introduced new methods for exploiting the peoples of other countries. On the other hand, the ram p of the forces which oppose imperialism today differs in size and strength. Its circumstances and level differ from What they were before World War II. The progressive movements in the world should realize these basic international facts which govern this historical phase. The Palestinian Arab liberation movement does not maneuver in a vacuum. It lives and fights within specific international circumstances which affect it and interact with it, and through which its future will be decided.

World War I was waged by the imperialist capitalist countries against each other with the aim of distributing world markets among themselves. It was not a revolutionary war waged by the working classes in the developed countries against the colonialist, exploiting capitalist classes. The same description applies to World War II. In other words their basic manifestation on the international level was the conflict that exists between the imperialist capitalist countries. The revolutionary forces the working class in the developed countries and the subjugated peoples were not in a position to transform these wars into revolutionary wars where the basic conflict would take, on the international level, its natural position between the exploiters and exploited. Yet the results of World War II and the events which took place later produced a new international situation. The forces of colonialism were grouped together and were crystallized in one camp, the camp of imperialism under the leadership of the US. On the other hand there was the camp of the socialist forces and the oppressed people.

The Soviet Union attained victory in this war. The socialist camp was enlarged to include a number of the East European countries. The enslaved peoples stood up to demand their rights to attain freedom and progress. The great Chinese revolution succeeded under the leadership of Mao Tse Tung and the Chinese Communist Party. This series of events and developments was the objective cause for the gathering together of the forces of capitalism and imperialism in the few years following World War II. The traditional colonialist countries Britain, France, Holland and Belgium were giving way under the burden of the war; and Germany, Italy and Japan were giving way under the burden of defeat. This situation enabled American capitalism to spread and infiltrate all these countries through the act of rebuilding which was witnessed by Europe immediately after World War II.

Through all this the picture of imperialism and its basic features became crystallized:

All the imperialist capitalist forces were grouped in one camp the camp of world imperialism under the leadership of the US.

The massiveness of American capital and its link with European capital is the objective basis for the unity of this camp and its interests. It is also the objective basis for the American leadership of this camp.

The conflicts between the partners of this camp which at times took the form of a conflict between traditional colonialism (Britain and France) and neo-colonialism (U S) remained partial conflicts in the face of the basic conflict which all these colonial forces began to face in their struggle against the socialist camp and the national progressive forces. Despite the accentuation of the partial conflicts between the US on the one hand, and Britain and France on the other (eg. the tripartite aggression on Egypt, the Algerian revolution, etc.), it continued to be dominated by the more important and more dangerous conflict between imperialism and the forces of revolution.

The attempts on the part of the France of De Gaulle to disentangle itself from this imperial framework have not yet formed any radical change in this picture.

The technical development and the major changes, which took (dace in the means of production and military equipment, resulted in strengthening the position of this camp with

335

regard to its control of the world markets, and to its ability to defend its presence and interests.

The US attempts to protect and defend its interests and confront the revolutionary camp with new methods. These differ from those of traditional colonialism which defended its interests by force and occupation. These new methods are the basic features of neocolonialism.

The US has established a series of alliance and defense agreements to resist the socialist camp, encircle it and pot down the national progressive movements. In addition to the policy of alliances, the US follows an economic policy in which local social forces participate in the profit which the US acquires through its exploitation of the peoples. The aim behind this policy is to make the social forces which are benefiting from the presence of imperialism the fortress behind which the US takes refuge in defending its influence and interests. Furthermore, the US attempts to embrace the national progressive movements by implementing the idea of coexistence with the nationalists and relinquishing certain benefits to them in an attempt to please their national pride on remain assured and condition safeguarded. The US also attempts, by alluding to the threat of a nuclear war, to push the Soviet U n k towards the policy of peaceful coexistence in an attempt to paralyze the effectiveness of the Soviet Union in supporting the peoples in their wars against imperialism. This will make it easier for the US to wage local wars on these isolated peoples.

The Vietnamese, Cuban, and Dominican experiences have pointed out that the US, in the event of the failure of these new methods, resorts to armed force to invade and occupy the countries in question to protect its influence, markets and interests.

The Palestinian people in their progressive march to recover their land and freedom are facing this unified imperialist camp.

The June war, what preceded it and what came after, is a manifestation of the above-mentioned. The US attempted to embrace the Arab progressive movement, bargain with it, and divert it from its organic link with the revolutionary world camp. It attempted to destroy it by using Israel and its military force. Then it attempted to embrace it anew while it was weak, and it is still attempting by using Israel and supplying it with all factors of power to keep the progressive movement at its mercy.

In order to face this situation, the Palestinian and Arab progressive movements should have: first, a clear view of matters; second, mobilize and assemble all their forces; third, draw up political, economic and military programs which will ensure such mobilization; fourth, adopt the method of a popular war of liberation in order to defeat the enemy's technological superiority; and fifth , form an alliance with all the forces of revolution on the international level. Such an alliance will ensure the establishment of the bloc through which well the oppressed peoples and all the anti-imperialist forces can create the force which is capable of defeating imperialism despite its strength at this juncture.

Our main friends are the oppressed peoples who suffer from colonization and its exploitation of their efforts and raw materials; or those peoples who live under the same danger represented by the US in its attempt to extend its influence on the developing nations. The peoples of Africa, Asia and Latin America are living under and daily suffering from conditions of misery, poverty, ignorance and under-development which accompany imperialism and its presence. The major conflict in the world of today is between world imperialism on the one hand, and the exploited peoples and the socialist camp on the other. The alliance of the Palestinian and Arab national progressive movements, the Vietnamese progressive movement, the Cuban and Korean revolutions, and the national progressive movements in the Asian, African and Latin American countries, is alone capable of creating the camp which can resist and defeat the imperialist camp.

The Palestinian and Arab progressive movements, in alliance with the national progressive movements in all the under-developed and poor countries, will find, in their struggle against world imperialism under the leadership of the US, a strong ally in Communist China which will strengthen their ability to resist

Communist China is still, objectively speaking, facing the semi danger; the attempt by the US. to isolate it and hinder its development. Communist China is still living under the effects of under-development caused by colonialism and is still confronting the same program and conflict. Furthermore, it adopts this analysis of the basic world conflict which governs the advance of history at this stage. In other words, it adopts the same progressive revolutionary strategy as that of the under-developed people in confronting colonialism. This similarity of strategy creates the objective basis for a revolutionary agreement which will increase our ability to face the enemy and defeat it. Communist China adopts the Palestinian Arab point of view in analyzing Israel as an imperialist base which should be destroyed.

In spite of the attempts by the US to isolate the Soviet Union and the East European countries and prevent them from allying themselves closely with our progressive advance, and despite the letters adoption of an attitude that is limited merely to forbidding Israeli expansion and any extension of its aggression and does not deal with the roots and basis of the aggressive nature of Israel, there still remains a contradiction between the socialist camp and the Zionist and imperialist presence in our homeland. This contradiction creates the possibility of alliance between us and the socialist countries. Our duty is to develop this alliance through the growth of the Palestinian Arab progressive movement and its final struggle with its enemies, in which the socialist countries will side with our progressive movement until the struggles decisive end.

Imperialism and the reactionary forces are trying to find a loophole in the relations between the progressive Palestinian and Arab nationalist movements and the Soviet Union and the countries of the socialist camp. Our duty is to prevent imperialism from succeeding in fulfilling this aim. The Soviet Union has been a main supporter of the Arab people in their war against imperialism and its plans in our homeland.

Through these alliances we will create the large bloc which will stand on our side in our war of liberation and will enable us to oppose the enemy bloc.

In addition to this basic series of revolutionary alliances we should also aim through our political and fighting effectiveness, and by clearly putting forward the view that our war is a national war of liberation and recruiting all the progressive forces in Europe, the US and other parts of the world.

Through such a strategy on the international level, we can encircle Israel, Zionism and imperialism, and mobilize all the forces of revolution to stand on our side in the war of liberation.

Such a view of the situation might look unrealistic in the light of the circumstances of the present stage of the Palestinian Arab progressive movement. Yet continued revolutionary action, and the movements attainment of true resistance within a long-term revolution will ensure its active existence. Effectuating all these alliances does not imply m oral support only, but actual true support, through which we can create the ability to resist and attain victory.

With this, the chart of our friends and enemies on the Palestinian, Arab and international levels becomes complete. A clear view of this chart will determine the aims of the war of liberation, its strength, general framework and location with regard to the historical dialectical movement which governs the present period.

How Do Weak Peoples Face the Technological Superiority of Imperialism? With a Popular War of Liberation and Not Conventional Military War

Oar confrontation with the enemy camp Israel, world Zionism, world imperialism and Arab reaction will be through a strategy which aims at assembling the forces of revolution on the Palestinian, Arab and international levels. This will enable us to confront the enemy through a revolutionary bloc which will outweigh it in size and number. But this is not sufficient to achieve victory. One of the basic points of the enemy's strength is its scientific and technological superiority. This superiority is reflected in the enemy's military abilities which we have to struggle against in our revolutionary war. How can we face this superiority and defeat it?

The question of the scientific technological and civilizations! Superiority of the enemy is neither easy nor secondary. This superiority, on the military level, is reflected in the ability of the enemy to mobilize quickly, the size of that mobilization, the level of training, the high qualifications of the military leaders, its war plans, and its general superiority in handling the moment.

Any scientific critical study of the 1948, 19)6 and 1967 wars will clearly point out the role played by the technological and civilizational superiority of the enemy. It is idiotc to explain the three military defeats of the Arabs superficially, and say that we would have won those wars if certain unexpected occurrences had not taken place and certain mistakes had not been committed. Our failure in confronting Zionism and, then, Israel during the last 30 years cannot be explained except by pointing out the weakness and sketchiness of our political, economic, social and military set-up in facing a movement and a society which are superior to us in the fields of science, technology and civilization; and except by admitting that the war of liberation and the strategy of opposition which have been adopted until now have been wrong. Our opposition to Israel and imperialism cannot lead to victory by waging traditional conventional military war between the army and the forces of the enemy, on the one hand, and our regular armies, on the other. Israel and imperialism will be able to win such w an. Their technological and military superiority, their ability to handle the modem war machine and their economic capabilities for supporting such war, will enable them to defeat us. Three experiences of this sort are enough for us to learn a lesson. The enemy puts its technological superiority into effect by waging a blitzkrieg conventional classical war which uncovers the

weak points of a primitive society. Our
dependence on the Soviet Union does not suffice
to fill this gap in the scientific, technological and
cultural levels. The question is not only a matter
of modem weapons and the acquisition of such
weapons. It is a question of the human beings
who are well-qualified to understand, control
and use these military weapons. This depends on
the technological and scientific level of the
people who are carrying such arms. At this stage
such a factor is not on our side. The conclusion
is that we cannot confront Israel (and the US
behind it which will actively participate in the
war if it develops to our advantage) by adopting
traditional military methods of warfare. The
weapons at the disposal of the weak nations in
facing the forces of imperialism and their
superiority have become known as a result of the
experiences of those peoples who have waged
wars of liberation in this age and achieved
victory over imperialism. The weak peoples
confront the technological and military
superiority of imperialism with guerrilla warfare
and popular liberation wars. Guerrilla warfare
prevents us from directly fighting the enemy,
and thus it will enable us to prevent its
technological superiority from inflicting a
blitzkrieg war and destroying our forces.
Guerrilla warfare, which concentrates on
attacking the weak points of the enemy, quickly
withdrawing and avoiding direct confrontation,
can inflict upon the enemy minor losses which
will accumulate day after day without enabling
the enemy to strike and destroy all our forces

with the superior war machine at its disposal. The application of this method will make the enemy feel that it is starting to lose its bask characteristic, thus the balance of power starts to change slowly at the beginning and then more quickly with the passage of time in favor of the forces of armed revolution. The continual waging of guerrilla' warfare against the enemy will strengthen our forces which will acquire more knowledge, experience, ability to resist and skill in warfare, and will become in numbers and standards capable of waging War against units of the enemy.

We cannot completely destroy the forces of the enemy and attain liberation through popular warfare. _But popular warfare is the first stage of a popular liberation war. Guerrillas will gradually develop into a revolutionary regular army, which will be able to defeat the enemy through a long-term war. This will require political enlightenment and close unity with the organized masses which support it and provide it with the human and material requirements. Moreover, there will be alliances with the world revolutionary forces and the support and aid which they provide it with, as well as the knowledge and experience which it acquires through fighting. Furthermore, there must be a dose unity with the revolutionary party which provides it with a clear view of matters and an organic link with all the forces of revolution at all levels. Finally there is the heroic determination of the Palestinian people generated by the years of misery, humiliation, wretchedness and exploitation practiced by Israel and imperialism in our homeland.

We are not drawing up a military plan for an extremely difficult long term war, but we are pointing out the general framework of this war on the basis that we are an under-developed nation facing Zionism and world imperialism with all its capacities and scientific and technological superiority.

We are putting forward the formula of a popular liberation war in place of that of a conventional war which the enemy waged in 1948, 1936 and 1967, and which resulted in our defeat.

The strategic political slogans put forward by the national liberation movements and the national democratic revolutions in the age of imperialism are the following: "'revolutionary ideology, "strong organizing party, "revolution led by workers and peasants," a wide united national front, and "a war of popular liberation and long term resistance."

The Aim of the Palestinian War of Liberation

That Israel is an aggressive state hostile to our people is indisputable. The creation of Israel has meant for our people their expulsion from their homeland, the seizure of What was built by their own efforts and toil, their dispersion in different parts of the Arab homeland and the world, and the gathering of the majority of the Palestinians, with no hope and future, in the camps of misery and wretchedness, scattered in Jordan, Syria and the Lebanon.

The fact that Israel is an expansionist imperialist state at the expense of the Arab land and its people is indisputable. As far as we are concerned, it is an experience which dissipates all false claims. The national home for the Jews in Palestine became the "state of Israel within the borders stipulated by the 1947 UN Partition Resolution, then it expanded to include Israel with the pre-June boundaries, larger than those drawn by the 1947 UN resolutions, and then it expanded to include the whole of Palestine, Sinai and the Golan Heights.

The fact that Israel is a base for imperialism and colonialism on our land, which they use to destroy the revolutionary movement and keep us sub servient to them in order to plunder and exploit our wealth and efforts, is obvious and indisputable. As far as we are concerned this is not a theoretical conclusion. It is a reality which we have lived during the 1956 tripartite aggression, the 1967 June war and which we will continue to live as long as Israel remains in our land.

The truth about our war of liberation has been distorted and will continue to be distorted as a result of the following: the creation of the Zionist movement has been linked to the persecution of the Jews by the Europeans; the establishment of the state of Israel has been linked to the Nazi persecution of the Jews during World War II; the domination of the imperialist and Zionist influence on great parts of world public opinion; the existence of certain political forces which claim that they are progressive and socialist in addition to the Soviet Union and other socialist countries which supported the establishment of the state of Israel; the mistakes committed by certain Palestinian and Arab leaders in the manner of their conduct of the war waged against Israel.

The Palestinian liberation movement is not racist or hostile to the Jews. It does not aim at the Jewish people. Its aim is breaking the Israeli entity as a military, political and economic entity based on aggression, expansion and organic unity with the interests of imperialism in our homeland, jit is against Zionism as a racist aggressive movement in alliance with imperialism which has capitalized on the suffering of the Jewish people to serve its interests and those of imperialism in this rich part of the world, which is the gateway to the countries of Africa and Asia. The aim of the Palestinian liberation movement is the establishment of a national democratic state in Palestine in which the Arabs and Jews can live as equal citizens with regard to rights and duties, forming an integral part of the democratic progressive Arab national existence which will live peacefully with all the progressive forces in the world.

Israel has carefully portrayed our war against it as a racist war aiming at the destruction of every Jewish national and throwing him into the sea. The aim behind this is the gathering together of all Jewish nationals and their mobilization for a war of life or death. A basic strategy in our war against Israel should aim at exposing such a falsification and addressing the exploited misled Jewish masses and pointing out the contradiction between their interest in living peacefully, and the Zionist movement and the ruling forces in the state of Israel. Such a strategy will ensure the isolation of the fascist group in Israel from the remaining progressive forces in the world. It will also ensure for us, alongside the growth of the progressive armed resistance and the classification of its identity, the widening of the gap in the contra diction which objectively exists between Israel and the Zionist movement, on the

one hand, and the millions of exploited and m
isled Jews, on the other.

The Palestinian liberation movement is a
progressive national movement against the
forces of aggression and imperialism. The link
between the interests of imperialism and the
continued existence of Israel will make our war
against the latter basically a war against
imperialism. On the other hand the link between
the Palestinian liberation movement and the
Arab progressive movement will make our war
against Israel that of 100 million Arabs in their
progressive, national and unitary struggle. The
battle of Palestine today, and all the objective
circumstances surrounding it, will make the war
a starting point for the attainment of the
interconnected aims of the Arab revolution.

Lastly the Palestinian war will be, as far as
the Palestinian and Arab people are concerned,
an introduction of the Arabs into the civilization
of the age and a transition from the state of
under-development to the requirements of
modem life. Through our war of liberation, we
shall acquire political awareness of the facts of
this age, and we shall throw aside delusions and
k am the value of facts. The habits of under-
development exemplified in sur render,
dependence, individuality, tribalism , laziness,
anarchy and extemporization will change,
through the war of liberation, into the realization
of the value of time, organization, accuracy,
objective thinking, the importance of collective
action, planning, total mobilization, interest in

education and acquisition of all its weapons, knowing the value of the human being, freeing woman half of society from the bondage of decadent habits and customs, the basis of nationalism in confronting dangers and the supremacy of this connection over tribalism and regionalism. Our long-term national war of liberation implies our fusion in a new way of life and our starting point on the road of progress and civilization.

General Comments

Generally speaking our view of the strategy of the liberation of Palestine is based on the above-mentioned. PFLP regards this strategy as a general guide for action. We should emphasize that the validity of any theoretical analysis is subject to its success in reality and practice. The revolutionary experience itself will give the scientific answer concerning the correctness or incorrectness of every theoretical political analysis. Any theoretical analytical attempt cannot provide, from the start and in a complete form, a comprehensive view of matters. The relationship between thought and action is dialectic. Thought directs revolutionary action which in turn creates results, circumstances and interactions which affect the theoretical view of matters. On this basis, as much as we insist on these strategic lines as a guide for our action, we insist, at the same-time, that we will not understand them as being inflexible and unchangeable. The experience itself will deepen, crystallize, enrich, compliment, develop and amend certain aspects of this view. Such a view of this strategy is the scientific dialectic one which is based on the following: rejection of inflexibility and petrification, undergoing criticism and self-criticism from time to time, benefiting from experience, actively and closely linking between thought and revolutionary action in order to develop and deepen the former which in turn will direct revolutionary action in a more correct form. Any other view of matters is actually idealist and inflexible and will lead to failure.

On the other hand this strategy represents the general view of the war of liberation and its basic tendencies. Thus it does not go into the details and complexities which will imbue every phase of the war of liberation and which will accompany every one of its aspects. For example, in defining the basic conflict between the forces of revolution and those of counter-revolution, and w anting that to focus our attention on this basic pattern , we did not pause to consider the other efficacious and existing conflicts among the forces of the enemy, on the one hand, and among the forces of revolution, on the other. Our specification of Israel, for example, as one of the enemy's forces does not imply a static and inflexible conception of this force. Israel does not represent a single homogeneous unit free of internal anomalies. In Israel there exists more than one social political force, and conflicts among these forces are present. These conflicts may be aggravated or subdued depending on the development of the war and the phase through which it is passing. Although the existing conflicts inside Israel between what are called the hawks and doves does not leave any important effects on the overall conception of the war, yet the more latent radical conflicts may emerge and intensify in the future. Furthermore, the organic link between Israel and imperialism does not imply the absence of partial conflicts between them. In addition, we are witnessing, in the present phase, a conflict between Israel and the reactionary regime in Jordan, which makes it look as if the latter considered its conflicts with guerrilla action less important than that with Israel. Moreover, we are witnessing the readiness of the Palestinian bourgeoisie, living outside the occupied territories, to provide guerrilla action with financial support

On the other hand there will also be other aspects of conflict. The existing conflicts among the armed Palestinian organizations are clear. Also, the alliance between the Palestinian liberation movement and revolutionary action on the regional and Arab levels will not be a harmonious alliance free of conflict. In putting the formula of popular liberation warfare as the revolutionary formula for confronting the enemy, we should not eliminate the concept that the traditional Arab armies of the nationalist regimes, through defending themselves, on the one hand, and carrying out tactical attacks, on the other, will play a military role for a long period. At times, this role might appear to be the main role in the course of events, although, strategically speaking, these armies will not be the revolutionary forces which will continue to resist Israel and imperialism until essential national liberation is achieved.

The basic pattern of conflict which was defined by the above-mentioned strategy is not a geometrically straight line which has two contradictory powers at either end. In fact it is a tortuous dialectical line of progression which contrasts a group of allied forces within which there exist conflicts. At some points such alliances become stronger and at other points the conflicts within them become greater, so that the picture it presents at certain phases becomes Mended, confused and interacting along both sides of the basic line of contradiction. It is equally important and bask that we should view each phase of the war in a detailed and exact manner, thus enabling us to determine our tactical steps in a scientific way. Similarly our detailed and tactical conception of each phase should be within the context of our long term strategy. Such a strategy will enable us to lead and direct the war and avoid committing mistakes caused by experimental and ill-planned actions, or following in the wake of events, being affected by them without taking any part in their direction.

In the light of such an understanding PFLP adopts this political strategic analysis to guide it in the war of liberation which it is confronting and preparing for.

PART II
Strategy of Organization

A popular war of liberation directed against imperialism with its technological superiority, production and economic capacities, long experience in colonizing, exploiting and suppressing the people, aborting their revolution by new and developed methods which fit the present age cannot be evolved, continue and succeed in an automatic manner. The revolutionary party which creates and leads the popular war of liberation to victory is a basic condition for any radical and true revolution in our age. The party provides for a sound view of the war of liberation and determines its strategy and tactics in the light of a scientific study of the forces of the war, the weak and strong points of these forces. The party makes provision for leading the war of liberation and puts forward the framework in which the capacities of the people will be mobilized and directed to ensure victory in the war and attainment of the goal. On this basis party problems (our understanding of the party, its basis, class structure, method of action, the institutions and the relations which govern the sub-structure and super-structure, its relations with the people) will not be secondary. The strategy of organization becomes an integral part of the war strategy. The theoretical dialogue which has been going on for a period of time between the revolutionary forces in Latin America the Castroist parties, on the one hand, and the pro-Soviet or pro- Chinese communist parties, on the other, concentrates primarily on problems pertaining to the creation of the revolutionary party which will lead the revolution.

The failure of the national leftist parties and communist parties in the Arab homeland reflects the failure of their structure and strategy and not the failure of the concept of the existence of a party as a basic condition for a revolutionary existence. This has been proved by the fact that in the 20th Century not a single revolution has been started and been able to continue, succeed, bring about radical changes in society, and give new life to the people without a party leading it and providing it with the ideological, class and social basis on which it objectively relies for its continued existence.

The Palestinian revolution requires a revolutionary Palestinian party.

A Revolutionary Party Requires a Revolutionary Ideology

The basis of a revolutionary party is the revolutionary ideology to which il is committed. In the absence of such an ideology the party would be a simple grouping of people whose movement is based on spontaneous reactions or experience. It cannot be a force which is capable of directing events. Revolutionary ideology implies a clear view of and a scientific method in understanding the analysis of events and appearances; in other words the ability to lead.

The revolutionary ideology that puts forward the problem s of man and the present age in a scientific and revolutionary manner is the Marxist ideology. It represents a unique attempt on the part of man to acquire knowledge of and understand life, society and history. Marxism has put forward an ideology that analyzes and explains nature, its evolution and the rules which govern the evolution by the direct method of scientific materialism. Marxism has applied this method to the study of society and its evolution, movement of history (historical materialism), and the structure, contradictions and dialectic of modem capitalist society (the theory of surplus value and scientific socialism). In other words, Marxism has put forward a scientific dialectical method which has raised the level of studying history, society and political developments to that of science. Natural sciences provide for man the means to study, control and exploit nature for his own interests. Marxism is the science which enables man to understand, direct and influence the development of societies and history. Lenin completed the scientific work of Marx by applying the same method to the study of capitalism in its development towards centralization, monopoly and colonization, explaining in this way all the developments and political events which accompanied the beginning of the 20th Century. Moreover, by relying on Marxism and the method of scientific socialism, he was able to lead successfully the first socialist revolution in history, draw up its strategy, face its problems and define the details of the revolutionary organization which he led on the road of victory. Thus Lenin gave the Marxist ideology its modem revolutionary applications, making Marxism-Leninism the science of revolution in this period of the history of man. It was able to pass, like all other scientific theories, the test of its validity through practical application. It has gained, during this century, all its factors as a science. The final trial for any theory or law is the conformity of experience to the theory or law. This was the case with Marxism. The October Revolution, the

Chinese, Cuban and Vietnamese revolutions, and the revolutionary existence at the international level, was based on the Marxist-Leninist ideology. The remaining revolutionary attempts which resulted in failure were not based on this ideology. It is not accidental that the Chinese, Cuban, North Korean, Vietnamese and East European countries revolutions were able to resist imperialism and succeed in overcoming or starting to overcome the state of under-development. While the countries of the third world which were not committed to the scientific ideology of socialism have remained paralyzed and lame.

Marxism, as a revolutionary ideological weapon, depends on its understanding, on the one band, and the validity of its application to a specific situation and phase, on the other. The essence of Marxism is the method which it represents in viewing, analyzing and determining the direction of events. A revolutionary understanding of Marxism implies its understanding as a guide for action and not as a constant, inflexible ideology. Lenin and Mao Tse Tung, and prior to them Marx and Engels, have recorded on more than one occasion the necessity to view Marxism as a guide for action and not as an inflexible ideology.

The essence of the Marxist view of society is that it is continuously evolving and changing. Thus any analysis put forward by Marxism for a specific period or situation cannot be the same with regard to a new situation emanating from the old one. The constant element in Marxism is its scientific dialectical method in seeing events While they are continuously moving and changing. This method is the revolutionary theoretical weapon that will enable us to view events in a scientific manner while they are continuously moving, developing and changing. The capitalism of today differs from that of the time of Marx. The class structure of an underdeveloped society differs from that of an society. The attempted nationalist phenomenon which to exploit in the service of its interests differs from that of the underdeveloped countries where the concept of nationalism acquires revolutionary connotations since it is the framework that mobilizes the subjugated peoples against imperialism, the highest form of capitalism. The true scientific understanding of the Marxist ideology is that which will enable us to understand those differences and benefit from all the theoretical efforts emanating from its adoption by which it has been enriched instead of remaining static and inflexible. In opposition to that will be the attitude of everyone who considers Marxism as a constant ideology. In Marxist understanding, theory is in a constant dialectic relationship with reality and practice. Such a dialectical relationship implies that it is in a state of development and change and not constant. The greatest danger which confronts us in our commitment to Marxist ideology is that it should be understood in a mechanical idealistic form; for in this way it would lose its ability to provide an explanation for living reality. The benefit we acquire from reading and comprehending the writings of Marx and Lenin is limited by the knowledge that was available to them at the time of their writing. The real knowledge to be gained from these writings is a true comprehension of the method which Marx and Lenin put forward to understand and explain society, history and revolutionary action. Marxism, as a means of analysis and i guide for action, is the weapon which we aspire to in order to understand the ideology. A Marxist-Leninist commitment will only lead to positive results if this ideology is applied and used to understand reality and draw up a strategy of action which will define the nature of the present phase, battle and struggling forces, and will help us to show the evolution of the struggle. Only by applying Marxism-Leninism to our present reality and battle will our commitment to it be something that will be meaningful and capable of realizing positive results. We will commit a great error if we think that a simple declaration of our commitment to Marxism-Leninism will be a magic wand that will lead us to victory. While on the one hand there have been cases of a Marxist-Leninist commitment leading to successful revolutions, eg ., the Chinese and Vietnamese revolutions, on the other hand there are others where this commitment has led to failure. The Arab communist parties which were committed formally and literally to Marxism-Leninism were unable to lead the revolution in our homeland because either their commitment to this ideology was verbal or their

362

understanding of it was constant and inflexible, or they lacked the ability to apply it to the present reality in such a way as to form a clear picture of the struggle and the correct strategy with which to lead it.

Unless our commitment to Marxism-Leninism is based on a mature understanding by the leading cadre and the rank and file of the party, it will be a mere verbal delusion and an escape from reality. Firstly, this can only be achieved by serious study over a long period. Secondly, the value of our commitment to this ideology depends on the nature of our understanding of it as a means of analysis, a method of dealing with the problem s of revolutionary action and a guide for such action, and not as an inflexible ideology. The aim of this study and effort should be to master Marxist- Leninist ideology. Thirdly, the value, in the final analysis, of this commitment is to apply k to our struggle so that we can formulate the strategy and tactics of the revolution. Unless we attain this level, the commitment will be that of intellectuals who use it in their conversations and not that of a revolutionary party, which will clarify the struggle. Finally, the ultimate benefit to be gained from all this depends on the great effort exerted in applying this strategy properly so that it does not remain at the stage of plans which are never put into effect.

A commitment, with this meaning and those results, will pave the way for the propagation of leftist revolutionary thought among our people and enable this thought to overcome any obstacles. The people will not decide their attitude towards scientific socialist ideology by an abstract theoretical judgement of it. The people will only decide their attitude to it as a direct outcome of the consequences of this thought in the struggle against their enemies and those who exploit them. When this thought can carry the Arabs and Palestinians into a developing people's war of liberation which will threaten the Israeli, Zionist, imperialist, reactionary existence in a manner similar to that of Vietnam, the people will realize that this ideology is their strongest weapon in their war against these enemies. Thus all difficulties, both real and apparent, confronting this ideology will disappear.

Since they are under the domination of reaction and imperialism, the dominant thought of the people is that of the right. Furthermore, the failure of the communist parties and the attitude they have adopted towards the of the peoples problems, e.g. unify, nationalism and Israel, have caused the people to confuse Marxist thought with such attitudes. In addition there has been a continuous attempt by reaction and imperialism to distort this thought and portray it as hostile to the peoples nationalism and traditions. Finally, we present to the people, who are still immature and undeveloped in political leftism, a distorted picture of Marxist-Leninist thought in a language which is incomprehensible to them, appears strange and does not deal with their immediate problems. Yet a true understanding and application of this thought will enable us to build our lives and our scientific understanding of life and modem values in a positive manner.

In this contest PFLP adopts Marxist-Leninist ideology as a basic strategy in the establishment of a revolutionary party. This party will have a positive ideology which will unify its thought and vision of the battle and enable the masses to concentrate their efforts in one direction, thus creating a positive force capable of attaining victory.

The Second Strategic Line: Class Structure of the Revolutionary Party

The revolutionary theoretical structure of the party should coincide with the class structure. The Palestinian revolutionary party must consist primarily of workers and peasants. When these classes form the basis of the party, then the solidarity of the party, its ability to resist, its correct attitudes and its revolutionary capabilities can be secured. But if its structure and its fundamental cadres come from the petit bourgeoisie, then it will reflect that class by its vacillation and lack of decision and half-baked ideas. There will then exist the likelihood of it giving way and being deficient in the face of challenges.

A true basis for a revolutionary party lies, first of all, in a thorough comprehension and commitment to scientific socialism; secondly, its class structure should be based on workers and peasants. This cannot be formed in a haphazard manner. Clear vision and much effort are required. A haphazard organization will lead to domination by the petit bourgeoisie because of its effectiveness and engagement in political activity in the present time compared with the workers and peasant's weakness and ineffectiveness and their political and class naivete.

PFLPs present political organization does not yet have in its fullest form a working down-trodden class structure which will make the objective material basis for the revolutionary aspect of the organization and its ability to carry on the revolution. Generally it can be described as being made up of a haphazard extension of the Arab Nationalist Movement, thus still dominated by the petit bourgeoisie. If this goes on without any planning, our organization will be limited to Amman and other cities with certain branch extensions in rural areas and the camps.

We should aim at putting our best elements of leadership in the camps and villages. There should be a thorough survey of the rural areas and camps and our efforts should be concentrated on these areas. Also we should recruit the youth in these areas and educate them in our organization and theory so that they form the majority of the leading cadre in a revolutionary class. The present existence of hundreds of the members of PFLP in the cities at a time when there is no relationship between us and many of the forces of the camps and labor groupings, however small numerically these groupings may be, is an indication of the haphazard development of our organization, its lack of revolutionary vision and effective revolutionary plans stemming out of this vision. These people should spread out and infiltrate to areas where there are true revolutionary groups and thus, after a period of time, we will find ourselves possessing a solid political organization composed of the poor down-trodden workers determined to carry on the revolution and resist all challenges. In this way we will be sure of the revolutionary nature of our organization and it will be politically a real aid in the fighting, by providing revolutionary fighters and security which will be politically linked to it. A political organization, dependent on the petit bourgeoisie and the intellectuals without roots in the villages, camps and alums of dries, cannot provide men for the fighting and security for the fighters. This is not all. For such a political organization might become a burden on the struggle; since it may aim to exploit its relationship with the armed struggle for benefits, both immaterial and formal, to take up leading positions and to indulge in personal and tactical contradictions which are sometimes hidden behind verbal arguments which bear no relation to problems of actual fighting.

We don't actually mean to shut the petit bourgeoisie out of our organization. What we mean is the at the basic material of our organization should be workers, peasants and the poor. In this way we will ensure that it has solidarity, the ability to resist and that it will really direct itself to the battle and the problem s of waging that battle. Under these conditions the organization will be able to recruit and mobilize the revolutionary sectors among the petit bourgeoisie without falling a victim to its indecision, vacillation, lack of strength and short-sightedness.

Revolutionary intellectuals are a basic element in the building of the party and the revolution. In defining revolutionary forces in the under developed countries modem socialist thought lists workers, peasants, soldiers and revolutionary intellectuals. The intellectuals provide the revolutionary forces with clear vision and through them political awareness is spread to the working classes. Furthermore, they are able to organize and plan different stages of the work in hand. In this their presence and organic link with the party is fundamental. However, their role in building the party and serving the revolution is conditional on their close association with the people, fighters and revolutionary action. They must also acquire through experience the ability to take part in resistance. Their presence, in isolation from the people and the fighting, might expose the party to gossip, which is contrary to the problems of teal work. They must be ready to live among the down-trodden people and the fighters, to learn from them whatever they teach them , and be able to live under the same conditions, to have comradely relations with both fighters and poor, avoid appearing greater than them , and avoid material and m oral benefits. Only in this way will the intellectuals be able to fulfill their role in the revolution.

Our second basic line in the building of the party will be to recruit its members from the classes of the workers, peasants, toilers and revolutionary intellectuals. Naturally this will not ensure the realization of this aim, unless effort is made to organize the workers, poor peasants and toilers. In other words, when our organization becomes actually that of the camps, villages and poor quarters of cities.

Third Strategic Line: The Party and the People

The party is the leader of the people. Thus party members and party cadres should be politically aware, and filled with enthusiasm. They must be ready to sacrifice themselves, submit to discipline, the regulations and principles of the organization. The patty should ensure that all its members set an example of (and be in the vanguard of) political awareness, energy, sacrifice and discipline. If the party and its members lose these qualities, it will lose its role as a political revolutionary organization. Inasmuch as the revolutionary political party should be an organization for politically aware elements who are sincere, energetic and prepared to follow regulations, so at the same timeshould the party be an organization for the people and of the people. It should live among them, fight for them, depend on them and realize its aims through them, of them and for them.

Mao Tse Tung says: "However active the leading group may be, its activity will amount to fruitless effort by a handful of people unless combined with the activity of the masses. On the other hand, if the masses alone are active without a strong leading group to organize their activity properly, such activity cannot be sustained for long, or carried forward in the right direction, or raised to a high level.

It would be useful for us to remember these words in our action. By understanding the dialectical relationship between the party and the people, we can understand the role of the party on the one hand and the role of the people on the other.

The peoples line is the third strategic line in building PFLP. In order to succeed in building PFLP as a peoples organization, its leaders should thoroughly understand that the aim behind our action is the people; their freedom, their dignity, their life, the provision of their needs and the security of their future.

To keep this aim in our mind, to deepen our members awareness of it and to remind them constantly of its importance will help us to guide our actions in the right direction. It will also determine our evaluation of our action, cadre, leadership and branches. Moreover, it will protect the organization from the danger of abstruseness, isolation, bureaucracy, arbitrary action, opportunism and nepotism. Furthermore, it will determine the nature of our activities and the direction of our effectiveness. Sometimes, our organization, or rather some of its branches or aspects, will limit itself to internal activities ie., meetings, education, discussions, criticisms etc. In the absence of a peoples problem in which the organization will be involved and in the light of the organization being isolated from the people and their problem s, its life will become abstruse and isolated. Thus sooner or later such an organization will become so involved in the complication of superficial administrative problems that it will almost completely lose its ability to undertake revolutionary action.

Our primary responsibility is to go to the people, tackle their problems and work for them. It is also to help the people to understand, analyze and adopt an attitude to their problem s. Moreover, we must help them to organize themselves and to act when confronted with their problems. This should be the aim behind our existence, and it is the only way to group the forces of revolution that are capable of accomplishing our goals.

The peoples line and the extent of its success will be a basic measurement of the revolutionary spirit of the members, the organization and its political set-up as a whole.

The revolutionary member is the one who establishes the best relations with the people around, looks for any opportunity to serve them and is a source of awakening and help to the people around him. It is incontestable that a member who harms the masses or lives in isolation from them cannot claim to be revolutionary. The branch of the organization which can be considered successful in manifesting the peoples line is the one which carries out the following: holds political debates; interacts with the people in solving their problem s and difficulties; serves the people through opening anti-illiteracy schools; helps them in reaping the harvest; directs them in establishing cooperatives; and leads them when they demand the construction of water or electricity projects or the opening of a road. On the other hand any branch of the organization which is separated from the people and concentrates only on its internal administration cannot be considered revolutionary.

The popular political revolutionary party is the one which mobilizes every man, woman, worker, peasant, student and youth for the revolution. It is also the one which directs and leads them in carrying out the revolution and the fight. It should be always remembered that the creation of such an organization cannot be accomplished in a short period.

Leading the people is not an easy responsibility. The success or failure of the party in leading the people depends on its ability to analyze the present situation, the slogans put forward, the nature of the problems confronting the method in which these problem s are put forward, and the methods of mobilizing and organizing the people. The party cannot lead the people if the questions put forward by it do not stem from among them, or the party's terminology cannot be comprehended by the people.

Our understanding of the peoples line and their role in forming the party should not be idealistic. We should organically link ourselves with the people in order to lead them and not emotionally follow them.

The working people are the basic material of the revolution. This material cannot be transformed into a political force capable of writing history except by possessing political awareness and by organization and discipline.

Our people, like those of the under-developed countries, are victims of decayed concepts, tribal and sectarian connections, and old traditions. Under such circumstances our people cannot be the capable force which can achieve victory over our enemy. Organizing the people in a party should be accompanied by a thorough program of political revolutionary education. The revolutionary party is the school where the people learn and change many of their habits, traditions and understanding. In this way they will be able to change all that is old and decayed for What is new, modern and revolutionary.

The working people because of their present material conditions and their subjection to exploitation and humiliation practiced by the counter revolutionary forces, form, without any doubt, strategically speaking, the true protection of the revolution from any vacillation, weakness and sloth. However, this should not imply that the people are always in the right in determining the tactics of political attitudes and draw ing up plans for them. The attitudes of the people sometimes reflect emotional evaluations of situations, which are both unscientific and lacking in objectivity. Thus it is wrong for the party always to agree with the people without trying to influence and direct them. It should always remember the dangers of haphazard political activity and that its role is to head the people not to be its tail.

Otherwise the party will lose every justification for its existence as a revolutionary political organization.

There is a dialectical relationship between the people and the patty. The party teaches the people and is taught by them; influences them and is influenced by them. The people provide the party with factual evidence and the party, in the light of its comprehension of this evidence, provides the right approach and program of work.

The strategy of armed struggle should reflect the building up of the party. This will reflect the advantages and requirements of the struggle. In turn, it will reflect the internal relations within the organization, its structure, leadership, educational, material and internal regulations.

The political aim of the Palestinian national movement is the liberation of Palestine. This can only be achieved through armed struggle and a peoples war of liberation. If this reality escapes our mind, it will cause a wide deviation in our party-political activity. A people's national Palestinian movement can only be built through fighting and the peoples awareness of the need for discipline, mobilization, and political activity that will aim at an escalation of the struggle the only way to liberation. Furthermore, no lasting escalation of the struggle can be achieved except through the basic essentials for it, i.e. arms, protection and human resources. This organically linked dialectical activity forms the true guide for action. This implies the following:

The military system engaged in the struggle should be formed in a politically mature manner. It is dangerous to limit our efforts to the mere mechanical form of a military system. A fighter who carries arms should know why, against whom and for what purpose. The people's ability to understand politically is what protects them from isolation from the forces of the revolution. It will enhance their ability to resist and avoid political chicanery and it will protect them from any action of political sabotage carried out by the enemy. Moreover, it will deter mine their relationship with every force that carries arms and mobilize them at specific times to carry out popular political activity that will benefit and fortify them in the fighting. A political fighter is able to carry on in a long harsh struggle such as we have today.

The political system should also be developed militarily. We should remember that this will be a reserve force for the fighters. The haphazard development of the political system will cause a serious deviation in that the organization will only benefit morally and politically through its form al connection with the struggle without being an integral part of the fighting system. If this is the case, it will cause a great conflict between the fighters and the politicians which will affect the revolution's development in a negative way and make the political organization a heavy burden on the fighters instead of being an asset. The political organization, that is linked to the struggle merely for the sake of the formalities of the struggles, i.e., identification with guerrilla action and wearing military uniform s, without being truly ready to join the fighting, will be an obstacle to revolutionary development and make the fighting party's and political sections. It should be built in such a way that it is always ready to join the fighting. Its responsibility should be military protection of the fighting (popular resistance). It should be subject to the same conditions as the fighters. In this way we can build a unified fighting party and avoid any serious conflicts between fighting and political action.

The party's leadership should be political and military. At intervals the political and military leadership should exchange positions in order to acquaint themselves with each other's problems.

The party's internal education should be both political and military. The cadres should be trained politically and militarily at the same time.

The leadership should direct its most strenuous efforts to the fighting to solve its problems, satisfy its needs, escalate it, strengthen its resistance, continuation and development. All the organizational, political, information and financial efforts should be related to the fighting, for its benefit and not at its expense.

The internal regulations of the party should be drawn up on the basis of the organic unity of the fighters and politicians.

The organizational picture which we are aiming at is that of a unified fighting party. Some of its members will be engaged in the fighting, others preparing for it, and a third part will form the popular resistance which will protect the fighting and assist it, a fourth will work among the people to explain the problems of fighting to move them to serve it, and a fifth will carry on the financial, administrative and information activities which will serve fighting. All these sections make up one organization which is led by the same leadership responsible for fighting, organization and political activity in a unified manner.

The slogan that "every fighter is a politician and every politician is a fighter will draw the basic strategic line for creating the fighting party in conformity. with the nature of our vision of the Palestinian national movement and the war of liberation.

The revolutionaries who meet around a revolutionary ideology, and a strategy for action, and are grouped in a political organization whose aim is to struggle for the sake of such an ideology, need to define the manner of organizing their work, e.g. the organizations leadership, the changing of this leadership when such a change is called for, the tasks of the different offices within the leadership and those of the rank and file membership, the method of solving the problems and conflicts of the organization, how to maintain discipline and unity in the party, how to have the party as a basic unifying factor for the members of the organization which will exclude family, personal and local relationship, giving those capable of holding responsibility the opportunity to fulfill this.

The definition of the party's method of organization in order to fulfill the above-mentioned is a basic requirement for the construction of the party's unity, development, effectiveness and coherence.

At this point we are not going to discuss in detail the internal regulations of PFLP and its organizational principles and activities. "What is important for us is to determine the primary basic principles from which will stem all the other organizational principles and on the basis of which all the other internal regulations of the party will be drawn up. This principle is that of democratic centralism.

Democratic centralism is the basic principle of all revolutionary parties in this century. Its validity is not only theoretical, but it has been proved practically in revolutions. Democracy within the party means the right of every member to know its strategy, political position, major plans and to discuss these matters and give his opinion on them. However, the members right to know everything about the party must be limited owing to the security situation. The right to discuss the strategy of the party and its attitudes and to criticize its mistakes is unconditional and absolute. It is fundamental to democracy.

Collective leadership is another important aspect of democracy within the organization. Moreover, it will prevent domination of the party by one man and its deviation. Also it will ensure that the leaders impose a personal censorship on themselves. Furthermore, it will ensure discussion of problems, and that they are examined from many angles so that the party's decision may be as correct as possible. Loopholes within the collective leadership will be overcome by a clear distribution of responsibility and authority and by giving the leader of the group a certain degree of authority.

The third important aspect of democracy within the organization is the members right to voice their opinions on their leaders or to give or withold a vote of confidence in those leaders. Thus the members will be able to change their leaders, if that leadership fails, or becomes im potent, or deviates, or misunderstands the concept of responsibility in a manner which is reflected in their relationship with the members. The election and changing of the leadership will be determined by the internal regulations. A leadership which does not enjoy the members confidence will be unable to mobilize them, discipline them and encourage them.

The members right to change their leaders will ensure the leaderships good behavior and sense of responsibility in every decision it takes and will develop their leaders capabilities for the offices they hold.

Only by constant democratic revolutionary education will its essence be attained and applied, and its positive aspects accomplished. It must be stressed that the leaders understanding of the importance of democracy and their application of that understanding should be greater than that of the members. In this way democracy a humanitarian revolutionary way of life will become its laws and internal regulations. Furthermore, democracy and centralism should carry importance in our organization. Democracy without centralism will lead to class deviation and indiscipline so that the party will be paralyzed and incapable of executing its plans.

The party must adopt attitudes, plans and regulations to accord with new developments. While discussing these things, more than one opinion will be put forward. The majority's decision should prevail. This is democratic centralisms real significance.

In order to counteract any mistake of any branch office of the leadership, the central leadership should be able to criticize them. However, this does not imply that the central leadership can interfere in all the party's activities, but only when that interference is necessary to protect the party.

The third thing that we understand by centralism is the leaderships absolute authority to execute and carry the responsibility for the execution of any democratic decision of the party. At the time the execution of any decision, democracy, discussion and debate end; obedience, discipline and complete subjection to orders start. Otherwise we cannot build up a disciplined revolutionary party capable of waging a long harsh war of liberation.

Democratic centralism provides a correct basis for all relations within the organization. It combines the members right and duties with freedom and order. If the members understand this, then they will ensure the creation of a revolutionary party capable of leading an armed revolt and a long harsh people's war.

Democratic centralism will be at the base of all other organizational principles governing the party (collective leadership, leadership of the members, interaction between the leadership and the rank and file, submission by the minority to the will of the majority, no different wings within the revolutionary party, submission of members to the organization, submission of all branches to the central committee, to execute action then discuss). This basic principle will determine the internal regulations of the party which will define relations, authority, responsibility, punishments and rewards. Thus the picture of the internal life of the party as a revolutionary, democratic, disciplined organization becomes clear.

The Sixth Strategic Line: Criticism and Self-criticism

Self-criticism by the leaders and members will help the party to discover its midair and correct them ; this will ensure the party's development, avoiding failure and impotency as a result of these mistakes. No party, nor individual, can avoid committing errors. By self-criticism, mistakes will be turned into things from which benefit can be gained and negative things will become positive. Evaluating our actions and the party's position, policies and activities, and following up the party's policies, programs and attitudes towards the revolution will provide the party with a revolutionary scientific mentality which will always overcome mistakes and develop work plans in the light of these results and lead the party on the road of success.

Sensitiveness and emotionalism in the face of criticism directed at the party by its members and the people will lead to introversion, and persistence in error through the failure to benefit from such remarks and will raise a barrier between the party and the people. A confident, honest leadership will welcome criticism, listen to it, think about it and benefit from it. It will admit the mistakes it makes and correct them and be constantly ready to develop and reform itself in the light of its experience and practice.

Mao Tse Tung says, Conscientious practice of self-criticism is still an other hallmark distinguishing our party from all other political parties. Criticism will strengthen the party if the following basic regulating it factors are taken into account:

(1) criticism should be objective;

(2) should be constructive and not destructive; and

(3) it should tackle basic problems of the party and not m in or personal problems.

This is the strategy of PFLP. By the above-mentioned lines, comprehension and adoption as our guide in building up the organization, we can make the front a revolutionary party a party of the workers, which adheres to the people and directs their movement. Moreover, such a party will be able to undertake an armed, democratic, disciplined and revolutionary struggle.

There is no doubt that our difficulties at present stem from the fact that the front has not been built on this strategy. A clear strategy of organization accompanied with long and hard efforts to build up the party along these lines, is the solution for our organizational problems. In fact these problems are common and general, in different degrees, among the political organizations presently grouped around guerrilla action.

This does not imply that the revolutionary party will ever be without problems. Such thinking is ideal and unscientific. Our aim is to overcome the problems of the present our aim is to overcome the problems of the present phase of the life of the organization in order to confront the problems of a more advanced and revolutionary phase.

At the time of its establishment the Popular Front for the Liberation of Palestine was composed of the Palestinian branch of the Arab Nationalist Movement, Heroes of the Return, the Palestinian Liberation Front (Ahmad Jibril), and other independent elements which formed a fourth grouping in the organization. In the light of this composition, the front did not plan to put forward, in the early stages of its development, a comprehensive left- wing political view of the war of liberation based on the ideology of scientific socialism. In fact it was tacitly understood that the front would put forward a general progressive liberal thought which would crystallize through experience. Moreover, the front did not plan to organize itself into a single party to be based on the above-mentioned strategic revolutionary lines of organization. Furthermore it was understood that, for some time, the organizations that made up the front would maintain their separate existence. At the same time plans were to be drawn up to coordinate these organizations and unify their educational material in order to pave the way for the unification of these organizations.

In the light of this picture, there had to be a dear distinction between the organization of the ANM's Palestinian branch on the one hand, and that of PFLP on the other. The ANM, in the light of the plans drawn up by its Central Committee in July 1967, possessed a revolutionary socialist liberation, whereas PFLP put understanding of forward a progressive liberal political thought. Moreover, the ANM represented a unified party which was ready to reshape itself according to a strategy of revolutionary organization, whereas PFLP represented a group of organizations with differing organizational structures. Thus the nature of PFLP and its the picture of an organization which possessed a revolutionary scientific view of matters and formed one front which put forward a progressive liberal thought and was composed of a group of independent organizations aiming at unity. Under such circumstances it was natural for the ANM to insist on its separate existence and role in the front.

This is the summary of the situation at the time of the establishment of PFLP. Yet the developments and divisions which PFLP witnessed have changed this picture.

The Palestinian Liberation Front (Ahmad Jibril) and the independent organizations have seceded is now composed of from PFLP. PFLP the ANM s Palestinian branch and the Heroes of the Return. This new development has enabled the ANM to put forward through the front its revolutionary method of analyzing the Palestinian situation and its comprehensive political view of the war of liberation, i.e., its political thought. Thus the picture of PFLP and the ANM is almost similar. PFLPs political thought is that of the ANM, and its structure, to a great extent, is that of the ANM. The organization of the ANM forms a high percentage of that of PFLP. Furthermore, if we take into consideration the nature of the establishment of the Heroes of the Return, the organization of its first leading cadres, it's thought, the nature of its comradely relations with the ANM , we will find that its structure is almost similar to that of the ANM. If the thought and structure are similar, it follows that any definite strategic distinction will become invalid. Any insistence on maintaining the Palestinian branch of the ANM as a separate entity independent of PFLP should be based on an objective, defined and direct distinction which proves that the ANM is one thing and PFLP is another. What is the distinguishing factor which calls for the independence of the ANM? Is it the political view of matters? PFLPs political view of the war of liberation is that of the ANM. Is it an organizational distinction? It is true that the presence of the Heroes of the Return within PFLP constitutes a special organizational subject. It is also true that the short time in which PFLP was organized made it, in certain aspects, less solid and disciplined than the ANM. But do such shortcomings justify our call for maintaining the separate existence of the ANM within PFLPs organization? In the light of this analysis the conference which was held in February drew up the line of strategy to organize, direct and guide the future relations between the ANM and PFLP. This line calls for the merger of the Palestinian branch of the ANM within the organization of PFLP, and to work, at the same time, for the merger of the Heroes of the Return within the organization of PFLP. Alongside plans should be drawn up to raise PFLPs organization to the level of a revolutionary, committed, disciplined and politically aware party. On this basis, our concept of PFLP will no longer be the same as it was at the time of its establishment.

PFLP, from the point of view of our present understanding of it and from our present development of its structure, is the revolutionary party based on the political and organizational strategy which has become clear from this report.

The right slogan which should be raised during the total merger between the Palestinian branch of the ANM and PFLP is that the AN M is in the service of PFLP and not PFLP in the service of the ANM.

Made in United States
Troutdale, OR
07/22/2024

21485115R00216